Believing by faith

# Believing by faith

*An Essay in the Epistemology and Ethics of Religious Belief*

John Bishop

CLARENDON PRESS · OXFORD

# OXFORD
UNIVERSITY PRESS

Great Clarendon Street, Oxford OX2 6DP

Oxford University Press is a department of the University of Oxford.
It furthers the University's objective of excellence in research, scholarship,
and education by publishing worldwide in

Oxford New York

Auckland Cape Town Dar es Salaam Hong Kong Karachi
Kuala Lumpur Madrid Melbourne Mexico City Nairobi
New Delhi Shanghai Taipei Toronto

With offices in

Argentina Austria Brazil Chile Czech Republic France Greece
Guatemala Hungary Italy Japan Poland Portugal Singapore
South Korea Switzerland Thailand Turkey Ukraine Vietnam

Oxford is a registered trade mark of Oxford University Press
in the UK and in certain other countries

Published in the United States
by Oxford University Press Inc., New York

© John Bishop 2007

British Library Cataloguing in Publication Data
Data available

Library of Congress Cataloging in Publication Data
Data available

Typeset by Laserwords Private Limited, Chennai, India
Printed in Great Britain
on acid-free paper by
Biddles Ltd., King's Lynn, Norfolk

ISBN 978-0-19-920554-7

10 9 8 7 6 5 4 3 2 1

# Contents

*Preface*                                                                     ix
*Acknowledgements*                                                            xi

1 Introduction: towards an acceptable fideism                                  1

  The metaquestion: what is the issue about the 'justifiability' of
  religious belief?                                                            4
  Faith-beliefs                                                                6
  Overview of the argument                                                     8
  Glossary of special terms                                                   18

2 The 'justifiability' of faith-beliefs: an ultimately moral issue            26

  A standard view: the concern is for epistemic justifiability                26
  The problem of doxastic control                                             28
  The impossibility of believing at will                                      29
  Indirect control over beliefs                                               30
  'Holding true' and 'taking to be true'                                      33
  A second—direct—locus of doxastic control                                   35
  Moral doxastic responsibilities                                             41
  The moral significance of faith-beliefs                                     47
  Linking moral to epistemic justifiability: reinstating the standard
  view?                                                                       48

3 The epistemic justifiability of faith-beliefs: an ambiguity thesis          53

  Plausibility of requiring epistemic for moral justifiability under a
  realist interpretation of faith-beliefs                                     53
  Interpreting the link principle: epistemic entitlement as requiring
  evidential justification                                                    55
  Evidentialist requirements specified by an implicit evidential practice    65
  Rational empiricist evidential practice                                     66
  Applying rational empiricist evidential practice to theistic
  faith-beliefs: an ambiguity thesis                                          68

4  Responses to evidential ambiguity: isolationist and Reformed
   epistemologies                                                        77

   Two strategies for defending the moral probity of theistic faith-belief
   in the face of evidential ambiguity                                   78
   Appealing to a special theistic evidential practice/improved
   epistemologies                                                        79
   An isolationist epistemology                                          79
   Reformed epistemology                                                 86
   Conclusion: the need for a fideist response to ambiguity              99

5  Faith as doxastic venture                                           101

   Agenda for a defence of doxastic venture                             102
   The nature of theistic faith                                         103
   The doxastic venture model                                           106
   The psychological possibility of doxastic venture                    111
   A Jamesian account                                                   112
   'Passionally' caused beliefs                                         113

6  Believing by faith: a Jamesian position                            122

   An initial hypothesis for a Jamesian thesis on permissible doxastic
   venture                                                              123
   The notion of a 'genuine option'                                     125
   A 'degrees of belief' challenge                                      128
   Evidentially undecidable forced options                              129
   Permissible doxastic venture: supra- not counter-evidential          135
   How theistic religion could present essentially evidentially
   undecidable genuine options: the notion of a highest-order framing
   principle                                                            137
   Restricting thesis ($J_i$) to faith-propositions: thesis ($J$)       145

7  Integrationist values: limiting permissible doxastic venture        151

   Can counter-evidential fideism be non-arbitrarily excluded?          151
   A coherence requirement and integrationist values                    155
   Moral integration of faith-commitments                               163
   Implications for reflective faith-believers                          167
   Coda: A reflection on Abraham as forebear in faith                   170

8  Arguments for supra-evidential fideism                                     174

   The importance of defending the epistemic permissibility of
   faith-ventures                                                             176
   Strategies for supporting fideism                                         178
   An 'assimilation to personal relations cases' strategy: experimental
   ventures in interpersonal trust                                           180
   The 'assimilation to personal relations cases' strategy: cases where
   'faith in a fact can help create a fact'                                  182
   A consequentialist strategy                                               185
   A note on Pascal's Wager                                                  187
   The *tu quoque* strategy                                                  189
   Is hard-line evidentialism self-undermining?                             190
   Attitudes to passional doxastic inclinations                             194
   Epistemological externalism again: a presumption in favour of
   fideism?                                                                   196
   Scepticism about passional doxastic inclinations as guides to truth:
   how passions may be schooled                                              197
   The significance of scientific theories of passional motivations for
   faith-commitment                                                          204
   An impasse?                                                                206

9  A moral preference for modest fideism?                                     208

   Implications of accepting (J+) for orthodox and revisionary theistic
   faith-ventures                                                             209
   The apparent fideist/evidentialist impasse and its implications          211
   Beyond impasse? Direct moral evaluation of the fideist/evidentialist
   debate                                                                     215
   Self-acceptance and authenticity                                          216
   Hard-line evidentialism as grounded in doctrinaire naturalism            220
   Coherence amongst moral and religious passional commitments              225
   Conclusion                                                                 227

*Bibliography*                                                                230
*Index*                                                                       237

# Preface

This is not the book I originally intended to write. My initial motive was to write on alternative concepts of God—alternative, that is, to the prevailing classical theistic concept of God as the supernatural, omnipotent, omniscient, omnibenevolent Creator *ex nihilo* (whom I have the somewhat irreverent habit of referring to as the 'omniGod'). People have too readily assumed that rejecting belief in omniGod excludes any kind of continuing theistic commitment. Yet believers could reject classical theism *as an inadequate theory* of the nature of God as revealed in the theistic religious traditions while still maintaining their faith: one should not, after all, confuse God's reality 'in itself' with a theory of the nature of God's reality. To continue to believe in God while an 'omniGod atheist' will, however, be an intellectually respectable position only if one has *some* idea of a viable alternative theory of God's nature. And it was my intention to explore further the possibility of concepts of God that were both clearly distinct from the classical theistic conception and religiously adequate for (at least some form of) theistic religious tradition. I thus set out to write a book inquiring into the question whether it could be justifiable to believe in God according to some alternative concept, expanding on a discussion already published ('Can There Be Alternative Concepts of God?' *Noûs*, 32 (1998): 174–88). I found, however, that I lacked a clear enough understanding of what it would be for *any* theistic commitment—revisionary or classical—to be 'justifiable'. My attempts to get this question out of the way in a short preliminary chapter increasingly became both long-winded and unsatisfying. The present book is the result of my desire to do the best I can to deal with this dissatisfaction.

Not, of course, that I am now fully satisfied! I have, however, come to a settled view on the following key points.

First, philosophers of religion have not fully appreciated a significant distinction between the belief-state of holding a proposition to be true and the action of taking it to be true in (practical) reasoning. The evaluation of the justifiability of religious beliefs should not therefore be confined to belief *states*, it should also include mental *actions* of practical commitment to the truth of what is believed.

Second, the question of the justifiability of taking a religious belief to be true in one's practical reasoning is ultimately a *moral* question, since religious beliefs (virtually by definition) influence morally significant actions and ways of life.

Third, there is a major issue about how the *moral* justifiability of taking a religious belief to be true is related to the *epistemic* evaluation of that belief, and of practical commitment to its truth. In particular, the question arises whether the *thesis of moral evidentialism* holds—if not universally, then, at least for religious beliefs and their ilk. According to that *prima facie* plausible thesis, practical commitment to the truth of a religious claim is morally justifiable only if its truth is sufficiently supported by the agent's total available evidence.

Fourth, it is important to take seriously the possibility that core theistic truth-claims are *evidentially ambiguous*, in the sense that our total available evidence is viably interpreted both on the assumption of their truth and on the assumption of their falsehood. The implications of this possibility need to be considered, even though many philosophers continue to work, more or less hopefully, in what has been historically the mainstream with the aim of 'disambiguating' either for or against theism.

Fifth, the question arises whether stepping outside the mainstream by accepting evidential ambiguity requires the defender of the moral justifiability of practical commitment to theistic truth-claims to reject moral evidentialism and defend some form of fideism (i.e. a claim to the effect that such commitment without adequate evidential support can sometimes be justifiable).

Sixth, the insight that the truth of theistic beliefs need not be evidentially ambiguous *relative to a specifically theistic evidential practice*—as expressed in different ways both in isolationist (or 'Wittgensteinian') epistemology and in Reformed epistemology—seems incapable of deployment in a moral evidentialist defence of theistic commitment. Such commitment can be justifiable under evidential ambiguity, then, only if practical commitment to a religious truth-claim without sufficient support from one's evidence can be morally permissible.

My reasons for accepting these six claims are set out in Chapters 2–4 of this book. The remaining Chapters (5–9) deal with the dialectical situation we face if the last of the six claims listed above is correct. For, it will then be reasonable to hold that anyone who accepts evidential ambiguity and wishes to defend theistic (or, for that matter, atheistic) commitment will be obliged to affirm *some* version of fideism. I have therefore attempted to articulate and defend a modest version of fideism inspired by William James's 1896 lecture 'The Will to Believe', and to consider whether such a version of fideism may ultimately be vindicated against evidentialists who regard any religious (or similar) faith-commitment as immoral.

## Acknowledgements

Some material in this book is reworked from two recently published articles: 'Faith as Doxastic Venture', *Religious Studies*, 38 (2002): 471–87, and 'On the Possibility of Doxastic Venture: a Reply to Buckareff', *Religious Studies*, 41 (2005): 447–51. I am grateful to the editor of *Religious Studies* and to Cambridge University Press for kind permission to adapt some passages from these articles for use here. An overview of material from Chapters 2–4 has already appeared in my 'The Philosophy of Religion: A Programmatic Overview', in Blackwell's online journal *Philosophy Compass*: my thanks for permission to use some passages from this electronic article in the present work. The critique of Reformed epistemology in Chapter 4 substantially repeats the argument published in my paper (co-authored with Imran Aijaz), 'How to answer the *de jure* question about Christian belief?' *International Journal for Philosophy of Religion*, 56 (2004): 109–29. The copyright for this article is held by Kluwer Academic Publishers, and parts of it are reused here with kind permission of Springer Science and Business Media. The passage on Abraham in Chapter 7 is substantially the same as already published in 'Believing by Faith and the Concept of God', in Ree Boddé and Hugh Kempster (eds), *Thinking Outside the Square: Church in Middle Earth* (Auckland: St Columba's Press and Journeyings, 2003), 1–11. I am grateful to the editors for permission to redeploy this material.

I am indebted to two anonymous readers for Oxford University Press for many excellent suggestions for improvements. I am also most grateful to six people who have helped me with the preparation of the present work: Andrei Buckareff, for valuable comments on chapter drafts, and the stimulus provided by his criticisms of my earlier published views in his article, 'Can Faith be a Doxastic Venture?', *Religious Studies*, 41 (2005): 435–45; Folke Tersman, who read the whole text in its penultimate draft and saved me from an error previously unnoticed; Richard Visković, who assisted with the preparation of the bibliography; David Garner who let me read the draft aloud to him over many weekly sessions, and gave me illuminating responses from a seasoned physicist's perspective; Imran Aijaz, who has been my main source of academic support, advice, and encouragement in this project and has supervised my research at least as much as I have supervised his; and Alastair Anderson, who advised on information technology, and, who, as my partner-in-life, patiently both tolerated and curbed my tendency to allow work on this book to crowd out other vital aspects of our lives. Finally, I express my gratitude to the University of Auckland for granting two periods of research and study leave to enable this project to proceed, to the Department of Philosophy at the University of Edinburgh who were my kind hosts during my leave from July to December 2000, and to my esteemed colleagues and students for providing, collectively, a context in which philosophical research flourishes.

John Bishop
Department of Philosophy
The University of Auckland
Auckland
New Zealand
June 2006

# 1

# Introduction: towards an acceptable fideism

My aim in this book is to contribute to rehabilitating an unpopular position in the epistemology of religious belief: I seek to defend a version of *fideism*.

The core issue in the epistemology of religious belief is generally taken to be the question of whether religious beliefs are epistemically justified, with 'religious beliefs' typically specified as the beliefs of classical theism. This issue provides the familiar territory for perennial philosophical debate between theists and atheists—the contest between natural theology and natural atheology to determine whether our total available 'natural' evidence (i.e. evidence that stands independently of any presumed revealed truths) supports the existence or the non-existence of a classical theistic God.[1]

Although this debate has often been assumed to be at the heart of Philosophy of Religion, there is also a long-standing view that it is a debate which neither side can win. This view may be expressed as *a thesis of evidential ambiguity* which accepts that the question of God's existence is left open—perhaps even necessarily—because our overall evidence is equally viably interpreted either from a theistic or an atheistic perspective. The question thus arises whether traditional theistic belief can nevertheless in some sense still be justified even if it is indeed beset by evidential ambiguity. Obviously enough, philosophers committed to theism who are inclined to

---

[1] For a useful survey of the Philosophy of Religion since the mid-20th century, see 'The Ethics of Religious Belief: a Recent History', in Andrew Dole and Andrew Chignell (eds), *God and the Ethics of Religious Belief: New Essays in Philosophy of Religion* (Cambridge: Cambridge University Press, 2005), 1–27. Dole and Chignell give a helpful account of the return to centrality of issues concerning the rational justifiability of religious belief.

accept the thesis of evidential ambiguity have an interest in being able to answer this question in the affirmative.

To that end, considerable attention has been paid to the idea that theistic beliefs might be, so to speak, good epistemic currency even though their truth is not supported by independent evidence. This idea is well developed in Reformed epistemology, which maintains that foundational theistic beliefs may carry epistemic worth even though they are held 'basically' (i.e. other than by inference from other epistemically justified, more basic beliefs). Indeed, Reformed epistemology has become a significant rival to the more traditional natural theological approach to the epistemic defence of classical theism.[2]

There has been less discussion, however, of an obvious response to intimations of the evidential ambiguity of theism—namely the fideist response that affirms that people may be justified in holding and acting on religious beliefs even though those beliefs lack sufficient evidential support, whether direct or inferential. To the extent that this response is considered, it is usually swiftly dismissed. And that is natural enough: to an epistemologist, fideism will seem on the face of it not even to be an option when it comes to defending the justifiability of religious belief. If there is any sense in which believing without epistemic certification—'believing by faith'—can be 'justified', it can hardly be an epistemic sense. Or so it seems.

Furthermore, there seem to be serious objections to the fideist proposal that believing by faith without sufficient evidential support might be justified in religious and similar contexts. In the first place, it is hard to see how believing by faith is possible psychologically or even conceptually—for surely belief is essentially a state of finding a proposition to be true through exposure to some form of evidence of its truth? In the second place, even if believing without evidential support is possible, it seems an epistemically—even morally—irresponsible thing to do. Believing by faith appears to be little more than wishful thinking, and to share the same loss of integrity. Once evidential guidance is left behind (if, indeed, it can

---

[2] The perspective of Reformed epistemology is set out in essays by William Alston, Alvin Plantinga, and Nicholas Wolterstorff in Alvin Plantinga and Nicholas Wolterstorff (eds), *Faith and Rationality: Reason and Belief in God* (Notre Dame: University of Notre Dame Press, 1983). Its most thorough development to date is to be found in Alvin Plantinga, *Warranted Christian Belief* (Oxford: Oxford University Press, 2000).

be), what limit is there to the beliefs that might be justified 'by faith'? How could there be any principled distinction between good and bad, better or worse, 'leaps of faith'? It seems that sheer subjectivity must reign: practising fideists will inevitably find themselves conjugating the following irregular verb: '*I* am a "knight of faith"', '*You* are an ideologue', '*They* are fanatics'.

These are weighty objections. And their weight may be acknowledged without any need to insist on an absolutist evidentialist position—that is, while admitting *some* restricted scope for acceptable believing by faith. (Everyday examples here might include taking a friend to be trustworthy beyond one's evidence, or believing one *can* succeed in a daunting task when the evidence suggests this is unlikely. A more philosophical example is accepting foundational claims—such as the existence of an external world and other minds, or basic arithmetical truths—while acknowledging that there are no rational means of refuting scepticism about their truth.) Objections to fideism with respect to religious commitments need not, that is, apply to *all possible forms* of believing by faith: they may be understood as *specifically directed* against religious (and relevantly similar) cases of it.

I am convinced, nevertheless, that *a version of fideism* can be defended against objections to believing by faith in religious and similar contexts. Furthermore, I believe that the most philosophically satisfactory response to the evidential ambiguity of theism (or, for that matter, to the evidential ambiguity of any relevantly similar religious, quasi-religious, or even non-religious system of beliefs) is correctly described as a fideist one—although not in the popularly prevailing sense in which to be a fideist is to ignore or reject the deliverances of reason.[3] In this book, I shall develop a modest, moral coherentist, 'supra-evidential' fideism (the meaning of these qualifying epithets will be explained in due course). This modest fideism is inspired by, though not confined to, William James's 'justification of faith' in his famous 1896 lecture, 'The Will to Believe'. I shall investigate the prospects for defending this modest fideism against its rival which I shall call (again, for reasons to be explained in due course) 'hard-line' evidentialism. My conclusion will be that there can be no decisive rejection of fideism

---

[3] The *Oxford English Dictionary* defines fideism as 'any doctrine according to which all (or some) knowledge depends upon faith or revelation, *and reason or the intellect is to be disregarded.*' (my emphasis). The fideism I shall defend does not fit this definition.

as epistemically irresponsible. Furthermore, although some favourite fideist arguments are not as successful as often supposed, fideism is open to certain forms of direct moral advocacy. It is an important question whether the morally best kinds of life admit making religious (and similar) commitments insufficiently supported by evidence, or whether, to the contrary, the highest morality is achievable only by resisting the temptation to make such leaps of faith. My conclusion will support fideist commitment to the former view.

As that conclusion suggests, my case for a modest fideism will not confine itself to epistemology. Indeed, I shall construe the fideist claim that religious (and relevantly similar) believing by faith can sometimes be justifiable as ultimately a *moral* claim. To motivate that construal, I shall re-examine the usual assumption that philosophical concern about religious beliefs is directed solely at their *epistemic* justifiability.

## The metaquestion: what is the issue about the 'justifiability' of religious belief?

My starting point, then, is the following metaquestion: what is it that concerns those who raise questions about the 'justifiability' of religious beliefs?[4]

To anchor that metaquestion, consider the following (quite varied) examples of situations in which people are aptly described as concerned about the justifiability, *in some important sense or other*, of their own or others' religious beliefs.

- An undergraduate from a closely knit conservative Evangelical community is challenged by his new friends in Philosophy 101 to prove his Christian beliefs. He is dismayed to find he cannot: he is able to detect flaws in each of the famous 'proofs' of God's existence he has studied, and can see no way to improve on them. He thus becomes concerned whether he could be justified in continuing to hold and act on his faith-beliefs in the absence of proof of their truth.

---

[4] The term 'metaquestion' is Plantinga's: see Plantinga, *Warranted Christian Belief*, 67. Although my own answer to it is quite different from his, I acknowledge the service Plantinga has done by drawing attention to the importance of this metaquestion.

- An eco feminist is convinced that people are morally in error in believing in God, since she thinks that such belief supports the evils of patriarchy and 'man's dominion over nature'.
- A scholar spends a lifetime considering all the available evidence for and against the existence of the Christian God and comes to the conclusion that the balance of probability supports such belief and so feels vindicated in his continuing orthodox Christian faith.
- A Christian woman has fallen in love with a Muslim man and wonders whether it would be right (or indeed, even psychologically possible) for her to convert to Islam out of a desire to share his faith just because it is *his* faith.
- A young man from a nation oppressed by an imperial power comes to think that God is calling him to be prepared to sacrifice his life to liberate his people, and takes that as overriding justification to join an armed struggle.
- A journalist interviews a pastor who is convinced that God is telling him to denounce homosexuality as perverted; she comes away stunned at the man's arrogance, yet reflects that she recently completed an admiring article on a Central American Archbishop martyred for acting on his conviction that God was calling him to denounce the violence of a military junta.

And, for a final example:

- An Anglican priest finds she can no longer believe in the supernatural God of traditional philosophical theism because she thinks it unwarranted to believe in a morally perfect and all-powerful being given the horrendous evils that blight our world. She is troubled as to whether she could conscientiously continue her priestly ministry with suitably revisionist views about the nature of God, or whether she should come clean as a post-Christian atheist who retains from Christianity only certain core moral values.

These examples form a complex and varied set. What they have in common—and further examples with this same common feature could be multiplied many times over—is that in each case people are concerned with, or have views or puzzles about, the 'justifiability' in one sense or another of their own or other people's religious beliefs. In some of these examples, the people involved simply have—perhaps quite dogmatic—opinions about the justifiability or unjustifiability of certain religious beliefs (the eco feminist, the 'freedom fighter'). In other examples, however, those involved are themselves concerned about the justifiability of beliefs they already hold, but might revise or abandon, or of beliefs they do not at present hold but which count as more or less live options for them (the undergraduate, the scholar, the Anglican priest). I shall refer to people in this latter category as *reflective* believers, taking that term to include reflective *would-be* believers also.

The justifiability issues with which reflective believers are concerned may, of course, be raised using many different normative expressions. For example, it may be asked whether religious beliefs are *rational* or *held reasonably*; or whether those who hold them are *warranted* in so doing, or *entitled* to take them to be true when they come to act. It may be asked whether people are *within their rights* in holding and acting on their religious beliefs; or whether, in so doing, they are *expressing* or *honouring salient virtues*; or whether holding religious beliefs is *intellectually* or *morally respectable*; or whether, in acting upon those beliefs believers are doing what they *ought* to do, or what it is *permissible* for them to do. Notice that sometimes the focus of these questions is on the status of people's religious beliefs themselves, and sometimes on what people do with, or in virtue of, their religious beliefs. I shall make more of that difference later. But for now I will refer to all such questions simply as questions about the *justifiability* of religious beliefs, though I recognize that the different normative terms I here place under one grand umbrella have often been recruited to make important distinctions—though by no means in uniform ways.

## Faith-beliefs

My inquiry concerns religious beliefs—but what do I take the scope of religious belief to be? I take as my paradigm religious beliefs in the theistic traditions—with the core belief of each such tradition being that God exists, and is revealed historically in certain specific ways that vary according to the tradition concerned.[5] Classical philosophical theism specifies the nature of

---

[5] Note that the term 'belief' is used here to refer to a certain kind of psychological state known as a *propositional attitude*. This usage is so familiar in the analytical tradition that the fact it is a technical

God as the omnipotent, omniscient, omnibenevolent, supernatural personal Creator *ex nihilo* of all else that exists.[6] It is an interesting question—though a question I shall not here directly pursue—whether that classical theistic concept of God is in fact adequate to the God who is worshipped in theistic religious traditions.

But there are, of course, *non-theistic* religious beliefs—and there may also be quasi-religious or non-religious beliefs about which analogous justifiability concerns arise. Indeed, my defence of a modest fideism will amount to a defence of believing by faith *any* propositional content that plays a relevantly similar cognitive role to that of theistic religious beliefs, and which exhibits the same evidential ambiguity as putatively affects theism. How that whole category of relevantly similar beliefs might be defined is an interesting question, to which I shall in due course return. Since theistic religious beliefs constitute the cognitive component of theistic faith, I shall sometimes describe them, and the general category to which they belong, as *faith-beliefs*, and their propositional contents as *faith-propositions*.[7] Whether, as fideists maintain, faith-propositions are ever properly believed '*by* faith' (in the sense that they are believed without sufficient evidential support) is, however, left entirely open under this description of them. For, there are, of course, important *non-fideist* models of theistic faith that take its cognitive component to consist wholly in faith-beliefs held *with* adequate evidential support.

---

one is often forgotten. (Also familiar is the use of 'the belief that p' to refer, by metonymy, to the proposition that is the intentional object of the attitude.) In the philosopher's technical sense, then, to have the belief that p is simply to have the attitude towards the proposition p that it is true. In this sense, believing that p is consistent with—indeed necessary for—knowing that p. In ordinary usage, however, believing and knowing may be contrasted: to say that one believes that p is sometimes implicitly to deny that one knows that p. Some practising theists may thus deny that they merely 'believe' that God exists—they affirm that they 'know' it. Theistic religious belief, furthermore, is centrally a matter of believing *in* God (in the sense of placing one's trust in God)—and, in this sense, to believe is obviously more than just to have a certain kind of attitude to a proposition.

[6] There is room for variation, of course, in formulated definitions of the classical theist's God. Compare, for example, Richard Swinburne's definition of God as '[a] person without a body (i.e. a spirit) who is eternal, free, able to do anything, knows everything, is perfectly good, is the proper object of human worship and obedience, the creator and sustainer of the Universe' (*The Coherence of Theism* (Oxford: Clarendon Press, 1977, rev. 1993): 1).

[7] A belief will be a *faith-belief*, then, in this stipulated sense, just in case it is held in, and has the right kind of relation to, some particular context in the same way that beliefs that make up the cognitive component of (e.g.) Christian theistic faith are held in and related to the context of Christian faith.

## Overview of the argument

So much by way of introduction. My attempt to defend fideism—or at least a certain modest version of it—begins at the start of the next chapter. I will supplement this introductory chapter with an overview of what is to come.

Chapters 2–4 deal with preliminaries needed to set the stage for my case for a modest fideism. In Chapter 2, I tackle the important metaquestion identified above. What notion or notions of justifiability are at issue in a reflective believer's concern? I shall outline a standard answer to this question: namely, that what is at issue is whether faith-beliefs are epistemically justifiable in the sense that it is reasonable to hold them on the basis of one's evidence of or for their truth. I shall argue that this standard answer fails to recognize that reflective believers' concern is ultimately for the *moral* justifiability of *taking faith-beliefs to be true in their practical reasoning*. Our control in relation to our beliefs—which seems presupposed if concern for their justifiability has any point—is exercised, I shall claim, at two 'loci': indirect control over what we *hold* to be true, and direct control over what we *take* to be true in our practical reasoning. Taking a belief to be true in practical reasoning is itself open to moral evaluation, I shall argue, whenever the actions to which such reasoning can lead are themselves morally significant—and this condition is clearly met in the case of theistic faith-beliefs, which pervasively influence how people live. I thus conclude Chapter 2 by noting the need for an *ethics of faith-commitment*—an account of the conditions under which it is morally permissible to commit oneself practically to the truth of a theistic (or any other) faith-belief.

The fact that it is the *moral* status of commitment to faith-beliefs that is ultimately at issue does not, of course, entail that epistemic evaluations are irrelevant. Indeed, in Chapter 3 I set out a plausible case for the *moral evidentialist* view that people are morally entitled to take faith-beliefs to be true in their practical reasoning only if they are *evidentially justified in holding* those beliefs (i.e. only if those beliefs are held on the basis of adequate evidential support for their truth). Moral evidentialism, I shall maintain, needs to be parsed into (1) the *moral-epistemic link principle* to the effect that people are *morally entitled* to take faith-beliefs to be true only if they are *epistemically entitled* to do so, in the sense they do so through the right exercise of their epistemic capacities, and (2) *epistemic evidentialism*, which holds that practical commitment to a belief's truth carries epistemic entitlement only if the belief is held on the basis of adequate evidential support for its truth. Epistemic evidentialism may be defended, I shall argue, even though it is conceded to epistemological externalism that beliefs may indeed have epistemic worth quite independently of their truth being supported by evidence accessible to the believer. My argument for that conclusion relies on an important distinction, not usually noticed but apparent in the light of the two loci of doxastic control identified in Chapter 2, between *agency-focused* and *propositional-attitude-focused* epistemic evaluations.

If theistic faith-beliefs are evidentially ambiguous—that is, if our total available evidence is equally viably interpreted on the assumption either of their truth or of their falsehood—then, under moral evidentialism, it will *not* be morally permissible to commit oneself in practice to their truth. Yet, as I argue in the remainder of Chapter 3, it is plausible enough that theistic beliefs *are* evidentially ambiguous for it to be important to consider whether this moral evidentialist verdict on theistic faith-commitment under evidential ambiguity is correct. My argument from here on, then, will remain within the scope of the assumption that all forms of theistic religious belief are indeed evidentially ambiguous.

Reflective theists who accept the evidential ambiguity of theism will naturally hope that their faith-commitments may nevertheless be morally vindicated. There are two broad strategies by which this might be achieved: one aims to avoid fideism, while the other embraces it (or, at least, some version of it). The strategy that embraces fideism seeks to show that believing by faith *can* be morally justifiable—or, as I shall prefer to put it, that it can be morally permissible to make a *doxastic venture*. *To make a doxastic venture is to take a proposition to be true in one's reasoning while recognizing that it is not the case that its truth is adequately supported by one's total available evidence.* I shall outline a doxastic venture model of theistic religious belief in Chapter 5 so as to prepare the ground for considering whether an exception to moral evidentialism may properly be made for faith-commitments of the kind made by theistic religious believers. My prior task, however, will be to consider whether the moral probity of evidentially ambiguous theistic commitment might be upheld without the need to attempt a defence of fideism in any shape or form.

In Chapter 4, then, I consider responses to the evidential ambiguity of theism that (*a*) note its relativity to a prevailing set of norms for assessing evidential support for beliefs—the norms of what I shall call *our rational empiricist evidential practice*—and then (*b*) maintain that those are not the right norms by which to judge the evidential justifiability of theistic faith-beliefs. Theistic faith-believers might thus turn out to be evidentially justified after all, relative to the properly applicable evidential practice.

I shall argue that this approach does not succeed in circumventing the need to defend a fideist position. It is true that theistic beliefs are subject to an at least partly distinct evidential practice (think, for example, of hermeneutic principles applied to sacred scriptures, which presuppose the existence of a God whose word is there revealed). So theistic faith-beliefs do form an identifiable *doxastic framework* within a person's overall network of beliefs. But this observation, I believe, cannot provide a satisfactory basis for defending the conformity of theistic faith-commitments to moral evidentialism.

I shall consider two proposed epistemologies of religious belief which might be thought to offer such a defence. The first is an *isolationist* epistemology, which takes theistic doxastic frameworks to be epistemically isolated in the sense that their 'framing principles' are *necessarily* not assessable in the light of evidence *from outside* the framework. (Isolationism, I shall observe, has a clearly principled basis for *non-realists*, who take theistic claims to have some non-assertoric function, such as expressing a community's core values and encouraging solidarity in respecting them.) It is true that, under isolationism, theistic faith-believers may be evidentially justified *from within* a theistic doxastic framework, but their commitment to its foundational principles will necessarily lack *external* evidential justification. Such commitment therefore requires doxastic venture, and can be morally justifiable only if doxastic venture is, in the relevant circumstances, itself morally justifiable.

The second attempt to uphold moral evidentialism appeals to *Reformed epistemology*, according to which holding certain theistic beliefs may be evidentially justified because their truth is *basically, non-inferentially,* evident in experience. Once within a theistic doxastic framework one may indeed treat the truth of some foundational theistic beliefs as non-inferentially evident; but that fact can provide reflective theists with no assurance that their commitment *to a framework of theistic beliefs as a whole* carries either epistemic or moral entitlement. I shall examine and find wanting two Reformed epistemologist attempts to avoid this conclusion. I shall argue, first, that the so-called 'parity' argument fails: lack of external evidential justification does indeed also affect (e.g.) our basic sensory perceptual beliefs, yet our commitment to them carries epistemic entitlement by default, since we cannot generally do otherwise than take (unoverridden) sensory perceptual beliefs to be true in our practical reasoning. The same does not hold of our basic theistic beliefs, however. The second Reformed epistemologist argument rests on an appeal to externalist epistemology. It is indeed true, I shall concede, that theistic beliefs held without inferential evidential justification *may* have epistemic worth. Yet, I shall argue, reflective theists may not, without begging the question, infer from the *conditional* truth that, if God exists, their basic theistic beliefs are (most likely) caused in such a way as to guarantee their truth, to the conclusion that they are *in fact* epistemically entitled to take those beliefs to be true. Accordingly, commitment to the truth of foundational theistic faith-propositions ventures beyond evidential support. Such commitment can be morally justifiable, then, only if doxastic venture in favour of faith-propositions can be morally justifiable. Reformed epistemologists, I thus maintain, need to come out of the closet as fideists—at least, fideists of a modest kind.

Once I have thus (as I shall claim) established that morally acceptable commitment to evidentially ambiguous faith-propositions can be defended only *via* some version of fideism, the preliminaries will finally be over. I will then occupy the remaining chapters, first, by seeking to develop a fideist thesis that specifies conditions for morally permissible believing by faith; second, by showing how a version of fideism based on that thesis avoids widely held objections; and, finally, by considering the prospects for vindicating my favoured version of fideism against a 'hard-line' moral evidentialism which insists that commitment to religious (and similar) faith-propositions without evidential support can never be justified.

Believing by faith tends to suggest *acquiring* or *inducing* by an act of will a state of belief recognized as evidentially unsupported. The fideism I seek to defend, however, understands believing by faith as, rather, a matter of *taking a proposition to be true in one's practical reasoning* while recognizing its lack of adequate evidential support. This latter notion is what I mean by *doxastic venture* (as already indicated)—and, in Chapter 5, I set out a doxastic venture model of faith, contrasting it with alternative models which locate the venture of religious faith elsewhere. I then provide a Jamesian account of how doxastic venture may be conceptually and psychologically possible. On this account, beliefs can, and often do, have 'passional' causes—where a passional cause is broadly understood to mean a 'non-evidential' cause: i.e. any cause of belief *other than* something that provides the believer with evidence of or for its truth. So, for example, religious beliefs resulting from enculturation or from desires (perhaps deep-seated and unconscious) will count as passionally caused. Where such a passional cause sustains belief even though the believer recognizes a lack of evidence for its truth, there is the opportunity for doxastic venture: the person concerned may, *if he or she so chooses*, practically commit him or herself to its truth. If such a doxastic venture is made, it will not amount to inducing a state of belief (either directly or indirectly); rather it will be a direct act of *taking to be true* in one's practical reasoning what one *already holds to be true* from passional, non-evidential, causes. (I shall concede, however, that commitment beyond one's evidence by faith might sometimes involve only *sub-doxastic* venture—that is, taking a faith-proposition to be true in one's practical reasoning with the weight that goes with believing it to be true, yet without *actually having* that belief.)

Whether commitment by faith is fully doxastic or not, however, it involves giving the truth of a religious (or similar) proposition full weight in one's reasoning while recognizing that it lacks sufficient support from one's total available evidence. The conditions under which such ventures may be permissible is the subject matter for Chapter 6. Using Jamesian resources (in particular, an interpretation of his notion of a 'genuine option'), I shall propose that doxastic (and sub-doxastic) ventures are permissible provided that the issue is 'forced', of sufficient importance, and *essentially* unable to be decided on the evidence. I shall observe that this proposal rules out *counter-evidential* ventures—i.e. taking beliefs to be true *contrary to* one's recognized evidence—and thus expresses a potentially more palatable *supra-evidential* version of fideism. This proposal faces a significant 'degrees of belief' challenge, however—to the effect that practical reasoning never forces us to choose starkly between taking a proposition to be true and not doing so; we may always give it *partial belief* according to the degree of probability the evidence affords its truth, so that there can be no cases where 'the evidence does not decide'.

I shall respond to this challenge by taking advantage of the appeal to doxastic frameworks already discussed in Chapter 4 in the context of isolationist and Reformed epistemology. Religious beliefs form a doxastic framework resting on distinctive framing principles. The foundational principles of theistic doxastic frameworks may well be highest-order (that would certainly explain the evidential ambiguity of theism and show it to be no mere contingency). Highest-order framing principles, however, present options for commitment that are both forced and persistently and necessarily unable to be settled by rational assessment of external evidence. One either does or does not 'buy into' a whole doxastic framework of theistic beliefs; and the notion of committing to the truth of the relevant framing principles with some intermediate degree of partial belief determined by their probability on the evidence can make no sense given that evidence is in principle persistently unavailable. Propositions that express highest-order framing principles function differently, of course, from ordinarily factual propositions: but it is, I shall claim, mere logical positivist dogma to insist that that function cannot have any assertoric aspect.

Having thus met the challenge that there can never be occasion for passional resolution of essentially evidentially undecidable options, I will next take up the task of defending my James-inspired supra-evidential fideist thesis. In the final stages of Chapter 6, I state this thesis—thesis (J)—as a claim about the permissibility of *faith-ventures*—that is, commitments under evidential ambiguity to *faith-propositions of the kind involved in theistic religion and relevantly similar contexts*. It will thus be clear that thesis (J) does not purport to provide necessary and sufficient conditions for permissible doxastic (and sub-doxastic) ventures *in general*.

Chapter 7 deals with a serious general objection to thesis (J), namely that it is too liberal, admitting faith-ventures that ought intuitively to be rejected as ethically dubious. One version of this objection alleges that it must be arbitrary to permit supra-evidential yet reject counter-evidential faith-ventures. But that objection, I shall maintain, wrongly assumes that supra-evidential fideism advocates 'the ethical suspension of the epistemic'. To the contrary, proponents of thesis (J) need to insist that the faith-ventures it counts as carrying moral entitlement *carry epistemic entitlement as well*. Supra-evidential fideists need to hold, that is, that permissible faith-ventures are made through the right exercise of epistemic rationality—a condition not met by counter-evidential faith-ventures, which necessarily fail to respect the coherence requirements of what I shall refer to as 'integrationist doxastic values'.

Commitment to the overall integration of one's network of beliefs—evaluative as well as factual—is also crucial in responding to a second, straightforward, version of the 'too liberal' objection. As (J) stands, it seems quite possible that an obviously morally objectionable faith-venture—say to the existence of the gods of Nazi religion—might fit its conditions. Such cases may be excluded, however, by augmenting (J) (now (J+)) with the requirement that both the content and the motivational character of a permissible faith-venture should cohere with correct morality. To assure themselves as best they can of the moral probity of their ventures in faith, reflective believers will therefore need to integrate those commitments with their best theories of how the world both is and morally ought to be—and I will follow Kierkegaard's example in using a reflection on Abraham, as forebear in faith, to illustrate how theistic faith-ventures develop in tandem with evolving moral commitments.

Finally, I will turn to consider what arguments may be advanced in favour of the modest, moral coherentist, supra-evidential version of fideism developed in Chapters 5 to 7. Some standard objections to fideism will, I hope, have been successfully set aside in the process of arriving at thesis (J+). But can this version of fideism be vindicated against a moral evidentialism which, though not absolutist, does take a hard line in its determination to exclude religious faith-ventures? In Chapter 8, I shall try to answer this question. As already noted, a full vindication of supra-evidential fideism would require showing that faith-ventures conforming to (J+)'s conditions carry *epistemic* as well as moral entitlement. That does not follow, however, *merely* from the special features incorporated in (J+): the importance, unavoidability, and essential evidential undecidability of an option presented to a person by a faith-proposition *does not simply entail* the epistemic permissibility of resolving it through passional motivation. But that conclusion might be thought to follow with further argument—and I shall consider three broad strategies for producing such further argument.

The first is an 'assimilation to personal relations cases' strategy. A widely acknowledged counter-example to absolutist moral evidentialism is the obvious moral permissibility of taking another person to be trustworthy beyond one's initial evidence: perhaps the permissibility of religious faith-ventures can be defended by assimilation to such cases? The analogy seems not to be close enough, however: evidence may subsequently emerge in the interpersonal case, whereas (on our assumption) it is persistently unavailable in the religious case. I shall note, however, that commitment to some forms of revisionary theism might be assimilable to cases where (as James puts it) 'faith in a fact can help create a fact', and (as James says) it would indeed be 'an insane logic' that refused to permit doxastic venture in such a case.[8]

A second strategy is to offer consequentialist justifications for faith-ventures. Apart from the usual general objections to moral consequentialism, this strategy faces the problem that it is ill-fitted to the defence of *supra-evidential* fideism, which resists the very overriding of epistemic considerations that will be involved in a consequentialist justification. Besides, any actual consequentialist defence of a particular faith-venture is likely to be question-begging—and I shall add a note to the effect that Pascal's Wager offers no real hope of overcoming this difficulty.

I shall pay most attention to a third, *tu quoque*, strategy, which seeks to defend fideism by showing that *everyone* unavoidably makes faith-ventures, *including evidentialists themselves*. This strategy looks promising, but it is difficult to make it work, since sensible evidentialists may concede fideist insights while maintaining a hard line specifically against religious and similar faith-ventures. Every sane person is committed beyond any *external* evidential support to the truth of the existence of an external world, other minds, and basic arithmetical propositions, for example; but such commitment is not optional in the way that religious and similar commitments are. Commitment *to evidentialism itself*, however, obviously is optional, and it is easy to suspect that it is passionally, rather than evidentially, motivated. Are there prospects, then, for decisively vindicating fideism on the grounds that hard-line evidentialism is self-undermining because its proponents must be making just the sort of faith-venture hard-line evidentialism prohibits?

Not obviously so. Even if commitment to hard-line evidentialism is passionally motivated, there is nothing *inconsistent*, I shall point out, in

[8] William James, *The Will to Believe and Other Essays in Popular Philosophy, and Human Immortality* (New York: Dover, 1956), 25.

holding that the only faith-venture permissible is the one which hard-line evidentialists themselves might need to make. That view may nevertheless seem unreasonable: surely our capacity for uncompelled doxastic venture could not be so singularly restricted in its proper exercise? Evidentialists might protest in reply, however, that they *do* recognize a wide enough scope for permissible doxastic venture. They concede its propriety in the interpersonal cases already discussed, for instance. They may concede also (if disinclined to be Kantians) that commitment to basic moral and other evaluative claims requires a venture beyond any possible evidential support. What they reject, they may argue, is venture beyond one's evidence in favour of religious and similar faith-propositions *that have factual content.*

This would be all very well if the venture that undergirds evidentialism did indeed consist in commitment to a purely evaluative claim—as it would if evidentialism did indeed rest on giving higher priority to the avoidance of irremediably erroneous commitments than to the chance of gaining commitment to evidentially inaccessible vital truths, as James himself in effect suggests. I shall argue, however, that such a preference cannot favour evidentialism over fideism *with respect to forced and in principle evidentially undecidable options*, since the risk of irremediable misalignment of one's commitments with the truth attaches to *both* ways of resolving such options.

I shall then suggest that evidentialism is in fact grounded in commitment to a key *factual* claim—namely, the claim that *passional doxastic inclinations cannot function as guides to truth even when the truth is essentially beyond evidential determination.* The truth of this key claim might seem self-evident (given that a 'passional' doxastic inclination is, by definition, not motivated by anything that could count as evidence for the truth of the belief concerned). I will argue, however, that its self-evidence may be parried by appeal to epistemological externalism; and its truth challenged by showing how, paradoxical though it may seem, aspects of epistemic rationality are involved in the making of passionally motivated faith-ventures in accordance with thesis (J+)'s constraints. I will also argue that any attempt to establish the truth of the evidentialist's key claim by appeal to scientific explanations of how religious passional doxastic inclinations can arise even though they are systematically false will beg the question; and I shall conclude that evidentialists' confidence in their key claim ultimately rests on a passionally motivated doxastic venture in favour of a purely naturalist view of the world.

On the other hand, however, once evidentialists admit that their prohibition of faith-ventures on foundational matters of fact must allow as a sole exception the doxastic venture they themselves need to make, fideists will hardly be able to accuse them of epistemic irresponsibility. For, the evidentialist's sole faith-venture would seem to meet (J+)'s first two conditions and thus, by fideists' own lights, carry epistemic entitlement. I will therefore conclude that the debate arrives at the following impasse: neither the evidentialist nor the fideist can decisively and non-question-beggingly establish the epistemic irresponsibility of commitment to the opposing position.

It may thus seem that the whole evidentialist/fideist debate must end in impasse, and, in Chapter 9—my final chapter—I shall begin by arguing that, even if this is the case, significant support has nevertheless been provided for the supra-evidential, moral coherentist, version of fideism expressed in thesis (J+). In the first place, fideism of this stripe has been defended successfully against objections: it gives no licence to self-induced direct or indirect 'willings to believe', making it clear that the venture of faith consists in choosing to take to be true in practical reasoning what one is *already* passionally inclined to hold to be true. Furthermore, (J+) places tight constraints on allowable faith-ventures: in particular, it permits no 'ethical suspension of the epistemic', excluding believing by faith *contrary to* one's evidence. It also requires permissible faith-ventures to be, both in content and motivational character, integrated with moral commitments. So this version of fideism can respond to the 'irregularly conjugated verb' problem posed at the outset, since it recognizes objective differences between good and bad faith-ventures. And it is—more than incidentally—an interesting question what verdict (J+) must pass, in particular, on classical theistic faith-commitments under evidential ambiguity. Arguably, taking the problem of evil into account, the version of fideism here defended *excludes* faith in the classical theist's omniGod, but leaves open the possibility of morally justifiable theistic faith-ventures under some alternative conception of the divine. It would be a further project to support that conclusion, however.

My rehabilitation of fideism amounts to more, however, than the articulation of a version of it that escapes the usual objections. For, as I shall argue next, if the debate does end in impasse, that suffices to secure the right to believe for those who make faith-ventures in accordance with (J+)—on the assumption, anyway, that either side of an essentially irresolvable moral disagreement ought to tolerate the opposing position. Such a broadly political solution will not be fully satisfying, however, for reflective faith-believers who seek reassurance that their commitments are morally right, not simply deserving of toleration.

I shall therefore conclude by indicating the only path available for moving beyond the impasse. Neither side of the fideist/evidentialist debate can show that the opposing side has an epistemically irresponsible position (i.e. one that issues from the improper exercise of epistemic capacities, or from an abandonment of proper epistemic concern). Perhaps, however, one of the opposed positions can be shown to be preferable directly *on moral grounds*. In considering this possibility, I shall do no more than canvas some moral considerations that appear to favour the fideist side—including the suggestion that evidentialists lack self-acceptance and that they are too dogmatically attached to a naturalist world-view (even to the extent of failing thereby in love towards others). I will also suggest that an evidentialist prohibition on those religious faith-ventures whose content affirms that the world is a moral order in which the pursuit of the good is not ultimately pointless will sit uncomfortably with any acknowledgment that basic moral truth-claims can themselves be accepted only through passionately motivated doxastic venture. Though these considerations do not give decisive independent moral grounds for preferring fideism to evidentialism, they do show that preference to be, not merely undefeated by evidentialist argument, but deserving of positive endorsement.

## Glossary of special terms

It will be clear from the preceding overview that I have found it necessary in the course of my argument to introduce some special terminology, and to use some existing terms in my own technical senses. So I will complete this introductory chapter by providing a short alphabetical glossary of terms. This glossary is not intended as a comprehensive guide to all philosophical terms used: rather, it picks out just those used in a special, or, it might be said, idiosyncratic, way. The glossary is given here mainly for reference, though it might also serve an introductory purpose in forewarning readers as to terminology that could otherwise be confusing. The reader may, however, pass over it without loss, since I do endeavour to explicate as fully as I can each item of specialist terminology in its proper context. My definitions are, of course, intended only as *locally* canonical: whether any of them might be more broadly useful is something readers may judge for themselves.

### absolutist moral evidentialism

Absolutist moral evidentialism is the thesis that, without exception, people are morally entitled to take beliefs to be true in their practical reasoning only if they are *evidentially justified* in holding those beliefs.

### agency-focused epistemic evaluations/propositional-attitude-focused epistemic evaluations

Agency-focused epistemic evaluations are epistemic evaluations of agents' (mental) actions in taking propositions to be true (with some given weight) in their reasoning; propositional-attitude-focused epistemic evaluations are epistemic evaluations of psychological states that consist in attitudes towards propositions (principally, states of belief).

### basically evident

See inferentially evident/non-inferentially (basically) evident.

### counter-evidential venture

A counter-evidential venture is a venture in practical commitment to a proposition's truth contrary to one's evidence. That is, people make a counter-evidential venture with respect to proposition p if and only if they make a *doxastic* or *sub-doxastic venture* with respect to p, while recognizing that p's falsehood is adequately supported by their total available evidence.

### counter-evidential fideism

Counter-evidential fideism is the thesis that *counter-evidential ventures* are sometimes morally permissible.

### doxastic framework

A doxastic framework is a framework of beliefs dependent on the acceptance of certain *framing principles*, in the sense that the evidential justifiability of any belief in the framework depends on accepting the truth of those principles. (For example, no specifically Christian theological belief could be regarded as evidentially justified except within the scope of the framing principle that God exists and is revealed in Jesus the Christ.) A doxastic framework has associated with it a specific *doxastic practice*.

*doxastic practice*
A doxastic practice is a complex of both habituated and voluntary behaviour relating to the formation, revision, and evaluation of beliefs within a given *doxastic framework*, including the assessment of the epistemic merit of beliefs in the light of evidence in accordance with an associated *evidential practice*.

*doxastic venture*
People make a doxastic venture if and only if they take to be true in their practical reasoning a proposition, p, that they believe to be true, while recognizing that it is not the case that p's truth is adequately supported by their total available evidence.
   See also *sub-doxastic venture*.

*epistemic entitlement*
People take proposition p to be true in their practical reasoning with epistemic entitlement if and only if they take p to be true through the right exercise of their epistemic capacities. (People take propositions to be true in their practical reasoning through the right exercise of their epistemic capacities if and only if they do so (i) having paid proper attention to the question of the truth of those propositions, (ii) having judged that issue properly (in accordance with the correct application of the objective norms applicable to such judgements), and (iii) having taken proper account of that judgement in committing themselves practically to the truth of those propositions.)

*epistemic evidentialism*
Epistemic evidentialism is the thesis that people take p to be true in their practical reasoning with *epistemic entitlement* if and only if they are *evidentially justified* in holding p to be true.

*ethics of faith-commitment*
An ethics of faith-commitment is an account of the conditions under which it is morally permissible to make a *faith-commitment*.

*evidential ambiguity*
The truth of a proposition, p, is evidentially ambiguous if and only if the total relevant evidence neither shows p's truth nor p's falsehood to be significantly more probable than not, where the total evidence is, furthermore, systematically open to viable overall interpretation, both on the assumption that p is true and on the assumption that p is false.

## evidential justification

People hold the belief that p with evidential justification (= are evidentially justified in holding that p) if and only if they hold p to be true on the basis of adequate evidential support for p's truth.

## evidential practice

An evidential practice is a practice that accepts certain norms for judging the degree of evidential support enjoyed by a given proposition.

A given evidential practice will (implicitly) specify *inter alia* logical norms governing the inferential transfer of evidential support, and norms specifying categories of propositions whose truth may be taken (under canonical conditions) to be non-inferentially or basically evident.

## evidential undecidability

The question of the truth of a proposition p is *evidentially undecidable* if and only if that question cannot be settled *purely* by judging correctly either that p's truth or that p's falsity is significantly more probable than not given the total available evidence. (This is a way of making more precise the vague notion of a question whose truth 'cannot be decided on the evidence'.)

## evidentialism

Evidentialism is the thesis that people are entitled to take beliefs to be true in their practical reasoning only if they are *evidentially justified* in holding those beliefs. (See also *epistemic evidentialism, moral evidentialism, hard-line evidentialism.*)

## faith-belief

A belief is a faith-belief just in case it is held in, and has the right kind of relation to, some particular context, in the same way that beliefs that make up the cognitive component of Christian theistic faith are held in and related to the context of Christian faith.

*Note:* this specifies the intended sense of 'faith-belief', but—evidently— does not provide a real definition of it. In the course of my argument three further features of faith-beliefs emerge, each of which would need to be included in a real definition.(I do not, however, purport to provide a full real definition.) First, a belief will count as a faith-belief only if that belief is existentially significant, in the sense that practical commitment to its truth has an important pervasive influence on the way people who make that commitment live their lives. Second, a belief will count as a faith-belief only if practical commitment to it is genuinely a matter of choice. Third, a belief that p will count as a faith-belief only if the *faith-proposition* that p is either a *highest-order framing principle* of a *doxastic framework* of faith-beliefs (in which case we may call it a foundational faith-proposition), or a proposition whose truth presupposes the truth of some relevant highest-order framing principle (in which case we may call it a derivative faith-proposition).

### faith-commitment
For a person to make a faith-commitment is for that person to take a *faith-proposition* to be true in his or her practical reasoning.

### faith-proposition
A faith-proposition is any proposition that is the content (or, intentional object) of a *faith-belief*.

### faith-venture
A faith-venture is a *doxastic* or *sub-doxastic venture* with respect to a *faith-proposition*.

### fideism
Fideism is the thesis that *faith-ventures* are sometimes morally permissible.

### framing principles
The framing principles of a *doxastic framework* are those propositions whose truth must be presupposed if any of the beliefs belonging to the framework are to be *evidentially justified*. (For example, the proposition that God exists and is revealed in Jesus the Christ is a framing principle of any specifically Christian theological doxastic framework, since no belief belonging to that framework could be evidentially justified unless that proposition is true.)

### full weight
See *taking a proposition to be true in one's practical reasoning with full weight*.

### hard-line evidentialism
Hard-line evidentialism is the thesis that people are morally entitled to take *faith-propositions* to be true in their practical reasoning only if they are *evidentially justified* in holding those beliefs.

   *Note:* Hard-line evidentialism is not as hard line as *moral evidentialism* could be, for it recognizes that it may sometimes be morally permissible (even obligatory) to make *supra-evidential* (or even *counter-evidential*) *ventures*. It is not, in other words, *absolutist moral evidentialism*. But it is 'hard line' because it does altogether reject all *faith-ventures* as morally impermissible—i.e. all ventures in favour of religious (or quasi-religious) *faith-propositions*.

### highest-order framing principle

A highest-order framing principle is a *framing principle* whose truth cannot be *evidentially justified* within any wider *doxastic framework* (on the basis of any higher-order framing principle).

### holding/taking a proposition to be true

For a person to **hold** a proposition, p, to be true is for that person to be in a psychological state that counts as a belief that p—i.e. a psychological state that consists in having the propositional attitude towards p that it is true; for a person to **take** a proposition to be true is for that person to take it to be true in his or her reasoning—i.e. to employ it as a true premise in reasoning.

### inferentially evident/non-inferentially (basically) evident

A proposition's truth is inferentially evident when its truth is correctly inferable (in accordance with the norms of the applicable *evidential practice*) from other propositions whose truth is accepted; a proposition's truth is non-inferentially (basically) evident, when it truth is acceptable (under the norms of the applicable evidential practice) without being derived by inference from other evidentially established truths.

### integrationist

Integrationists generally value connecting things so that they can influence each other rather than separating them into isolated spheres or compartments. Those who accept integrationist doxastic values accept the ideal of overall coherence amongst their beliefs, and will therefore reject the view that *doxastic frameworks* can be epistemically insulated from a person's overall network of beliefs.

### isolationist epistemology of religious beliefs

An isolationist epistemology of religious beliefs takes religious *doxastic frameworks* to be epistemically isolated in the sense that belief in the truth of their *framing principles* is necessarily not epistemically assessable in the light of evidence from outside the relevant framework.

### moral coherentist fideism

Moral coherentist fideism is the thesis that *faith-ventures* are morally permissible only if they are properly integrated with (correct) moral commitments.

### moral evidentialism

Moral evidentialism is the thesis that people are morally entitled to take beliefs to be true in their practical reasoning only if they are *evidentially justified* in holding those beliefs.

*Note:* Moral evidentialism may be factored into the *moral-epistemic link principle* and *epistemic evidentialism*.

### moral-epistemic link principle

People are morally entitled to take their beliefs to be true only if they are *epistemically entitled* to do so.

### naturalism

The metaphysical thesis that the world is just as depicted according to our best—or, perhaps rather, our ideally completed—scientific theories.

### non-evidential causes of beliefs

See *passional causes of beliefs*.

### non-inferentially evident

See *basically evident*.

### passional causes of beliefs

A passional cause of a belief is any cause of that belief other than a cause that provides the believer with evidence for its truth.

*Note:* This usage is derived from William James. To avoid confusion, I often describe passional causes of beliefs as 'non-evidential' causes. I also sometimes refer to potential passional causes of beliefs as 'passional doxastic inclinations'.

### rational empiricist evidential practice

Rational empiricist evidential practice is the evidential practice that assumes deductive and inductive standards for inferential evidential support, and allows as basically evident only incorrigible and self-evident truths (including fundamental logical and mathematical truths) and truths evident in sensory perceptual experience under 'normal' conditions (i.e. in the absence of recognized overriders such as conditions known to create sensory illusions, etc.).

### sub-doxastic venture

People make a sub-doxastic venture with respect to the proposition p if and only if they take p to be true in their practical reasoning, while recognizing that it is not the case that p's truth is adequately supported by their total available evidence, yet without believing that p—i.e. without actually holding that p is true.

### supra-evidential venture

A supra-evidential venture is a venture in practical commitment to a proposition's truth beyond, but not contrary to, one's evidence. That is, people make a supra-evidential venture with respect to proposition p if and only they make a *doxastic* or *sub-doxastic venture* with respect to p, while recognizing that neither p's truth nor p's falsehood is adequately supported by their total available evidence. (One may also say that a supra-evidential venture is a doxastic or sub-doxastic venture that is not a counter-evidential venture.)

### supra-evidential fideism

Supra-evidential fideism is the thesis that *supra-evidential ventures* are sometimes morally permissible.

### taking a proposition to be true in one's practical reasoning with full weight

People take the proposition p to be true in their practical reasoning with full weight if and only if they take p to be true, not with some intermediate degree of partial belief, but with the kind of weight that naturally goes along with straightforwardly believing that it is true that p.

# 2

# The 'justifiability' of faith-beliefs: an ultimately moral issue

Reflective believers are concerned about the justifiability of their faith-beliefs. But what notion of justifiability is here involved? When, for example, people reject traditional Christian beliefs as 'unjustifiable', yet hope to retain a revised core of Christian belief to which they may be 'justifiably' committed, what notion or notions of justifiability matter to them? And how does such concern arise? Is this a kind of concern that people *ought* to have about their various religious (and similar) faith-beliefs, and, if so, why?

## A standard view: the concern is for epistemic justifiability

I begin with a standard answer to the metaquestions just raised: I will then explain how I believe this standard answer needs to be reassessed.

This standard answer is that concern for the justifiability of faith-beliefs is the concern to hold faith-beliefs that are *epistemically* justifiable in the sense that *it is reasonable to hold them true on the basis of one's evidence of or for their truth*. According to this standard answer, the issue of the justifiability of *faith*-beliefs is just a special case of the general issue of epistemic justifiability that arises with respect to any belief. And what is that general issue of epistemic justifiability? It is the question whether beliefs have *the kind of justification* necessary for them to count as *knowledge* of the truth.[1]

---

[1] Hence the term 'epistemic': Greek *episteme* = knowledge.

Why, though, should we care in general about the epistemic justifiability of our beliefs? Because, the standard answer maintains, our beliefs influence how we act. Since we are generally more likely to succeed in fulfilling our intentions if our beliefs are true, we should be concerned to hold our beliefs with epistemic justification—that is, with the kind of justification relevant to their *worthiness to be taken to be true* when we reason towards further beliefs or towards action.[2] Not all justification is *that* kind of justification, of course. Some beliefs might count as justified in the sense that holding and acting on them serves the believer's interests, or in the sense that holding and acting on them has, or is likely to have, generally good consequences. Other beliefs might be described as justified because they conform to prevailing attitudes in a given cultural, professional, or academic context. Being justified in any of these senses gives no indication, except quite accidentally, as to the truth of these beliefs; justification in any of these senses, then, contrasts with *epistemic* justification.

What it is, precisely, for a belief to be epistemically justified (or, held with epistemic justification) is, of course, controversial. The standard answer just given takes epistemic justification to be a matter of evidential support (a notion usually labelled *internalist*, because it makes a belief's justification depend on something internal to the believer—namely, the evidence cognitively accessible to him or her and consisting in his or her relevant experiences and other beliefs).[3] This internalist notion obviously stands in need of an account of what it is for a belief to have evidential support sufficient for epistemic justification—and there is much scope

---

[2] 'Worthiness to be taken to be true', that is, relative to the canonical context in which all that matters is that the propositions we take to be true should in fact be true. There may arguably be situations where concern for the truth of the propositions on which one acts is morally overridden (e.g. when it is more important to act out of loyalty than to act on what one holds to be the truth—in such a situation an epistemically unjustified belief may be worthy of being taken to be true). I shall have more to say later about circumstances in which moral considerations may override epistemic concern (Chapters 6 and 8).

Note that, despite the obvious conceptual connexion between epistemic justification and knowledge, understanding a belief's epistemic justification as the extent to which it deserves (in the canonical context) to be taken to be true in reasoning enables discussion of the nature of epistemic justification without any need to try to define knowledge itself.

[3] Cf. Alvin Plantinga, 'The basic internalist idea ... is that what determines whether a belief is warranted for a person are factors or states in some sense internal to that person ... ' (*Warrant: The Current Debate* (New York: Oxford University Press, 1993), 5); and Earl Conee and Richard Feldman, 'In our view the primary strength of internalism consists in the merits of a specific internalist theory, evidentialism, which holds that epistemic justification is entirely a matter of internal evidential factors.' ('Internalism Defended', in Earl Conee and Richard Feldman (eds), *Evidentialism: Essays in Epistemology* (Oxford: Clarendon Press, 2004: 53)).

for controversy on that matter.[4] Some epistemologists, however, advocate an *externalist* account that 'locates some important feature of a belief's justification outside the mind of the one whose belief is justified'. On a reliabilist view, for example, epistemic justification attaches to beliefs produced by a mechanism that is a reliable producer of true beliefs.[5] And the key epistemic notion in Alvin Plantinga's Reformed epistemology is the externalist notion of a belief's 'warrant', defined (roughly) as a matter of its resulting from properly functioning cognitive faculties that have a 'design plan' 'successfully aimed at truth'.[6] I shall not pause here to elaborate upon (let alone try to settle) these controversies in epistemology, since the issues involved may become clearer after I have succeeded—as I hope I shall—in reassessing the just stated standard view of what it is to be concerned about the justifiability of one's faith-beliefs.

## The problem of doxastic control

The reassessment I hope to achieve results from considering an obvious question that arises once we accept that we should be concerned about the justifiability of our faith-beliefs—whatever account we may ultimately come to give of that justifiability. Such a concern has point only on the assumption that one *ought to* hold faith-beliefs *only if* those beliefs are justified. But if we ought to hold beliefs only when they are justified then surely it must be true that we have a capacity to control our beliefs so as at least to try to meet that requirement? The question thus

---

[4] For example, foundationalists hold that the truth of some beliefs is non-inferentially evident (i.e. that it need not have its evidence inferred from the truth of other epistemically justified beliefs), whereas coherentists maintain that all evidential relations are inferential, so that evidential support for the truth of any particular belief is always a matter of its coherence with that of other beliefs. Amongst foundationalists there is controversy over what categories of belief count as non-inferentially evident. And, then, of course, there is room for much debate over what the norms are that govern relations of evidential support, what counts as 'adequate' evidential support, etc.

[5] The cited definition of externalism is from Earl Conee, 'The Basic Nature of Epistemic Justification', in Conee and Feldman (eds), *Evidentialism*, 46. For a defence of reliabilism, I follow Conee in referring the reader to Alvin Goldman, 'What Is Justified Belief?' in George Sotiros Pappas (ed.), *Justification and Knowledge: New Studies in Epistemology* (Dordrecht, Holland: D. Reidel, 1979), 1–23; reprinted in Jack S. Crumley (ed.), *Readings in Epistemology* (Mountain View, CA: Mayfield, 1999), 364–77.

[6] For the full definition of Plantinga's notion of warrant, see *Warranted Christian Belief*, 156. For useful discussions see Jonathan L. Kvanvig, *Warrant in Contemporary Epistemology: Essays in Honor of Plantinga's Theory of Knowledge* (Lanham, MD: Rowman & Littlefield Publishers, 1996). I will discuss Reformed epistemology in Chapter 4.

arises whether we do indeed have such a capacity.[7] Concern for the justifiability of our faith-beliefs appears to rest on the assumption that we have doxastic responsibilities: but do we have the doxastic control that those responsibilities would presuppose?

The question of what control we may exercise with respect to our beliefs and believing has been widely debated. I shall not here attempt any thoroughgoing review of that debate. Nevertheless, I do maintain that to understand reflective believers' concern for the justifiability of their faith-beliefs, we must recognize the importance of *our having direct control over what we take to be true in our reasoning, especially our practical reasoning.* This kind of control is—or at least encompasses—a kind of control aptly described as 'doxastic', that is, as a form of control with respect to our beliefs. As this claim is pivotal to the account of believing by faith I will be proposing, I do need now to say enough about the question of doxastic control generally to articulate this pivotal claim clearly and provide it with argumentative support.

## The impossibility of believing at will

Beliefs are a species of psychological state generically known as 'propositional attitudes' because they consist in a person's having a certain attitude to a proposition. The type of attitude characteristic of belief is, of course, the attitude *that the proposition is true.* We do not have an expression in ordinary English which means, stably and solely, that because a person has the attitude towards a given proposition, it is true. Notoriously, 'believes' in ordinary language does *not* have just this meaning, often carrying connotations of a lack of knowledge or certainty about the truth of the proposition concerned. To get at the more neutral meaning intended we may say that the person 'regards' the proposition as true, 'finds' it to be true, 'considers' it true, perhaps—or (my own preference) that he or she *holds* the proposition

---

[7] This question could be avoided by denying that 'ought' implies 'can' in the case of doxastic obligations. Since I believe that we *can* provide an account of doxastic control that meets what is plausibly required to ground doxastic responsibilities, I shall proceed on the plausible assumption that such a ground is indeed required. I shall return (see n. 27 below) to consider Richard Feldman's claim that deontological epistemic judgements can be true even if we lack control over our beliefs. See his 'The Ethics of Belief', in Conee and Feldman (eds), *Evidentialism*, 166–95.

true. Each of these expressions, however, carries additional connotations of its own—different connotations in different contexts, furthermore. I shall nevertheless take the last expression mentioned as canonical: to believe that p is, I shall say, to *hold* that the proposition p is true, where 'M holds p true' is technically to be understood as conveying no more and no less than that person M has the attitude towards proposition p that p is true. Belief is thus, I shall say, a state of *holding true*.

Beliefs understood as 'holdings-true' are *responsive* attitudes, and, as such, are neither formed nor revised under the direct control of the will. One cannot simply 'decide' to believe; one cannot form any particular belief just 'at will'. Whether this is a conceptual or merely psychological impossibility may perhaps be disputed. For myself, I accept Bernard Williams's explanation of it as a conceptual impossibility.[8] The nub of his argument comes, I think, to this: to want to believe is to want to believe *what is true*; yet, if we did (*per impossibile*) have the capacity to believe directly at will, we would realize that exercising that capacity would yield the desired belief *whether it was true or not*, thereby frustrating our desire. The desire to believe that p—which would be needed to motivate a putative act of directly forming the belief that p—is, in other words, essentially a desire *to be somehow acted upon or affected* so that one comes to *find it true* that p. It is therefore a desire unable to be satisfied by any *direct* action on the part of the desirer. (One might perhaps compare the desire to be tickled, though the analogy is not exact. Wanting to be tickled is essentially wanting to be *made to react to* bodily touch in the characteristic way—and something about our psychology ensures that it has to be someone else's touch. Similarly, wanting to believe that p is essentially wanting to be *made to hold* that p is true—and, in this case, it is a feature of the very nature of belief that ensures that something other than our own will is required to bring this about.)

## Indirect control over beliefs

The impossibility of direct believing at will does not, however, rule out the possibility of doxastic control altogether, nor the doxastic responsibilities

---

[8] Bernard Williams, 'Deciding to Believe', in id., *Problems of the Self: Philosophical Papers 1956–1972* (Cambridge: Cambridge University Press, 1973), 148.

that presuppose it. For we do have some *indirect* control over the formation, retention, and revision of our beliefs. What we believe depends on the functioning of our cognitive capacities, and *some* aspects of their exercise are under direct voluntary control. We have some indirect control, for example, over our perceptual beliefs (we can stop our ears, look away, fail to pay attention, and so on). More generally, we have considerable control over the processes of inquiry that influence our beliefs; for example, we may control the extent to which we seek out and pay attention to relevant evidence and argument.[9] An agent may thus *intentionally* form a belief on a particular question (say, the current state of the weather) by exercising direct voluntary control (looking out the window)—though her action will be intentional only under the description 'forming a belief on the current weather', and not under the description 'forming the belief that it is raining' (as the case may be).

We do, then, possess indirect control over what faith-beliefs we hold, and this is enough to show that it is coherent to claim that we ought to care about their justifiability. So—to return now to the standard view that takes justifiability to be epistemic, and epistemic justification to be a matter of evidential support—it may be maintained that our doxastic responsibility is to use our indirect capacities over what faith-beliefs we hold in order to ensure, so far as we may, that those beliefs are held with proper evidential support. According to this standard view, then, our responsibilities on questions of faith amount just to an application of our doxastic responsibilities generally: we should, that is, seek out, attend to, and assess relevant evidence in such a way that the faith-beliefs we thereby form have the kind of evidential support that confers epistemic justification. In exercising our doxastic responsibilities, we need to respect the virtues and norms of critical rational inquiry that govern attempts to settle the truth on the basis of argument and evidence—and it is, of course, a major project to determine exactly what these norms and virtues are. The standard view assumes, however, that we do, as rational beings, have an implicit practical

[9] This indirect control over belief formation is widely recognized. See, for example, Lorraine Code, *Epistemic Responsibility* (Hanover, NH: University Press of New England, 1987), 85; Plantinga, *Warrant: The Current Debate*, 24; and Paul Helm, who writes 'Although Hume was firmly of the view that beliefs are not subject to the will, he could hardly have said, 'the wise man proportions his belief to the evidence' unless he also held that there is also a sense in which they are; and, like Hume, I think that while single beliefs about straightforward matters of fact are not subject to the will, belief policies are' (*Faith with Reason* (Oxford: Oxford University Press, 2000), 93).

grasp of these norms—sound enough to ensure that, by and large, if we exercise it properly, we will not form beliefs, faith-beliefs included, unless they possess the epistemic justification that comes from adequate evidential support.

We do enjoy direct control, then, over actions which may significantly affect what beliefs we form, retain, or revise: through our exercise of this direct control we may then be indirectly responsible for what beliefs we hold. We have here, then, a *locus of doxastic control*, albeit indirect. We are able to exercise control at this locus in ways which seek to respect the rational norms and virtues of good inquiry. But we are also sometimes able to exercise this control in ways that neglect these norms. Indeed, we may sometimes, if we choose, deliberately defy such norms altogether—in an attempt, for example, to produce in ourselves particular beliefs which we desire to have (because they are comforting or empowering, for example). Such attempts may sometimes succeed. We are sometimes in a position to adopt means—necessarily independent of the proper exercise of our epistemic rationality—for getting ourselves to hold a desired belief. For example, we may induce a desired belief by having ourselves hypnotized, by taking psychotropic drugs, or by behavioural conditioning through regularly acting *as if* we held the belief concerned.[10] (Note that the psychological feasibility of such projects may depend on special conditions—e.g. conditions that allow self-deception about how the desired belief, once acquired, actually came about.) So, though we cannot directly believe that p at will, we may sometimes be able indirectly to bring it about that we believe that p. (Compare: I cannot tickle myself, but I can get myself tickled.) However, to the extent that it matters to us to be epistemically justified in our belief on a given question, we will accept that we should act with the intention to come to believe what is true on that question by respecting the norms of critical rational inquiry.

---

[10] Richard Feldman has observed that one may sometimes be able intentionally to acquire a particular belief by bringing about a given state of the world—namely, just when that state is reliably tracked by one's beliefs. For example, I can intentionally make myself believe that the light is on by switching it on. (See Feldman, 'The Ethics of Belief', 171) This kind of indirect control over beliefs is not, of course, 'independent of the proper exercise of our epistemic rationality'. The types of indirect control I have mentioned, however, are so independent, and they are the kinds of indirect control we will need to exercise in order to fulfil any desire to believe that p, where it is not under our control whether p obtains.

On this standard view, then, concern for the justifiability of theistic faith-beliefs is a concern that they be held with epistemic justification. To meet this concern, one should subject theistic beliefs to critical rational inquiry with a view to ensuring that they will be retained only to the extent that their truth is supported by the evidence and arguments thereby uncovered. The standard view thus yields a familiar understanding of the central task of Philosophy of Religion: namely to arrive at a systematic rational assessment of the evidence for and against core theistic belief (God's existence), and so reach a verdict on the question whether theistic belief can be epistemically justifiable.

## 'Holding true' and 'taking to be true'

It is necessary, I believe, to move beyond the view that the reflective believer's justifiability question has to do just with the *epistemic* justifiability of theistic belief (and therefore beyond the familiar view of the core task of Philosophy of Religion). As I shall now seek to show, the justifiability question as it applies to faith-beliefs is ultimately a question about *moral* justifiability, and, in particular, a question about the moral justifiability of *taking those beliefs to be true in one's practical reasoning*.

To develop my argument for this claim, I begin by considering the standard answer already sketched above to the question *why* we ought to care about the epistemic justifiability of our faith-beliefs. According to that answer, we should care about their epistemic justifiability because we should intend, in *all* our believing, to grasp truth and avoid error. And why should we have that general intention? Because of the *practical* consequences of our beliefs. Belief is the state of *holding* a proposition true. It is also a disposition—a disposition towards suitably 'matching' behaviour, to be sure, but also, more proximately, a disposition towards *taking the proposition believed to be true in one's reasoning* — both in one's theoretical reasoning and in one's practical reasoning from desires and intentions to action. Now, we are (much) more likely to achieve our intentions in general if the beliefs on which we rely in our practical reasoning are true. So, given our obvious general interest in practical success, we generally have good reason to try to ensure that the beliefs we take to be true in practical reasoning are indeed true beliefs. And that grounds the imperative to ensure, so far as we may, that our beliefs are epistemically justified.

Believing does, then, typically involve both *holding true* and *taking to be true in reasoning*, whether theoretical or practical.[11] For example: Mary believes her pet tortoise is liable to roam, so, while she shows it off to her guests during tea on the lawn, she keeps a wary eye on it so as to avoid lengthy searching in the undergrowth at the bottom of the garden. ('You would think you could put a tortoise down, forget about it, and expect it to be in the near vicinity ten minutes later. You would be wrong.') Here Mary holds true the proposition that her tortoise can hide itself surprisingly quickly, and—now that she has set her tortoise at large—this belief becomes salient given her intention not to lose it. Through an effortless piece of practical reasoning in which, *inter alia*, she *takes* this proposition about the tortoise to be true there results Mary's action in keeping a close eye on it.

In developing the version of fideism I seek to defend, I want to make much of the—obvious enough—distinction just illustrated between holding a proposition true and taking it to be true in reasoning. This distinction has not, I think, received the recognition it deserves.[12] Holding

[11] The term 'taking to be true' might, of course, be used in a range of different senses: I note, for example, its use in explaining Locke's distinction between knowledge as awareness of some fact, and belief (assent, judgement) as 'taking some proposition to be true' even though one lacks such awareness. See Nicholas Wolterstorff, *John Locke and the Ethics of Belief* (Cambridge: Cambridge University Press, 1996), 13 and 46. What Wolterstorff calls 'taking some propositions to be true' counts on my terminology as 'holding true'—at least until the proposition concerned is employed as a premis in reasoning. As already emphasized with respect to 'holding true', I am here introducing my own technical terminology—in the hope, however, that it will prove apt for the important distinction that needs to be marked.

[12] An important exception is Jonathan Cohen, who draws a distinction between 'belief' and 'acceptance'. 'To accept that *p*,' Cohen says, 'is to have or adopt a policy of deeming, positing, or postulating that *p*—i.e. of including that proposition ... among one's premisses for deciding what to do or think in a particular context, whether or not one feels it to be true that *p*' (L. Jonathan Cohen, *An Essay on Belief and Acceptance* (Oxford: Clarendon Press, 1992), 4). Accepting that p, for Cohen, is thus (in my terms) being disposed (or coming to be disposed) to take the proposition that p to be true in one's reasoning. In his, 'Belief, Acceptance and Religious Faith', in Jeff Jordan and Daniel Howard-Snyder (eds), *Faith, Freedom and Rationality: Philosophy of Religion Today* (Lanham, MD: Rowman & Littlefield, 1996) 3–28, William Alston takes up the belief/acceptance distinction, and argues that 'attention to [it] will powerfully affect our understanding of the cognitive aspect of religious faith' (27). In particular, Alston argues, authentic Christian faith may require only acceptance of the core Christian credal claims, and not necessarily the belief that they are true (see 21–4). This claim is not as radical as it may seem, given that Alston (unlike Cohen) understands 'accepting that p [as involving] a more positive attitude toward that proposition than just making the assumption that p or hypothesizing that p' (11). Indeed, Alston says that 'to accept that p is to regard it as true' (11): Alston

a proposition true, in the sense defined, is a *state*—the belief-state a person is in when he or she has the attitude towards the relevant proposition *that it is true*. Taking a proposition to be true, on the other hand, is an *event* which occurs in reasoning. Holding true and taking to be true are connected (at least) thus: the belief-state of holding a proposition true is a disposition to take that proposition to be true, whenever salient, in one's reasoning. Both holdings-true and takings-to-be-true may be either conscious or unconscious. Conscious holding true involves the characteristic, responsive, 'cognitive feeling' that the proposition concerned is true. But one may, of course, hold many propositions to be true without any such conscious feeling. Conscious taking to be true occurs in deliberate, reflective reasoning—but a vast amount of taking propositions to be true in reasoning occurs without deliberation or conscious awareness.

## A second—direct—locus of doxastic control

Taking a proposition to be true in reasoning is always a mental *event*. I now wish to argue, furthermore, that it may also be a mental *action*, in which the agent exercises direct voluntary control. Accordingly, I shall maintain, it is necessary to revise any assumption that the source of our doxastic responsibilities is just our capacity for indirect control over what beliefs we hold. For, if takings-to-be-true can indeed be actions, in addition to this first locus of indirect control there is a *second* locus of *direct* control over how beliefs are *used* (rather than over how they are acquired, maintained, and revised). Granted this second locus of doxastic control, I shall argue that it follows that (for some kinds of beliefs anyway) the question of the *moral* justifiability of taking them to be true in practical reasoning can arise. In this way I will vindicate my claim that we need to shift away from supposing that reflective believers' concern for the justifiability of their faith-beliefs is exclusively an epistemic concern.

thus seems to think of acceptance as a species of holding true, differing from belief in so far as it lacks the cognitive feeling characteristic of belief, and (hence) being under direct voluntary control. I suspect (but will not here try to establish) that this notion of acceptance is confused, and that, though Alston is right to recognize the importance of the belief/acceptance distinction, his departure from Cohen's understanding of it is a mistake. My present concern, however, is just to emphasize the importance of the holding-true/taking-to-be-true-in-reasoning distinction, which clearly is presupposed by Cohen's belief/acceptance distinction.

An agent who holds that p is true is, as already noted, thereby disposed to take p to be true in salient practical reasoning. This need not, however, be a disposition to 'mere' behaviour: a person's having the belief that p does not simply entail that he or she will take p to be true in practical reasoning whenever p's truth is salient. Rather a person's having the belief that p is a disposition *to perform a certain kind of (mental) action over which that person may exercise direct voluntary control.* When agents act on their beliefs, they *use* the propositional contents of those beliefs in their practical reasoning. Furthermore, they give the propositions concerned *that degree of commitment or weight that fits their responsive attitude of holding them true.* (Evidently, these claims can be generalized to allow for 'partial beliefs' or 'credences' if we wish to admit them.[13] Under this generalization, the holding/taking to be true distinction is that between the degree to which the agent holds p's truth probable, and the weight the agent affords to p's truth in salient practical reasoning.) Thus, my claim is that when agents act on their beliefs (or partial beliefs) those agents may be more than just the arena in which the causal influence of their doxastic dispositions plays out along with that of their desires and intentions: agents may *control* their practical commitment to truth-claims, so that a proposition's being employed in a chain of practical reasoning may be something which agents themselves *bring about.* There can thus be, conceptually anyway, an irreducible element of what has come to be known as *agent-causation* involved in what agents take to be true, and with what degree of confidence, in their practical reasoning.[14]

---

[13] On the regimenting assumptions of Bayesian decision theory, degrees of *partial belief* (or, *credences*) are understood as a continuum of degrees of confidence that p is true (representable on the real interval $[0,1]$). What degree of confidence agents give to p's truth in their practical reasoning will then influence their action—and the decision-theoretic apparatus using the notion of expected utility is a way of making precise the operation of this influence. Neither decision theory nor the notion of partial belief is wholly unproblematic, however. For example, the notion of partial belief seems to displace the ordinary notion of belief, since there are obstacles to regarding believing it true that p as equivalent either to giving p credence 1, or to giving p a credence over some threshold near enough to 1. See Mark Kaplan, *Decision Theory as Philosophy* (Cambridge: Cambridge University Press, 1996), for discussion of these obstacles, and an attempt to respond to what he calls 'the Bayesian challenge' to replace talk of beliefs altogether with talk of degrees of belief.

[14] Agent-causation is a causal relation between an agent (as cause) and an event or state of affairs (as effect). If—as I am here suggesting—acting on a belief does involve a *conceptually* irreducible element of agent-causation, it need not follow that any *ontologically* irreducible agent-causal relation is involved. See my *Natural Agency: An Essay on the Causal Theory of Action* (Cambridge: Cambridge University Press, 1989), 96.

To support this claim, I maintain that we can make sense of cases in which a person holds that p but does *not* take p to be true in reasoning to which p's truth is nevertheless salient. Such cases show that people can have the capacity to do otherwise than take to be true in salient reasoning what they hold to be true—and this establishes that taking a proposition to be true in practical reasoning is (or, at least, sometimes can be) an action under the agent's control.

Here are three examples to illustrate this possibility. There is a kind of weakness of will that results in acting only tentatively on what is held intellectually to be clearly true on the evidence. I feel convinced that certain medical advice is correct, yet when it comes to putting it into practice I hedge my bets. The weight I afford the truth of the advice in my reasoning does not match the degree of confidence with which, intellectually, I hold it true. Or—an example where the failure to act on what is held true shows strength rather than weakness—I may come to suspect that certain beliefs of mine arise purely from prejudice and so refrain from taking them to be true in my practical reasoning, even though I cannot immediately shake myself free of the attitude of holding them true. For example: so strong is my father's influence that I cannot shed his inculcated belief that a man who wears suede shoes or keeps his loose change in a purse is not to be trusted, but I do not have to take this to be true when I come to act. Or—an example where my playing a specific procedural role is salient—as a juror I may follow the judge's instruction that certain evidence is inadmissible, and so studiedly refrain from taking to be true in my reasoning towards a verdict what I hold *in propria persona* to be clearly the case.

Admittedly, these cases are not typical. Takings-to-be-true are, as already noted, very often neither deliberate nor conscious. Furthermore, the triggering of the belief disposition (the holding-true that p) to yield a taking-to-be-true that p is usually quite automatic. But the fact that, for someone who holds that p, taking p to be true in salient reasoning is typically unconscious and automatic does not preclude its counting as an action in which the agent exercises his own control. Exercises of agent-control can be unconscious and automatic—not, of course, in the sense in which automatic means 'automa*ted*'; but rather, in the sense in which automatic means 'habituated'. Thus, cases such as my overriding my prejudice against suede-shoe wearers—where agents hold that p, but, through conscious reflection, do not take p to be true in their practical reasoning—are cases where the strongly habituated connexion between holding and taking to be true is intentionally broken and so revealed to be a locus of agent-control.[15]

To describe the connexion between holding and taking to be true as 'strongly habituated' might yet seem still to understate the matter. Arguably, belief could not have evolved to be what it is without a highly reliable dispositional relation between holding and taking a proposition to be true. Surely, then, our 'habit' of taking to be true in salient reasoning what we hold to be true is so entrenched that it *is* pretty well automated? Well, I think the kinds of examples I have adduced suffice to show that we can voluntarily go against the habituated flow from what we hold to what we take to be true—*at least in some important cases*. There are, of course, always significant psychological limits on the real possibility of our doing other than what we are habituated to do. And habits are sometimes so ingrained that there is no real possibility of going against them. Furthermore, with respect to some important categories of beliefs such as our perceptual beliefs, it is arguably altogether impossible in particular cases not to take to be true what we hold to be true: the regularity is so deeply habituated as to be 'hardwired'. (For example, it seems psychologically impossible to override one's current proprioceptive beliefs about the position of one's own limbs and body when one comes to carry out intentions to perform bodily movements.) But all that is important to my argument is that it be agreed that, *with some kinds of beliefs* (including, crucially, those beliefs I am classifying as faith-beliefs), voluntarily doing otherwise than taking them to be true in practical reasoning *is* a real psychological possibility—and, when it is, then the agent concerned meets the control condition for responsibility for the use of the contents of those beliefs in reasoning.

---

[15] If I intentionally take it to be true that p in my reasoning while still holding it true that not-p, then the question arises: with what intention do I do so? The answer is, I think, that I do so with some higher-order general intention—such as, for example, not to take to be true what I find I hold to be true only on the basis of what I judge to be mere prejudice. Appeal to standing general intentions of the sort characteristic of the properly functioning rational practical agent seems to be necessary in order to defend the status of certain kinds of mental events as mental actions under a standard causal theory of action. For further discussion, see my 'Naturalising Mental Action', in Ghita Holmström-Hintikka and Raimo Tuomela (eds), *Contemporary Action Theory, Volume 1*, Synthèse Library (Dordrecht: Kluwer Academic Publishers, 1997), 251–66. Problems with appeals to higher-order intentions have recently been discussed in David-Hillel Ruben, *Action and its Explanation* (Oxford: Clarendon Press, 2003), 150–4.

THE 'JUSTIFIABILITY' OF FAITH-BELIEFS    39

Someone might object to the examples I have used to illustrate this psychological possibility, however, by maintaining that a person who does not take p to be true in salient reasoning cannot 'really' believe that p. If I do practically commit myself to the truth of the proposition that this suede-shoe wearer is trustworthy, then surely (such an objector might maintain) I cannot at the same time continue to hold it true that all men who wear suede shoes are untrustworthy?

Now, there is, of course, a conceptual link between what one holds true and what one would sincerely avow on the question concerned. This objection may therefore stand only if the possibility is discounted that I might quite sincerely avow that (regrettably) I still find myself holding it true that only an unreliable cad would wear suede shoes, while resolutely *not* taking this to be true when I come to act. That possibility should not, I think, be discounted: it will be useful, however, to have recourse to a further line of argument to deal with a persistent objector who does insist on discounting it. I shall therefore bolster the conclusion that our taking our beliefs to be true in reasoning can be an exercise of direct, voluntary agent-control, by placing this capacity in the wider context to which it belongs.

It is clear that we possess a relatively unrestricted voluntary capacity to take propositions to be true in our practical reasoning. We are certainly sometimes able directly to take to be true in our practical reasoning propositions that we do not believe to be true: so practical commitment to p's truth cannot simply be equated with 'really' believing that p. We may be disposed to take a proposition to be true in our reasoning without that disposition counting as a case of holding it true.[16] We may, for example, treat a proposition as an assumption or working hypothesis—and we may then be disposed to take that proposition to be true in our reasoning without actually holding that it is true. Though some degree of partial belief in its truth may be needed for us to take it seriously as a hypothesis, when we act experimentally on it we may need to do so, at the outset anyway, with wholehearted commitment to its truth (otherwise, the hypothesis will not 'get a fair go'): the weight we afford its truth in our practical reasoning then exceeds the degree to which we 'feel' it to be true. (When

---

[16] Such a disposition will count, in Cohen's terminology, as *accepting*, rather than *believing*, the proposition's truth. (See his *An Essay on Belief and Acceptance*.)

we test our 'pet' hypotheses, of course, we antecedently give their truth high credence—but not all hypotheses are pet hypotheses.) Pretending to believe shows a similar profile—and here I have in mind not play-acting, but situations in which it is vital that others take one to hold true what one knows to be false (for example, to protect the fugitive I'm sheltering in my attic I must resolutely pretend to believe that he fled elsewhere when the police raid my house). But to pretend to believe that p successfully, agents must come to be disposed to act as if they genuinely believed that p. Thus, in the practical reasoning they carry out while pretending, they must consistently and confidently take p to be true, though, of course, they actually hold p false.[17]

Once we recognize our voluntary capacity to take propositions to be true in our practical reasoning without believing them, it is no great stretch to accept that we are able, at times, to block the habituated flow from holding a proposition true to taking it to be true in our reasoning. Within certain limits, we possess direct voluntary control over what propositions we take to be true in our practical reasoning, and what weight to afford their truth. The capacity for this control may be exercised in respect of propositions to which we have any of a wide range of possible attitudes other than belief. But now, could it be the case that we possessed such a general capacity to take to be true in reasoning what we do not believe, yet *lacked* the capacity ever to withhold practical commitment in reasoning to the truth of a proposition that we *do* believe to be true? That is a barely logical possibility—but it is not plausibly, I suggest, a natural psychological one. A voluntary capacity for taking propositions to be true in reasoning independently of belief would seem naturally open to occasional deployment in resisting the usual dispositional pressure of salient beliefs on practical reasoning. (How, one wonders, could a feasible process of natural cognitive evolution have arranged it otherwise?) If I am capable of taking proposition p to be true in my practical reasoning as an experimental hypothesis without believing that p, then surely I must also be capable of such an experiment under conditions in which actually I believe that not-p? And, indeed, there do seem to be cases of just that sort—as when I commit myself to this suede-shoe wearer's trustworthiness while

---

[17] Pretending to believe that p is not *generically* different from acting confidently on the assumption that p: it is so doing while actually believing that not-p and having the intention to deceive others into believing one believes that p.

still holding my prejudiced attitude, or reach a verdict through reasoning that ignores an inadmissible truth of which I am well aware.

I maintain, then, that our wider capacity to decide what propositions to take to be true in our reasoning (and what weight to give their truth) can be deployed as a capacity for control over our beliefs—a locus of direct voluntary control over how beliefs are used in practical reasoning. It is true that, *described generically*, this capacity is not doxastic: but it does involve a specific capacity for a control that *is* properly described as doxastic, since it *may be used to determine whether or not beliefs* qua *held attitudes get given their due weight in salient practical reasoning*. Doxastic control—control with respect to beliefs—is thus not simply a matter of indirect control (at the 'first locus') over what beliefs one acquires, retains, or revises: it may also be a matter of direct control (at the 'second locus') over the use made of what is believed in reasoning.[18] There is a natural, strongly habituated flow from holding p true to taking p to be true in practical reasoning; but this is an habitual flow which—for some beliefs under some circumstances, anyway—may be stemmed by the exercise of the agent's voluntary control.

## Moral doxastic responsibilities

Recall that, on the standard view, (*a*) reflective believers' concern for the justifiability of their faith-beliefs is understood as the concern that

---

[18] I do not wish to suggest that these are the *only* two loci of control with respect to beliefs. Obviously, language users possess control over the avowal of their beliefs, and some philosophers regard this capacity as essential for a genuine believer—for example, Bernard Williams, who maintains that 'for full-blown belief, we need the possibility of deliberate reticence, not saying what I believe, and of insincerity, saying something other than I believe' (*Problems of the Self*, 147). There is also a philosophical tradition (found, for example, in Aquinas and Descartes) that uses the notion of 'inner assent' to a proposition. May the capacity to exercise such inner assent give rise to a further locus of doxastic control? The notion of inner assent might, of course, simply reduce either to holding a proposition with assent (in the sense of with the attitude that it is true) or to assenting to the proposition's truth in one's reasoning (in the sense of taking it to be true in reasoning). A further possibility, however, is that assenting to p's truth is *adopting a policy* of taking (i.e. actively coming to be disposed to take) p to be true in one's reasoning whenever salient. Assenting to p's truth would then be equivalent to accepting that p, on Jonathan Cohen's definition cited above. My current line of argument would not, however, be affected if it turns out that there *are* good grounds for the view that acting on beliefs may sometimes provide occasion for not one but two exercises of direct voluntary control—*first*, giving inner assent to the proposition held true, and, *second*, taking the proposition to be true in practical reasoning. For, my ensuing argument for the view that our doxastic responsibilities can sometimes be moral responsibilities rests just on establishing that taking beliefs to be true in practical reasoning is *a* direct locus of doxastic control.

those beliefs be epistemically justifiable in the sense of being adequately evidentially supported; (*b*) the assumption that we ought to believe only what it is epistemically justifiable to believe is taken to rest on our general interest in acting on beliefs that are true of the context in which we act; and (*c*) our capacity for meeting this requirement is understood just as our capacity for indirect control over belief-formation and revision (and, hence, over what beliefs we hold) through our ability to (try to) meet the norms and practise the virtues of critical rational inquiry in our searching and attending to relevant evidence and argument.

The standard view, then, understands our concern for the epistemic justifiability of our faith-beliefs as arising from the fact that those beliefs are dispositions to take the propositions believed to be true in our reasoning towards action. I have now argued, however, that, for some important kinds of beliefs anyway, the takings-to-be-true in reasoning to which they dispose us are subject to direct voluntary control. I have argued that agents can genuinely believe (= hold true) that p, while yet being able to control whether they take p to be true in their salient reasoning, and thus, if they wish, refrain from practical commitment to truths they nevertheless hold. I have appealed to plausible cases where agents refrain from taking to be true what they hold true. And I have also offered an argument from the premise that we have a general capacity to decide to take to be true in our practical reasoning what we do not hold true—for example, when we act experimentally on an assumption, or when we pretend to believe. Refraining from taking to be true what we hold to be true seems to be no more than a special application of this general capacity. What adjustments are required to the standard view, once it is recognized that, with certain important kinds of beliefs (including faith-beliefs), taking them to be true in practical reasoning is under direct voluntary control?

First, it is necessary to recognize that doxastic responsibilities can arise at the second locus of doxastic control that obtains in virtue of our active capacity to take propositions to be true in our practical reasoning. As well as our responsibilities over how we indirectly control the formation, retention, and revision of our beliefs (*qua* held attitudes), we may also have responsibilities over how we directly control what we take to be true—and how confidently we take it to be true—in our practical reasoning. So it is possible to succeed or fail in our doxastic responsibilities at two different loci. But what are those responsibilities? On the standard view, our doxastic responsibilities are epistemic, with epistemic evaluation to be clearly distinguished from other dimensions of evaluation, including practical and moral evaluation. While agreeing that practical, moral, and epistemic evaluation are indeed not to be confused, I nevertheless wish to argue that—at least when it comes to faith-beliefs—it is reasonable to hold that our doxastic responsibilities are ultimately *moral* responsibilities.[19] This important fact is, I think, readily discerned in the light of recognizing our direct control over what we take to be true in our practical reasoning.

As I have noted, our exercise of control over what we take to be true when we come to act—and the weight we afford its truth—need not have anything to do with what we actually believe. We can take a proposition to be true in our practical reasoning while treating it as a mere assumption. And we may sometimes be able to take a proposition to be true while pretending to believe it—that is, we can take it to be true with the intention of deceiving others into the false belief that we hold it true. Now, when practical reasoning in such contexts leads to morally significant action, it seems quite clear that our taking the proposition concerned to be true is *itself* open to moral evaluation. Consider a 'pretending to believe' example: suppose I am morally obliged to safeguard the fugitive I am harbouring, and so obliged to try to deceive his pursuers. I may then be under the further derived moral obligation to pretend to believe that he 'went that-a-way'. To act effectively as if I had that belief while under the eye of the pursuers, I must actually take it to be true as a definite assumption in some of my practical reasoning (giving its truth just that weight that I would if I did genuinely believe it). And that 'must' seems clearly to be a derived *moral* 'must'.

Cases of this sort, however, may seem exceptional. Most of the time—it may be claimed—our responsibility in exercising our control over what we take to be true in our practical reasoning is purely epistemic. But, if that responsibility is taken to be the duty to take to be true in our reasoning only those propositions that we are epistemically justified in holding true, then the question arises how such a duty may be supposed to arise. *Why* should we serve epistemic ends in our active takings-to-be-true? If we

---

[19] Note that this claim definitely does not entail that epistemic evaluation of beliefs is, somehow, itself a kind of moral evaluation—a claim which I take to be erroneous and confused. The question of how moral and epistemic doxastic *responsibilities* may be related is an important one, to which I shall shortly return.

ought (subject to exceptions, such as the above 'pretending to believe' case illustrates) to take to be true only what it is epistemically justified to take to be true, what sort of 'ought' is that?

One could, perhaps, reply that this 'ought' is an epistemic 'ought'. But that reply is, in effect, a way of refusing the question—or it is tantamount to answering it with the implausible essentialist claim that it is just in our nature as believers that we accept these epistemic duties. (Of course, one can define the role of the believer so that playing that role *just is* accepting such duties—but then the question shifts to the question why we ought to play that role.) In any case, as I have already indicated in sketching the standard view, it is usually accepted that epistemic duties rest on our general interest in trying to ensure that we have true beliefs about the situations in which we act, itself dependent on a general interest in satisfying our intentions—and that general interest might, more plausibly, be regarded as essential to being an intentional agent. Our alleged epistemic duties in relation to our control over our takings-to-be-true in practical reasoning seem thus to be grounded on our having the higher-order general end of achieving our intentions. If we ought (in general) to take to be true only our epistemically justifiable beliefs, this 'ought' seems, then, to be a *practical* 'ought' (although a deeply entrenched one, if the higher-order intention is indeed essential to intentional agency).

When the actions towards which our practical reasoning is directed are (or may be) morally significant, however, there is a strong case for holding that our mental actions in taking certain propositions to be true in such practical reasoning are *themselves* open to moral evaluation. It then follows that there *is* such a thing as an 'ethics of belief' in the sense (at least) of an ethics that governs our taking propositions to be true in our practical reasoning. It is thus a mistake to adhere to the common view that beliefs and the agent's employment of them in practical reasoning are open only to epistemic evaluation, with moral evaluation applicable only to the action which is the outcome of the practical reasoning.

Consider, for example, the case of the Inquisitor who believes that heretics must be burnt to death if they are to avoid everlasting fiery punishment, and who acts on that belief.[20] The Inquisitor's action (we may

---

[20] Belief of this kind is by no means historically confined to the Catholic side of Christianity. Consider, for example, the case of 'Servetus (1511–1553) whom the Calvinists in Geneva burned over green wood so that it took three hours for him to be pronounced dead'. In considering the

readily assume) is morally wrong. But does his moral fault lie solely in his action of having heretics burnt at the stake? Suppose, as may be, that the Inquisitor's *intention* in burning heretics is itself morally impeccable: suppose his intention is to serve their ultimate interests, which implies the derivative intention to do whatever necessary to preserve them from everlasting fiery torment. Then, it seems clear that the Inquisitor's taking it to be true in his practical reasoning that heretics will burn everlastingly if they are not burnt briefly here must *itself* be a morally wrong action. For, all that was necessary for the Inquisitor to derive the immoral intention to burn the heretics from his prior morally sound intention was that he should have taken that belief to be true—and taken it to be true with sufficient weight for his decision-theoretic reasoning to have yielded the conclusion that having the heretics burnt was all things considered the right thing to do. Therefore, his taking it to be true that heretics unburnt here burn for eternity in Hell was *itself* morally wrong, and a failure to meet his moral responsibilities—assuming, of course, that it was indeed under his control whether he took his dogmatic belief about heretics to be true in his reasoning. For then he *could have* reflected on the justifiability of holding his belief with the high credence needed to support his drastic course of action. And so he *could have* formed a (justified) second-order suspicion about the epistemic status of his dogmatic belief, and, through having the right higher-order intentions, accordingly decided not to take to be certainly true in his practical reasoning what he may nevertheless have continued to feel was indeed true. Admittedly, 'the circumpressure of his caste and set'—to use a nice expression from William James[21]—makes any such happy outcome most unlikely. Nevertheless, that the Inquisitor did not do any of this, but, rather, unreflectively took his dogmatic belief to be true was the source of his terrible misdeed in arranging the horrific deaths of fellow human beings.[22]

---

right response to heresy, Augustine asks, rhetorically: 'What then is the function of brotherly love? Does it, because it fears the short-lived fires of the furnace for a few, therefore abandon all to the eternal fires of hell?' (*De Correctione Donatistarum*, 14). I take these references from Chapter 3 (25, 27) of Thomas Talbott's excellent defence of Christian universalism (usually itself regarded as a heresy) in his *The Inescapable Love of God* (USA: Universal Publishers, 1999), and thank Imran Aijaz for drawing my attention to this book.

[21] James, *The Will to Believe*, 9.

[22] Compare Clifford's example of the shipowner whom he claims to be morally at fault for believing without sufficient evidence that his ship is seaworthy ('The Ethics of Belief', in Leslie Stephen and Frederick Pollock (eds), *Lectures and Essays of the Late William Kingdon Clifford, Volume 2* (London:

I maintain, then, that responsibilities relating to the exercise of direct control over what one takes to be true in practical reasoning are not, fundamentally or as such, epistemic responsibilities. The obligations concerned are moral obligations—or, if the resulting action is not of moral significance, they are purely practical obligations. When a belief does have the potential to influence morally significant action, then the believer's action in taking the proposition believed to be true in practical reasoning is open to moral evaluation and the believer bears moral responsibility for it. For, no belief can influence action unless the proposition believed is taken to be true in the agent's salient practical reasoning. The exercise of control over such takings-to-be-true is thus a locus of direct control over the influence of one's beliefs—and is therefore a source of moral responsibility in relation to beliefs of the sort that can affect morally significant outcomes.

Of course, our moral responsibility for taking beliefs to be true in our practical reasoning is undoubtedly importantly connected with epistemic evaluation of those beliefs and with epistemic responsibilities we have for them. (Our Inquisitor, we might well suppose, would not have been at risk of making the moral error of taking it to be true that unchastened heretics burn for eternity in hell had he properly exercised his epistemic responsibilities in acquiring and maintaining that belief.) Careful consideration is needed, however, to determine quite what these connections between moral and epistemic doxastic evaluations and responsibilities are—and I shall have more to say about this in due course. My present point is just to affirm that our responsibilities in exercising doxastic control at its second locus when engaged in practical reasoning towards morally significant actions are not *fundamentally* epistemic but at root practical or moral responsibilities. Accordingly, there must be *a morality* applicable to our exercise of direct control over what we take to be true in practical

---

Macmillan, 1879), 178). On my account, the shipowner is morally responsible for his mental action in taking it to be true in his practical reasoning that his ship is seaworthy, given the obvious moral significance of the ensuing action. The shipowner's belief-state itself is epistemically unjustified (but is not, as such, open to any meaningful moral evaluation). The shipowner may well, however, have failed in his epistemic responsibilities in allowing himself to form and maintain this belief—and that failure may also be seen derivatively as a moral failure, since it places him at risk of moral error. But (assuming that his intentions are themselves morally acceptable—e.g. to engage in legitimate trade) it is his *taking this belief to be true in his reasoning towards action* that is at the core of his moral offence. Had he not suppressed reflection on the question whether his belief in the ship's seaworthiness really was justified on the evidence, he might have refrained from wrongly sending the ship to sea and endangering its crew—even if (be it noted) he had continued to feel that the ship *was* seaworthy.

reasoning towards morally significant action. I shall consider in the next chapter what that morality might be, and how epistemic evaluation may be implicated in it. For the present, it is enough to have shown that when agents take propositions to be true in their practical reasoning, their doing so will be open to *moral* evaluation whenever the potential outcome is itself of moral significance.

## The moral significance of faith-beliefs

Now, it is undeniable that taking theistic faith-beliefs to be true does indeed result in outcomes of moral significance. Acting on one's beliefs about God and his will gives rise not only to particular religious rites and practices but also to whole ways of living as individuals and in community—and those practices and ways of living are evidently open to moral evaluation. Furthermore, to the extent that certain morally significant actions or ways of living would not have come about had it not been for the theistic faith-beliefs of the agents concerned, their taking those beliefs to be true in their practical reasoning carries considerable moral weight. Consider some of the examples mentioned in Chapter 1: from the ecofeminist's perspective, conservative Christians are morally in error when they act on their belief that God has given human beings dominion over other animals and the earth's ecosystems. The actions consequent on that belief are obviously morally significant; and so the required mental action of taking it to be true that God grants man dominion over nature is also open to moral evaluation. Similarly, the moral status of the violent deeds of a freedom fighter/terrorist reflects that of his faith-belief that God commands such deeds and will reward him if he is martyred. Indeed, the moral justifiability or unjustifiability of what he does may in some cases turn *wholly* on the moral justifiability or unjustifiability of his taking these faith-beliefs to be true—as in the case of the Inquisitor, where the immorality of his action depends solely on the immorality of his confidently taking it to be true in his practical reasoning that heretics will burn for ever in Hell if not first cleansed by fire here on Earth.

Since the question 'how should we live?' is fundamental to ethics, there is thus an ethical question as to whether we should live in accordance with theistic faith-beliefs. Or, at least, this is so to the extent that it makes a pervasive difference to the way we live our lives whether we do or do not take it to be true that God exists. But, then, it is surely essential to belief in God counting *as a faith-belief* that it *does* make such a pervasive difference? To those for whom belief in God is merely assent to a metaphysical hypothesis with no significance for how they live their lives, theistic belief is outside any context of faith. I shall take it, then, that faith-beliefs necessarily have existential significance.[23] (This is, then, a step towards a substantive general characterization of my target category of faith-beliefs, of which I have taken Christian faith-beliefs as the indicative paradigm case. A belief will count as a faith-belief according to the intended notion only if that belief is existentially significant, in the sense that taking it to be true will have an important pervasive influence on the way a person acts and lives his or her life.) Given this defining feature of faith-beliefs, it follows that the question whether one should take *any* faith-proposition to be true is an ethically important one—whether that faith-proposition be theistic or not, religious or not.

## Linking moral to epistemic justifiability: reinstating the standard view?

In this chapter, I have argued that, by contrast with a widely-held standard view, reflective believers' concern for the justifiability of their faith-beliefs should be regarded primarily as a concern about whether it is *morally* justifiable to *take faith-beliefs to be true in one's practical reasoning*. If that is correct, then Philosophy of Religion should not focus ultimately on the epistemic status of theistic faith-beliefs, but rather on the moral status of practical commitment to the truth of those beliefs. What we require is a *moral* evaluation of acting on and living by faith-beliefs, and of agents in so far as they exercise their agency in such ways.[24]

---

[23] Faith-beliefs are thus 'thick' beliefs in Paul Helm's sense. For Helm's contrast between 'thick' and 'thin' beliefs see Paul Helm, *Faith with Reason* (Oxford: Oxford University Press, 2000), 103–10.

[24] Joshua Golding has argued for a similar shift from a focus on 'having theistic beliefs' to 'being a religious theist', which essentially involves practical commitment. Golding takes the focal question to be *the rationality* (rather than the morality) of being a religious theist, however. See Joshua L. Golding, *Rationality and Religious Theism* (Aldershot, Hants and Burlington, VT: Ashgate, 2003).

This inquiry into the justifiability of faith-beliefs takes it origin, then, in the situation of *reflective faith-believers* (or would-be faith-believers) who are interested in the question whether they are morally justified in taking, or continuing to take, the relevant faith-beliefs to be true in their practical reasoning. This justifiability question presupposes that reflective faith-believers have control over whether they commit themselves practically to the truth of their faith-beliefs. This question is naturally posed as a *de jure* question—that is, as a question about whether they are *within their rights* in taking the relevant faith-beliefs to be true, whether they are *entitled* so to do. It has been the burden of my argument in this chapter that this *de jure* question should be identified as a question about *moral* entitlement.[25] I believe I have shown that reflective believers' interest ultimately is in whether they are *morally* within their rights if they take, or continue to take, the relevant faith-beliefs to be true in their reasoning towards action.[26]

Not all faith-believers are 'reflective', of course. And my conclusion in this chapter pertains to what happens when faith-believers *do* become reflective: it is the claim that, in becoming reflective, what faith-believers come to be concerned about is the moral justifiability of practical commitment to the truth of the relevant faith-beliefs. Nevertheless, this conclusion does have implications for all faith-believers, whether they are reflective or not. For, practical commitment to the truth of faith-beliefs is *always* in

[25] Alvin Plantinga draws a distinction between *de facto* and *de jure* objections to Christian belief in the preface to his *Warranted Christian Belief*. *De facto* objections are 'objections to the truth of Christian belief' (viii), while *de jure* objections he describes as 'arguments or claims to the effect that Christian belief, whether or not true, is at any rate unjustifiable or rationally unjustified, or irrational, or not intellectually respectable, or contrary to sound morality, or without sufficient evidence, or in some other way rationally unacceptable, not up to snuff from an intellectual point of view' (ix). While a claim that a person is not morally entitled to take Christian faith-beliefs to be true will count as a *de jure* objection according to Plantinga's usage of the term, Plantinga certainly does not take it that what reflective believers are fundamentally interested in is their moral entitlement to practical commitment to the truth of their faith-beliefs. Indeed, he argues that all that can reasonably be up for debate is a question about the epistemic status of Christian belief which he formulates as the question whether it has 'warrant'. On my account, however, the *de jure* question about Christian belief is ultimately just the question of moral entitlement to take Christian beliefs to be true; for Plantinga, the *de jure* question about Christian belief is the question whether *de jure* objections to Christian belief can be met—and those objections are a mixed bag, not all of them focusing on deontological issues such as the believer's 'entitlement'.

[26] It may perhaps be helpful to note that I am taking each of the following locutions as equivalent to one another, where M is an agent variable and p a propositional variable: 'M is morally justified in taking p to be true', 'It is morally justifiable for M to take p to be true', 'It is morally permissible for M to take p to be true', 'M takes p to be true in accordance with her moral obligations', 'M takes p to be true with moral probity', 'M is within her moral rights in taking p to be true'. Further variant equivalent locutions—for example, of a kind characteristic of virtue ethics—may also be admissible.

fact open to moral evaluation, whether or not those who make it have become reflectively concerned for the justifiability of their commitment. But it need not follow, I think, that *every* faith-believer *ought* to become reflective—a life of 'simple faith' may (under some conditions, anyway) be at least blameless and even fully virtuous. What may follow, however, is that a faith-tradition would be impaired if it did not make a place for reflective believers who raise justifiability questions and are at least respectfully regarded for so doing. Be that as it may, my present aim is to develop an account of the conditions under which faith-believers *are* morally justified in their commitments—that is, to try to provide an *ethics of faith-commitment*.

I shall develop my account of the ethics of faith-commitment from the perspective of reflective faith-believers (and would-be faith-believers) who seek to satisfy themselves, so far as they can, that their actual or envisaged faith-commitments are morally permissible. Reflective faith-believers thus need an account of the conditions under which it is morally justified to take faith-beliefs to be true. They will need to ask themselves *how they can check* whether they are indeed morally entitled to their commitments; so they will need an ethics of faith-commitment to provide criteria against which such a check can be made. (And perhaps we may understand a reflective believer with a particular—say, theistic—faith-belief as representatively raising on behalf of all faith-believers of that ilk the question of moral justifiability that applies equally to them all. In deciding that question for him or herself, the reflective believer will then, be 'deciding for them all'—though not, of course, in the sense of pre-empting anyone else's free decision.)

Reliance on a general account of the conditions for morally justifiable faith-commitments will meet the concern of reflective faith-believers, of course, only to the extent that they can satisfy themselves that those conditions are met in their particular cases. There may well, however, be a gap between the objective satisfaction of the conditions for morally justifiable faith-commitment and a situated reflective faith-believer's capacity to judge whether those conditions are met in his or her own case. Achieving a philosophically respectable account of morally justifiable faith-commitment may not *guarantee*, then, that reflective faith-believers with their own particular commitments will be able to be completely sure whether or not they stand on firm moral ground. If a satisfactory ethics of faith-commitment is forthcoming, however, reflective faith-believers will at least be able to make a judgement as to the moral status of their particular commitments—and the fact that a favourable judgement will fall short of a guarantee need be no more undermining here than anywhere else in morality.

My conclusion that the reflective faith-believer's concern is ultimately a moral one would, of course, be resisted by anyone who doubted that we had the kind of doxastic control required for it to make sense to raise questions about whether one is believing within one's rights (moral or otherwise). But I have argued in this chapter that we *do* have the required kind of doxastic control.[27] I have maintained that we may exercise doxastic control at *two* loci: direct control over what we take to be true in practical reasoning, and indirect control over what we hold to be true. Our direct control over what we take to be true is, I have argued, subject to moral evaluation—at least when beliefs are involved that may potentially influence morally significant actions, as is the case by definition with all faith-beliefs.

That conclusion might be conceded—and yet my presenting it as a reassessment of a standard view rejected as overdramatic. For, many philosophers might admit that taking faith-beliefs to be true in action is ultimately open to moral evaluation, yet still maintain that the focal task in assessing the justifiability of such beliefs is epistemic rather than moral. They might take this view because they think that the required moral evaluations

---

[27] As already noted (*n.* 7 above), an alternative response would have been to maintain that questions about our entitlement to beliefs can make sense even if we do not have any voluntary doxastic control. Richard Feldman has recently argued that 'deontological epistemic judgements can be true even if doxastic voluntarism [*sc.* the thesis that we have control over our beliefs] is false' by appealing to the possibility that 'epistemic oughts … describe the right way to play a certain role' and claiming that 'role oughts' can apply to those who are unable to do what they ought to do. (See Feldman 'The Ethics of Belief', 175.) While Feldman may be correct in holding that role oughts provide a counter-example to the rule that 'ought implies can'—maybe it does remain true, for example, that an incapacitated father ought *as a parent* to care for his children even if he is unable to do so—it does not follow that an agent can be responsible for outcomes over which he has no control (if the father's incapacity did not result from anything over which he had control, then we do not regard him as responsible for his neglect of his children). The applicability of *deontological judgements* (thus broadly understood) is one thing, that of *judgements of agent responsibility*, another. In fact, Feldman does go on to suggest that agents may properly be held responsible in the absence of agent-control, by claiming that 'we do praise and blame people for attributes, such as beauty, that they are unable to control'. This suggestion is unconvincing, however: we may *admire* or *celebrate* a person's beauty, but to *praise* someone for his beauty in the sense of giving him credit for it we would have to assume that he had some part in bringing it about. In any case, the arguments I have advanced in this chapter vindicate a certain kind of doxastic voluntarism—namely the thesis that, for some important kinds of beliefs including faith-beliefs, we do have direct control over whether we take our beliefs to be true in our salient practical reasoning.

*effectively reduce* to epistemic ones. They might admit that there is an ethics of faith-commitment, but claim that it amounts straightforwardly to the principle that *it is morally justifiable to take proposition p to be true in practical reasoning only if the belief that p is itself epistemically justifiable (or, more generally, that it is morally justifiable to give p's truth only that degree of confidence in our practical reasoning as is epistemically justified)*. If this principle is correct, then the core task in achieving moral probity in our faith-commitments will be to do what we can to ensure that the faith-beliefs we hold (and thus act upon) are epistemically justified. The standard view in Philosophy of Religion about the nature of concern about the justifiability of theistic belief will then be near enough to the mark. Maybe *ultimately* reflective believers need to answer a *de jure* question about the morality of practical commitment to theistic faith-beliefs, yet the really important philosophical business will still be to determine the epistemic status of theistic belief—most importantly, by evaluating arguments that purport to settle the *de facto* question whether such belief is true.

It is important to consider whether this claim is true—and I will take this issue up in the following chapter. What reasons are there for supposing that the moral justifiability of commitment to the truth of faith-beliefs is essentially linked to their epistemic justifiability? Indeed, how exactly should this claimed link be formulated? If moral entitlement to take faith-beliefs to be true turns out *not* to be strictly equivalent to practical commitment to epistemically justified faith-beliefs, then the recognition that reflective concern is ultimately for the moral justifiability of practical commitment to the truth of faith-beliefs will prove to be no merely peripheral matter.

# 3
# The epistemic justifiability of faith-beliefs: an ambiguity thesis

The reflective believer's concern about the justifiability of faith-beliefs of the kind exemplified in theistic religion is, I have argued, ultimately concern about whether one may be *morally* justified in *taking* such beliefs to be true in one's actions and way of life. To meet that concern we need an *ethics of faith-commitment*. That is, we need to know whether it is ever morally justifiable to take faith-beliefs to be true in practical reasoning, and, if so, under what conditions.

In this chapter, I will pursue the question of the ethics of faith-commitment within the limits of the assumption that taking faith-beliefs to be true will be morally justified only if it is epistemically justified.

## Plausibility of requiring epistemic for moral justifiability under a realist interpretation of faith-beliefs

A key issue for an ethics of faith-commitment is whether the moral justifiability of taking a proposition to be true in one's practical reasoning depends on the epistemic justifiability of taking—and, therefore also, of holding—that proposition to be true. I stand by my claim in the previous chapter that the ultimate issue is the moral justifiability of practical commitment to the truth of faith-beliefs. But, as I there acknowledged, it might well be supposed that—unless, exceptionally, ethical suspension of the epistemic is required (as when one ought to act out of loyalty to a friend rather than on what one holds to be the truth)—it is morally justifiable to take beliefs to be true in our reasoning only when it is epistemically justifiable to do so. This 'moral-epistemic link' principle may be thought to apply to faith-beliefs because it seems plausible, at least on certain assumptions, that a necessary condition for living morally well is that, if one does have a basic faith-orientation to the world, it should be a correct one. Let me explain further.

With theistic faith-beliefs taken as the paradigm case, it seems apparent that faith-beliefs make existentially important claims *about what sort of a world it is to which we belong.* That is, theistic faith-beliefs seem to need a *realist* interpretation, according to which they function as assertions or truth-claims about 'mind-independent' reality: for example, 'God exists and is revealed in Jesus the Christ' is either true or false, and what makes it true or false, as the case may be, is independent of the beliefs and attitudes on this question that happen to be held by any person or group.[1]

If theistic faith-beliefs are about mind-independent reality, and our acting on them has an important effect on how we live, then the ethical value of acting on them will surely depend on their conveying *truths* about the world. The *general* reason for caring about whether our beliefs grasp truth and avoid error must surely apply 'in spades' here, when it comes to faith-beliefs that set a whole framework for interpreting our experience and making decisions about our personal, social, and political lives. Surely, we will most likely fail to live morally well if we steer by faith-beliefs that are not true of our world?

This argument is not decisive, however—as its repeated use of the 'surely' modifier betrays. It may be contested whether people who live by faith-beliefs that do *not* correspond to reality will necessarily fail to live morally flourishing lives. There *are* perspectives from which *getting it right* about what divinities exist, if any, is irrelevant to moral health. But such

---

[1] Realism with respect to a given class of beliefs cannot unproblematically be defined as the thesis that those beliefs involve claims about mind-independent reality. One may surely be a realist about beliefs that attribute psychological states, yet, obviously, such beliefs are not about 'mind-independent' reality. So care is needed in formulating the thesis of realism. Here is a more promising formulation: to be realist about the belief that p is to take it that what makes p true (if p is true) is independent of anyone's belief or attitude on the question of the truth of p. (Such a claim typically is true of beliefs about mental states. Even if there is an intrinsic relationship between my believing, e.g. that I am in pain and my being in pain, it is usually not my—let alone anyone else's—belief that I am in pain that constitutes the truth-maker for my belief that I am in pain.)

perspectives either deny the moral import of theistic belief, or else interpret it in a *non-realist* way (i.e. by assigning to theistic beliefs a function distinct from that of making assertions about a mind-independent world—e.g. the function of *expressing* a community's commitment to its core values).[2] On a non-realist view, commitment to faith-beliefs will indeed be ethically important—but not because of anything to do with whether those beliefs grasp the truth about mind-independent reality.

Nevertheless, for those who take the common-sense view that theistic beliefs are existentially significant and also need a realist interpretation, it will seem obvious, for reasons already rehearsed, that one could not live successfully by such faith-beliefs unless they were true. From this common-sense perspective, it will follow that taking faith-propositions to be true will be morally justifiable only if it is epistemically justifiable.

I will return in Chapter 4 to discuss non-realist perspectives on theistic faith-beliefs; in the meantime, however, I will retain the commonsensical realist perspective, and consider the prospects for determining the moral justifiability of theistic faith-commitment on the assumption, well motivated from that perspective, that the moral-epistemic link principle does indeed apply.

## Interpreting the link principle: epistemic entitlement as requiring evidential justification

My question now is this: what conditions does the moral-epistemic link principle place on the moral justifiability of taking faith-beliefs to be true? How exactly should the link principle be understood?

For an answer, I build on the results of the previous chapter. There I distinguished between a person's *state* of *holding* a proposition true, and a person's mental *action* in *taking* a proposition to be true in his or her

---

[2] Don Cupitt expresses a non-realist understanding of theistic beliefs—for example, in the following passage from his *Taking Leave of God* (London: SCM Press, 1980):

I continue ... to pray to God. God is the mythical embodiment of all one is concerned with in the spiritual life. He is the religious demand and ideal ... the enshriner of values. He is needed—but as a myth. (180)

This passage is quoted by Charles Taliaferro in a helpful summary of the reasons that may be given in favour of theological non-realism. See his *Contemporary Philosophy of Religion* (Malden, MA: Blackwell, 1998), 40–5.

reasoning. I argued that people's mental actions in taking propositions to be true in their practical reasoning will themselves be *morally* assessable whenever the outcome is itself a morally significant action. Given that faith-beliefs influence not just certain actions but whole styles of living, that condition will hold for all faith-beliefs, properly so called. I thus concluded that the reflective believer's question about the justifiability of faith-beliefs is ultimately the question of the *moral* justifiability of *persons taking to be true in their practical reasoning* the faith-propositions that are the contents of their faith-beliefs—of acting on those beliefs, committing themselves to their truth, and living them out.

What, now, is the effect of applying the moral-epistemic link principle to this question? At its core the principle claims that the moral evaluation of an agent's taking a faith-proposition to be true depends on an epistemic evaluation. But an epistemic evaluation *of what*, exactly? Of the agent's *belief*, surely? That will indeed be involved, but I want to argue that there is something conceptually prior that is open to a certain kind of epistemic evaluation—namely, the agent's *action* in taking a faith-proposition to be true in practical reasoning. I have emphasized that reflective faith-believers care about the moral justifiability of their *practical commitment* to the truth of their faith-beliefs. They want to know whether they may (continue to) make that commitment with a clear conscience. And the moral-epistemic link principle, at its most basic, may thus be interpreted as claiming that their moral conscience can be clear only if, so to speak, their epistemic conscience is clear also: people may be morally justified in practical commitment to the truth of their faith-beliefs only if, I shall say, that commitment carries *epistemic entitlement*.

This notion of taking faith-propositions to be true with epistemic entitlement is an *agency-focused* notion. Epistemic entitlement can be carried—or not, as the case may be—only by agents' exercises of control in taking a proposition to be true in their reasoning. The assessment of epistemic entitlement is thus an assessment of agents' mental actions of practical commitment to propositions and (equally) of agents in so far as they exercise their control in this way.[3] This agency-focused notion of

[3] Note that the distinction I am here drawing between agency-focused and propositional-attitude-focused notions of epistemic evaluation is not to be confused with the distinction between virtue-theoretic *agent*-focused notions and epistemic evaluations of belief-states. My drawing attention to the agency-focused notion of epistemic entitlement is thus not in itself a virtue-theoretic move (though

epistemic entitlement is to be distinguished, of course, from the notion of the *epistemic justifiability of beliefs*, which is, by contrast, a *propositional-attitude-focused* notion, involving evaluation of a person's *state* of holding a proposition true. What do I mean, then, by a person's taking a proposition true with epistemic entitlement—and what relationship does this bear to the more familiar notion of the epistemic justifiability of that person's belief? (For, it might be suspected that to say that a person's practical commitment to p's truth carries epistemic entitlement means essentially the same as to say that the belief that p on which the person acts is epistemically justified. I shall need to show that claim to be false.)

For an explanation of the notion of taking a proposition to be true with epistemic entitlement, consider again the situation of the reflective faith-believer. On my account, reflective believers raise for themselves the question of the moral justifiability of their taking faith-beliefs to be true. My suggestion is that, assuming the moral-epistemic link principle, answering that question requires establishing whether their practical commitment to the truth of their faith-beliefs carries epistemic entitlement. For it to do so, I maintain, is for it to be *made through the right exercise of their epistemic capacities*. And the right exercise of those capacities comes to this: reflective believers will need to have paid proper attention to the question of the truth of their faith-propositions, to have judged that issue properly (in accordance with the correct application of the objective norms applicable to such judgements), and to have taken proper account of that judgement in deciding to commit themselves practically to the truth of their faith-propositions.

Now, properly judging the question of the truth of faith-propositions requires properly judging whether, and to what extent, one's *evidence* supports their truth. (Such judgements are governed by objective norms—and there is, of course, room for debate as to what these norms are. Suffice it for now to note that these norms will include (1) norms governing relations of evidential support—that is, norms for judging to what degree a given body of evidence indicates that a given proposition is true; (2) norms governing *in*

---

it would leave such a move open). Virtue epistemology foregrounds assessments of agents' characters, typically as they bear on their exercise of doxastic control at the first locus, namely indirect control over the formation, retention, and revision of beliefs. (For a thorough survey of recent work in virtue epistemology, see John Greco, 'Virtue Epistemology', in Edward N. Zalta (ed.), *The Stanford Encyclopedia of Philosophy (Winter 2004 Edition)*, <http://plato.stanford.edu/archives/win2004/entries/epistemology-virtue/>.)

*general* what may count as evidence; and (3) norms governing what counts as 'the' evidence, or 'all the' evidence, that a person has in any particular situated case.)[4]

Judgements of evidential support are judgements of what one's evidence shows to be true—or, more or less probably to be true. But they also amount to judgements *about beliefs,* and we may say that a person's belief is, more or less, evidentially supported to the extent that its truth fits the person's evidence. When, furthermore, a person holds a proposition true *on the basis of* the support of his or her evidence, we may say that that person's belief is *evidentially justified*—or, at least, that it possesses a certain degree of evidential justification.[5] (This notion of a belief's evidential justification is, of course, a propositional-attitude-focused notion.)

For their faith-commitments to carry epistemic entitlement, reflective believers need to make those commitments in a way that *takes proper account of* their evidence-based judgements as to the truth of their faith-beliefs. If their faith-beliefs *are* evidentially justified in the sense just defined—that is, the truth of those beliefs does fit their evidence, and they hold them on the basis of that evidential support—then that *suffices* for their practical commitment to the truth of those beliefs to carry epistemic entitlement.

The crucially important question is, though, whether that condition *is also necessary*: does epistemic entitlement in committing to the truth of one's faith-beliefs *require* that those beliefs be evidentially justified? Does it turn out that the agency-focused notion of taking a faith-proposition to be true with epistemic entitlement materially coincides with the propositional-attitude-focused notion of the corresponding faith-belief's possessing (adequate) evidential justification? And is there, then, an *evidentialist* constraint on faith-commitments carrying epistemic entitlement?

---

[4] I will return to the question of what these norms may be in the following section when I introduce the notion of an *evidential practice*.

[5] Compare Conee and Feldman's notion of a belief having epistemic justification, and, in particular, their recognition of the need for a notion of 'well-founded' belief 'to characterize an attitude that is epistemically both well-supported [sc: fits the believer's evidence] and properly arrived at [sc: formed on the basis of that evidence]' (Conee and Feldman, *Evidentialism*, 93). I am deliberately speaking in terms of *evidential* justification rather than 'epistemic' justification, in order not to beg the question against externalist accounts of epistemic justification as consisting in factors independent of evidential support cognitively accessible to the believer.

The evidentialist view that these questions need an affirmative answer is presumably driven by the following thought: if a person holds that p *other than* on the basis of evidence giving sufficient support for its truth, then that person's belief that p will surely have a 'non-epistemic' cause—such as, for example, wanting p to be true, or thinking it would be good if p were true, or wanting to conform to a cultural context where the assumption that p is entrenched. So, if the person then goes on to take p to be true in practical reasoning, he or she would not be doing so with epistemic entitlement, even though it may remain open that such an action might yet, under certain conditions, be morally justified. Now, as I observed in Chapter 2, people are naturally habituated to take to be true in their reasoning what they hold true. So, no doubt, most people who have beliefs that lack evidential justification go on to take them to be true in their reasoning without consciously considering the issue of their evidential support. And, often, such people can hardly be blamed for this omission—and so they may, *in some sense*, be within their rights in taking to be true what they are not in fact evidentially justified in holding true.[6] When it comes to *reflective* faith-believers whose beliefs are evidentially unjustified, however, considerations of this kind are unavailable. If reflective believers commit themselves to the truth of faith-beliefs *consciously recognized* as lacking adequate evidential support, then surely their action in so doing cannot carry epistemic entitlement—even if there might (perhaps) be some overriding moral justification for their so doing?

But are these considerations really sufficient to establish the principle of what I shall call *epistemic evidentialism*: namely, that people may take

---

[6] The practical commitment of such unreflective non-epistemically-justified believers may (under certain conditions, anyway) be *inculpable*—and they may commit themselves 'within their rights' in *that* sense—but that is not sufficient to establish that their commitment carries epistemic entitlement, which requires not simply the *blameless* exercise of the relevant epistemic capacities, but their *right* exercise. Under what conditions, though, will *unreflective* believers take their beliefs to be true *with epistemic entitlement*? The evidentialist view is that those beliefs must be evidentially justified. Now, it is clear what evidential justification of a belief amounts to *for a reflective believer*: namely, its being held on the basis of the believer's (correct) conscious judgement of adequate evidential support for its truth. But what does it amount to for an *unreflective* believer? How can a belief be 'based on' evidential support for its truth when no conscious judgement is made? There is something uncomfortable about invoking unconscious or counterfactual judgements in order to supply an answer. My project's focus on the situation of the *reflective* faith-believer absolves me from having to resolve this issue, however, since reflective believers (who accept evidentialism) will obviously have to *make a conscious judgement* about evidential support for the truth of their beliefs. I do need to make it clear, however, that I make no claim to provide fully general conditions for a person to hold a belief with evidential justification, and concede that this may prove difficult to achieve satisfactorily.

propositions to be true with epistemic entitlement if and, more importantly, *only if* they are evidentially justified in holding those propositions to be true? Some might object that the argument just given begs the question against an externalist account of what it is for people's beliefs to have epistemic justification. The above argument for epistemic evidentialism seems to assume that beliefs not caused by the believer's recognition of evidential support for their truth must have non-epistemic causes—'non-epistemic' in the sense that they could not contribute to those beliefs possessing epistemic worth. But that assumption is contestable. According to externalist epistemology, beliefs may have epistemic worth through causes quite independent of the believer's recognition of any evidential support for their truth—such as production by a mechanism that is a reliable producer of true beliefs, or whose 'proper function' is to yield true beliefs.[7] May it be, then, that anyone who takes the principle of epistemic evidentialism seriously just has not caught up with the externalist move in epistemology?

I think not. The argument as it stands is indeed open to the objection stated; yet, even if we accept that epistemic worth may be conferred on a person's belief through causes other than the believer's recognition of evidence for its truth, *prima facie* grounds remain for affirming the epistemic evidentialist principle that reflective believers may take their beliefs to be true with epistemic entitlement only if they judge their truth to be adequately supported by their evidence. Externalist theories are theories about what it is for agents' *beliefs* to have epistemic worth—and that is a propositional-attitude-focused notion. The notion of epistemic entitlement, however, is, as I have emphasized, an agency-focused notion. And it does not follow *in general* from a person's belief having epistemic worth that the person may take that belief to be true with epistemic entitlement. That entailment *does* hold when the person's belief has epistemic worth *due to its being held on the basis of the person's (correct) judgement of sufficient evidential support for its truth*. But, when the person's belief has epistemic worth *from some other*

---

[7] I put the externalist view in terms of 'epistemic worth' rather than 'epistemic justification', since some externalists, not unnaturally, associate the term 'justification' with the evidence-focused internalist views they are concerned to reject. Externalists typically claim that a belief's having the right kind of cause is sufficient (granted its truth) to confer on it the status of *knowledge*. That claim is, of course, contestable: the weaker claim that *some sort of epistemic worth* is conferred on a belief by its having the right kind of cause is much more secure—and this provides a further reason to conduct the discussion in terms of epistemic worth rather than knowledge.

*cause*, as externalism urges us to acknowledge it may, the entailment breaks down (and it is thus entirely clear that 'M takes p to be true with epistemic entitlement' is *not* synonymous with 'M's belief that p on which M acts has epistemic justification').

To illustrate. Suppose God exists and plants the belief that p in me intending to ensure that I believe the truth on the question whether p. Its origin in the exercise of intentional divine omniscient power *by itself* ensures that my belief that p has epistemic worth, since its having this cause guarantees its truth. But now suppose that God does not give me any evidence from which I could myself judge that p is true. I might yet be epistemically entitled to take p to be true—but only if God gave me adequate evidence for the divine origin of my finding myself believing that p is true. So, if, finally, we suppose that God does *not* give me that kind of indirect evidence for p's truth either, and if I do raise for myself, reflectively, the question of p's truth, then surely my taking p to be true cannot carry epistemic entitlement? My situation would be that I—so far as I can tell, unaccountably—hold p to be true; but when I reflect on it I find I have no inferential or direct experiential ground whatsoever for holding it true, and therefore, surely, I can hardly regard myself as *epistemically* in the clear if I commit myself practically to its truth?[8]

There is motivation, then, for adhering to epistemic evidentialism even though one accepts that beliefs may have epistemic worth (even, perhaps, the status of knowledge itself) under externalist conditions independently of their being evidentially justified. To hold that people may take their beliefs to be true with epistemic entitlement only when they hold those

---

[8] Compare Laurence BonJour's case of Boris in whom God has implanted a cognitive module designed to ensure that he has a correct belief about the Second Coming (see his 'Internalism and Externalism', in Paul K. Moser (ed.), *The Oxford Handbook of Epistemology* (New York: Oxford University Press, 2002: 255–6). Compare also BonJour's case of Norman who 'is in fact a reliable clairvoyant with respect to the geographical whereabouts of the president of the United States', but 'has no belief or opinion at all about the cognitive process involved' (Laurence BonJour, *Epistemology: Classic Problems and Contemporary Responses* (Lanham, MD.: Rowman and Littlefield, 2002: 230). BonJour takes this case as posing a problem for reliabilist (and, more generally, externalist) accounts of epistemic justification. His suggestion that one might be led to the conclusion that Norman's belief, on a particular occasion, about the President's whereabouts is not epistemically justified by 'asking whether Norman would be justified in *acting*' (231) on such a belief is on the brink of recognizing the significance of the agency-focused notion of practical commitment to a belief's truth carrying epistemic entitlement. On my view, clarity about such a case is achieved when we recognize that Norman's *belief* may indeed have epistemic worth (a propositional-attitude-focused dimension of epistemic evaluation) without *his taking it to be true* carrying epistemic entitlement (an agency-focused dimension of epistemic evaluation).

beliefs on the basis of adequate evidential support does not, therefore, entail commitment either to any internalist or to any deontological theory of the propositional-attitude-focused notion of epistemic justification. Indeed, adherents to the epistemic evidentialist principle will need to allow that a person's belief that p may sometimes be evidentially justified *via* a second-order judgement to the effect that it has been caused in such a way as to confer epistemic justification on it despite the absence of support for its truth from direct, first-order evidence accessible to the person him- or herself. Holding p true on authority is a familiar case in point. In such a case, the belief that p is not based on the believer's judgement of evidence that directly shows p to be true; yet it remains based on a judgement of the believer's evidence in a wider sense that includes evidence for the authoritativeness of the belief's source—that is, for its having been caused in a manner that confers epistemic worth. But where the believer *neither* has direct evidence for p's truth, *nor* indirect evidence for his belief that p having been caused in a way that confers epistemic justification, then his belief will not be evidentially justified and—under the evidentialist principle—he will not be epistemically entitled to commit to it, even if, in fact, it *does* possess epistemic worth through having the right kind of causal history.

To sum up, then. We have seen that reasonable grounds may be given for taking it that people will not be epistemically entitled to take beliefs to be true unless those beliefs are evidentially justified—the principle that I have named *epistemic evidentialism*. When that principle is combined with the moral-epistemic link principle (i.e. people can be morally justified in taking beliefs to be true only if they do so with epistemic entitlement), we get what I shall call *moral evidentialism*: the principle that people are morally justified in taking beliefs to be true in their practical reasoning only if those beliefs are evidentially justified (i.e. only if the beliefs fit the believers' evidence, and are held by them on the basis of that evidence). These evidentialist principles are open to an obvious generalization to take into account that people may have and act upon partial beliefs in which they afford a certain degree of probability to a proposition's truth. Thus generalized, epistemic evidentialism holds that people are epistemically entitled to take propositions to be true with that degree of weight that corresponds to their judgement, in accordance with the applicable norms, of the extent to which their evidence renders probable the truth of the propositions concerned. And generalized moral evidentialism, of course, places that same condition on the moral justifiability of taking propositions to be true in one's reasoning. (In what follows, I will not keep mentioning this generalization to allow for partial beliefs, unless the context makes it especially salient.)

There is, of course, a long history of support for 'evidentialism', construed broadly as the requirement that beliefs, if they are to be legitimate, should be adequately supported by, or proportioned to, the evidence.[9] The articulation of evidentialism that I have just given differs from most previous accounts in two significant ways. First, my account attaches the evidentialist imperative primarily to agents' *actions* in *taking the propositional content of their beliefs to be true in their reasoning*, whereas most previous discussions take evidentialism to focus on people's *beliefs*. Those discussions typically understand evidentialism as a thesis about what it is for beliefs to have epistemic justification, and, in so far as they recognize an evidentialist imperative, it is interpreted as a principle about the proper use of our indirect control over the formation, retention, and revision of our beliefs.[10] These accounts notice only what I have called (in Chapter 2) our 'first locus of doxastic control'. My present account maintains, however, that the

[9] Nicholas Wolterstorff makes the case for the claim that it is John Locke who is, '*on this issue*, the father of modernity' (*John Locke and the Ethics of Belief*, xiv). Wolterstorff attributes to Locke a 'Principle of Proportionality': 'adopt a level of confidence in the proposition which is proportioned to its probability on one's satisfactory evidence' (79), and then gets into some difficulty considering how we could have it in our power to do what this principle requires (see 109–18). These difficulties are, I think, overcome once the Principle of Proportionality is understood as referring to the action of taking a proposition to be true, with some more or less specific weight, in practical reasoning. It is beyond my present scope, however, to consider the scholarly question whether Locke himself may fairly be understood as interpreting the Principle in this way.

[10] See, for example, Earl Conee and Richard Feldman, who maintain that 'in its fundamental form … evidentialism is a supervenience thesis according to which facts about whether or not a person is justified in believing a proposition supervene on facts describing the evidence that the person has' (Conee and Feldman, *Evidentialism*, 1).

Note that Jonathan Adler argues that there is no conceptual space for an 'evidentialist imperative' at all—though he concedes that his version of evidentialism 'diverges from the tradition'. According to Adler, 'one must believe in accord with evidentialism, and it is a serious error to maintain … that adherence to evidentialism is an option that one can decide to take rightly or wrongly …'; '… it is incoherent to recognize oneself as fully believing both that p and that one's reasons do not establish p … ' (*Belief's Own Ethics* (Cambridge, MA: MIT Press, 2002), 2 and 249). If that is correct, it is hard to see how evidentialism can constitute an *ethical* position at all. The kind of evidentialism with which I am here concerned is, by contrast, quite explicitly an ethical thesis, and assumes that it is (at least sometimes) within our power whether or not we follow its requirement to take a particular proposition to be true in our reasoning only to the extent of its evidential support. I shall comment further on Adler in Chapter 5 in the context of defending the conceptual and psychological possibility of doxastic venture (see Chapter 5, *n*. 25).

evidentialist imperative should be construed as applying also—and, indeed, primarily—to our direct control (at 'the second locus') over what we take to be true (and with what weight) in our practical reasoning. And I take that imperative to be, not simply a *practical*, but also a *moral* imperative whenever such exercises of control can have morally significant effects, as is always (by definition) the case when faith-beliefs are taken to be true in practical reasoning.

The second notable feature of my present account is that I parse moral evidentialism into two component principles—the moral-epistemic link principle and epistemic evidentialism. Previous discussions often recognize a distinction between evidentialism as a moral position and as a—in itself morally neutral—claim about the requirements for epistemically rational or reasonable belief. My account indicates how these may be connected—at least for the case of faith-beliefs and all other beliefs capable of influencing morally significant actions.[11]

In this section, then, I have put forward some grounds in favour of an *evidentialist ethics of faith-commitment*—that is, in favour of accepting that moral evidentialism does apply to practical commitment to the truth of faith-beliefs. These grounds are weighty enough for it to be important to consider how reflective faith-believers fare (in our paradigm case of theistic belief) if moral evidentialism is indeed correct. The grounds here given for moral evidentialism, however, are by no means decisive. And it will, in particular, be worth keeping in mind the fact that—if externalist insights about how beliefs may possess epistemic worth are correct—people could, under some conditions, commit themselves practically to the truth of beliefs for which they have neither direct nor indirect evidential support yet which are, in fact, of high epistemic worth, albeit discernibly so only from a cognitive perspective necessarily external to theirs. The relevance of this to the question of the moral permissibility of doxastic venture (i.e. practical commitment to truths judged *not* to possess evidential support)

---

[11] Compare Jeff Jordan's discussion of evidentialism in 'Pragmatic Arguments and Belief', *American Philosophical Quarterly*, 33 (1996), 409–20. Jordan distinguishes between '*ethical* evidentialism'—represented by W. K. Clifford's famous claim that 'it is wrong always, everywhere, and for anyone, to believe anything upon insufficient evidence'—and '*cognitive* evidentialism', as found in both 'Locke's claim that "there is one unerring mark by which a man may know whether he is a lover of truth for truth's sake: the not entertaining any proposition with greater assurance than the proofs it is built upon will warrant" and in Hume's dictum that "the wise man proportions his belief to the evidence" ' (412).

may already perhaps be apparent. I will return to this important point later (in Chapter 8).

I shall now proceed, then, to consider what assessment of theistic faith-commitment results from assuming an evidentialist ethics. This consideration will in due course lead to questioning whether the principle of moral evidentialism should—or even can—be held to apply to faith-commitments.

## Evidentialist requirements specified by an implicit evidential practice

What is the status of theists' faith-commitments under an evidentialist ethics? According to moral evidentialism, for those commitments to be morally justified, they must carry epistemic entitlement, and that requires the relevant faith-beliefs to be evidentially justified (held on the basis of adequate evidential support for their truth). As already noted, judgements of evidential support are governed by objective norms, including norms determining what counts as a person's (total) evidence and what it would be for that evidence to support the truth of the belief concerned. People do not come to be evidentially justified in their beliefs just by sincerely judging the truth of those beliefs to be supported by what they take to be their evidence. Evidential justification is not open to subjective guarantee. Evidential justification requires that the relevant judgement of evidential support be made correctly, in accordance with the applicable norms.[12] But objective norms of the relevant kind do not simply appear in articulated form (as it were, on tablets of stone): rather, they are implicit in the practice of communities who generally seek to respect a requirement to conform belief to evidence. Such communities thus have an *evidential practice* in which certain norms for evidential support are implicit. There can thus be

---

[12] As already noted in *n*. 6 above, agents who sincerely but incorrectly judge the truth of their beliefs to be supported by their evidence may, in a particular context, be epistemically and morally *blameless* in taking that belief to be true in their reasoning—suppose, for instance, that they are simply unable, through circumstances beyond their own control, to appreciate the force of a given part of their evidence. In such cases, however, the agents' beliefs will remain evidentially unjustified, and, under evidentialist ethics, they will neither be epistemically entitled nor morally justified in taking them to be true. They will be 'within their rights' in so doing, or 'entitled' to do so, only in the sense that their doing so is inculpable.

contested theories about the norms of 'the right' evidential practice—and it may even be envisaged in some quarters that there is no such thing as *the* correct evidential practice, but that, rather, different evidential practices apply relatively to different contexts.

Any viable theory of evidential practice will specify logical norms, both deductive and inductive, governing the *inferential* transfer of evidential support. But, obviously, not all evidential support can be inferential, on pain of a vicious infinite regress or circle. A theory of evidential practice will thus need to specify categories of propositions whose truth may be taken (under canonical conditions) to be *non-inferentially* or *basically evident,* that is, evident, yet without deriving its evidence by inference from other evidentially established truths. Under a viable evidential practice, people will thus sometimes be evidentially justified in holding a given belief other than on the basis of judging its truth inferable from other evidentially secure truths. Typically, in such cases the truth will seem self-evident or evident in experience itself—as, for example, with perceptual beliefs, or arithmetical and logical beliefs, including beliefs about norms of inferential evidential support. The notion of a belief's being evidentially justified must thus include not only its being properly held in accordance with inferential evidence, but also its being properly held through its truth being found to be basically, non-inferentially, evident.[13]

## Rational empiricist evidential practice

Under evidentialist ethics, the faith-beliefs of those who make faith-commitments need to be evidentially justified. Evidential justification requires a belief to be based on a correct judgement of its truth's evidential support. Such judgements can be made only from within some evidential practice that implicitly specifies the applicable norms. When

---

[13] The need to distinguish between a broad and a narrow, 'inferential', sense of evidence is helpfully articulated by Stephen J. Wykstra, who further notes that it is evidence in the broad sense that constitutes the 'natural' sense of the word. See his 'On Behalf of the Evidentialist: a Reply to Wolterstorff', in D. Z. Phillips and Timothy Tessin (eds), *Philosophy of Religion in the 21st Century* (New York: Palgrave, 2001), 66–7. Note how important it is that the holding of basic relations of evidential inferential support should be basically evident—otherwise every claim to the effect that p's truth supports q's will *itself* require evidential support, leading to a vicious regress. People's beliefs that inferential relations obtain must therefore sometimes be *non-inferentially* evidentially justified.

reflective theists come to judge evidential support for their faith–beliefs, what evidential practice should they take to apply?

It has been widely, if by no means universally, assumed that reflective theists should assess evidential support for their beliefs from within what I shall call our *rational empiricist evidential practice*.[14] This practice assumes deductive and inductive standards for inferential evidential support, and allows as basically evident only incorrigible and self–evident truths (including fundamental logical and mathematical truths) and truths evident in sensory perceptual experience under 'normal' conditions (i.e. in the absence of recognized overriders such as conditions known to create sensory illusions, etc.). The admission of just these categories of basically evident truths is not *ad hoc*, since claims in these categories are open to wide intersubjective agreement. Furthermore, under this evidential practice, judgements of evidential support for theistic beliefs are to be made taking into account *all* the evidence that 'we' have available that could conceivably be relevant to their truth: attending only to a restricted part of 'our' total evidence will not be warranted.[15] 'We' here grandly signifies the widest possible community of inquiry—no less than the entire human race over its full history to date. Reflective theists who accept this evidential practice, then, do their limited and fallible best to judge evidential support for theism on behalf of that all–encompassing community of inquiry.

Rational empiricist evidential practice is, broadly speaking, foundationalist—though it may well also meet key holist or coherentist insights.[16] But

---

[14] This practice might also, in a broad sense of 'scientific' be called our 'scientific evidential practice'. In a narrower sense of 'scientific', however, where that term means 'what is proper to natural and social scientific disciplines', what I am calling rational empiricist evidential practice contains, but is not identical to, 'scientific' evidential practice.

[15] Sometimes, of course, beliefs will be evidentially justified relatively to what is in fact restricted evidence because that restricted evidence will nevertheless count as all the evidence that is accessible to believers in their particular situation—all the evidence that those believers 'have'. It is quite difficult to say, I think, just what the criteria are for a given body of restricted evidence to meet the requirement of being *all the evidence a particular situated believer has*. These difficulties are avoided in the present case, however. Reflective believers must aim to judge against the evidence of all humanity—which may *include* evidence that may be private to them or to some local community to which they belong, but cannot be *restricted to* such evidence.

[16] It might be objected that the distinction here drawn between inferentially held (non–basic) beliefs and non–inferentially held (basic) beliefs assumes 'foundationalism' without giving the rival 'coherentist' or 'holist' position a proper hearing. Could not the looming vicious regress be avoided alternatively, by granting that our beliefs form a 'network' that 'meets the tribunal of experience as whole', in Quine's famous phrase? It is quite clear, however, that some beliefs are held without being consciously derived from already secured beliefs. Yet acknowledging that the distinction between basically and

it is not foundationalist in a Cartesian sense, since it allows more than just deductive inference to count as providing sufficient rational evidential support, and it need not buy into 'the myth of the given' by attaching certainty to any of the beliefs it allows as properly basic. (Rational empiricist evidential practice need not, that is, be held hostage to various—failed—historical attempts to construct extreme idealizations of it.) It is a fallibilist practice, because it allows that people may be evidentially justified in holding beliefs that yet remain open to future revision.

I shall not try to specify rational empiricist evidential practice any further. (Anyway, to do so comprehensively would be a daunting task—arguably, at present impossible, given the gaps in our understanding of the nature of ampliative forms of inference.) Rational empiricist evidential practice is, of course, open to sceptical objections. But I will not try to defend it against scepticism. Nor will I try to defend it as 'the right' practice to conform to under an evidentialist ethics of faith-commitment—indeed, in the next chapter I shall pay attention to epistemologies of religious belief that contest this very claim. I here do no more than observe that many philosophers have assumed that evidential support for the truth of theistic faith-beliefs should be evaluated from within rational empiricist evidential practice. That is enough to make it pertinent to inquire into the outcome of such an evaluation. And such an inquiry may be conducted competently, I think, even though no comprehensive canonical articulation of rational empiricist evidential practice is available. All we need is a practical grasp of its norms good enough for us to appreciate their implications when applied to theistic beliefs.

## Applying rational empiricist evidential practice to theistic faith-beliefs: an ambiguity thesis

How do theistic faith-beliefs fare when evaluated according to rational empiricist evidential practice? For present purposes, it suffices to consider

---

non-basically held beliefs is well founded is quite consistent with the essential holist point that a basic belief cannot be evidentially justified in isolation from other beliefs—e.g. my belief that there is a (real) tree in front of me cannot be evidentially justified unless I have a large number of other beliefs that are also evidentially justified (e.g. the belief that there are such things as trees, the belief that there is an external world, etc.).

this question just with respect to *core* theistic belief—the belief that God exists (according to the classical conception). Theistic faith-beliefs always do, of course, expand into the varied frameworks of belief of the historical theistic religious traditions. Arguably, some beliefs distinctive of such traditions are empirically verified—for example, historical beliefs about the lives of prophets such as Jesus and Mohammad.[17] The question is, however, whether what we may arguably take to be facts about the lives of certain historical persons are rightly interpreted as revelatory of a classical theistic Jewish, Christian or Muslim God, and how our evidence bears on *that* question. If we are to determine the bearing of our evidence on any particular, 'expanded' set of theistic religious beliefs, it will be economical first to consider how our evidence bears on the core beliefs of classical theism that (as is widely assumed) are held in common amongst these traditions.

Assessing all the available evidence relevant to the question whether a classical theistic God exists in accordance with rational empiricist evidential practice, might have any of three possible outcomes. It might show the truth of the claim that God exists to be significantly more probable than not; it might show the truth of the denial of the claim that God exists to be significantly more probable than not; or it might show neither the truth of the claim that God exists nor the truth of its denial to be significantly more probable than not. Under the first outcome, assuming evidentialism, epistemic—and presumably also moral[18]—entitlement to theistic commitment will be vindicated; whereas, on either of the other two outcomes, under that same assumption, people will be neither epistemically nor morally entitled to take core theistic belief to be true in their practical reasoning.

---

[17] The existence of any of the historical prophets is certainly falsi*fiable*—even if it is, on current evidence, reasonable to take it to be veri*fied*. If, to take an imaginary example, it should ever be established that Jesus was a purely mythical figure, orthodox Christian belief would then be falsified. The discovery of decisive evidence for Jesus's non-existence would not, of course, falsify classical theism—nor even certain revisionary forms of Christianity for which a mythical Jesus (invented perhaps by St Paul?) might be enough.

[18] Being epistemically entitled to take a proposition p to be true may well not *in general* be sufficient for being morally justified in so doing—it may be, to continue with the example already mentioned, that the demands of loyalty should sometimes override one's evidence-based judgements of (e.g.) a close friend's conduct, making it morally wrong to act on what one correctly judges justified on the evidence. In the particular case where one is epistemically entitled to take it to be true that God exists, however, the fact that God possesses moral perfection surely ensures that there could be no overriding moral reason for withholding active commitment to that belief?

Some philosophers maintain that a proper assessment of all the available evidence (under our rational empiricist evidential practice) yields the first outcome: in their view, though demonstrative proof of God's existence may not be possible, the overall evidence makes it significantly more probable than not that the God of classical theism exists. Richard Swinburne is a leading example of a contemporary philosopher who has provided impressive support for this view (and, indeed, the further view that the evidence supports the existence of *the Christian* God).[19] Other philosophers, however, of equal integrity and acumen, maintain that the weight of the evidence supports atheism—that is, makes it significantly more probable than not that the God of classical theism does not exist. J. L. Mackie is a notable case in point: his *The Miracle of Theism*, over twenty years since it was first published, remains a first-rate presentation of the philosophical case for atheism.[20] And the debate continues, it seems unabated.[21] But this is not the kind of debate where the more it continues the more doubtful each side becomes; to the contrary, each side remains convinced that the other is seriously in error.[22]

In this climate, it is hardly surprising that, amongst philosophers, a *thesis of the evidential ambiguity of theism* has become attractive. This thesis first asserts

---

[19] Swinburne is the author of a trilogy defending generic theism—*The Coherence of Theism* (1977), *The Existence of God* (1979; 2nd edn, 2004), and *Faith and Reason* (1981; 2nd edn, 2005)—and a tetralogy further defending specifically Christian theism—*Responsibility and Atonement* (1989), *Revelation: From Metaphor to Analogy* (1992), *The Christian God* (1994), and *Providence and the Problem of Evil* (1998)—all published at Oxford, Clarendon Press.

For examples of philosophers who go against the trend by holding that demonstrative proof of God's existence *is* possible, see William Lane Craig, *The Kalām Cosmological Argument* (New York: Barnes and Noble, 1979), David Braine, *The Reality of Time and the Existence of God: The Project of Proving God's Existence* (Oxford: Oxford University Press, 1988) and Barry Miller, *From Existence to God: A Contemporary Philosophical Argument* (London: Routledge, 1992).

[20] J. L. Mackie, *The Miracle of Theism: Arguments For and Against the Existence of God* (Oxford: Oxford University Press, 1982).

[21] See, for example, J. J. C. Smart and John Haldane, *Atheism and Theism* (Oxford: Blackwell, 1996; 2002 2nd edn); and, for a sample of current debate on the Argument from Evil, Daniel Howard-Snyder (ed.), *The Evidential Argument from Evil* (Bloomington, IN: Indiana University Press, 1996).

[22] As Robert McKim puts it, 'for every Richard Swinburne who adds up what he thinks to be the relevant evidence and gets a result that supports theism, there is a J. L. Mackie who gets an entirely different result, and, in general, for every theist to whom the facts of her experience appear to confirm that God exists there are apparently equally well-qualified nontheists, including members of nontheistic religions, agnostics and atheists, to whom the facts of their experience have no such significance' (Robert McKim, *Religious Ambiguity and Religious Diversity* (Oxford: Oxford University Press, 2001), 24). Such a situation is not untypical of central philosophical debates. Consider, for example, debates between various forms of realism and anti-realism, or the debate between compatibilists and incompatibilists over the free-will problem.

that, under our rational empiricist evidential practice, our total evidence leaves it open whether or not the classical theistic God exists. That is, the evidence is 'open' in the sense that it neither shows the truth of the claim that God exists nor the truth of its denial to be significantly more probable than not. The thesis then further describes this situation of open evidence as 'ambiguity' by making the claim that the total available evidence is systematically open to two viable competing interpretations—in a sense of 'viable' that is hard to make fully precise, but may be compared by analogy to the sense in which the drawing of the duck-rabbit is open to two viable perceptual *Gestalts*.[23]

The fact that, after centuries of debate, equally intelligent and well-informed thinkers continue to disagree about how to assess the evidence for and against God's existence does suggest—though, of course, it does not prove—that the evidence on this question is indeed ambiguous. Further support for this claim might be drawn from a closer analysis of attempts at 'disambiguation', both by theists and atheists. I myself incline to the view that the arguments of both natural theology and natural atheology typically exhibit epistemic circularity by resting on hidden presuppositions acceptable only to those already convinced of their conclusions—and, if that is correct,

---

[23] Compare John Hick's thesis of religious ambiguity, according to which our universe 'is capable from our present human vantage point of being thought and experienced in both religious and naturalistic ways' (*An Interpretation of Religion: Human Responses to the Transcendent* (London: Macmillan, 1989), 73). In part two of this work, Hick makes a case for concluding that this ambiguity is 'systematic', and must serve as the starting point for any defence of the rationality of religious commitment (124).

Note that if Hick's thesis is understood with 'capable' interpreted to mean *'justifiably* capable', then it takes a step beyond what I am here calling the thesis of the evidential ambiguity of theism. For, the evidential ambiguity thesis goes no further than affirming that theist and atheist/naturalist interpretations provide equally viable *Gestalts* on the totality of facts that constitute the evidence. One might grant evidential ambiguity, and yet deny that either the religious or the naturalist interpretation of the world is justifiable—by maintaining, of course, that the only justifiable attitude is suspension of belief.

The thesis of the evidential ambiguity of theism (as here understood) also needs to be distinguished from the claim that 'if God exists, God is hidden to a considerable extent from all human beings at almost all times' (McKim, *Religious Ambiguity and Religious Diversity*, 12). God could be hidden in the sense that his existence (if indeed he does exist) is not, either directly or inferentially, obvious to normally situated human beings, and yet it turn out that, on reflection, we *are* able to uncover evidence which more or less decisively settles the question of God's existence.

For further recent discussion of religious ambiguity see Stephen T. Davis, *Faith, Skepticism, and Evidence: An Essay in Religious Epistemology* (Lewisburg: Bucknell University Press, 1978), 179–82; Terence Penelhum, 'Reflections on the Ambiguity of the World', in Arvind Sharma (ed.), *God, Truth, and Reality: Essays in Honour of John Hick* (New York: St Martin's Press, 1993), 165–75, and *Reason and Religious Faith* (Boulder, CO: Westview Press, 1995), ch. 6, 109–43; and Daniel Howard-Snyder and Paul K. Moser (eds), *Divine Hiddenness: New Essays* (Cambridge: Cambridge University Press, 2002).

the case for the evidential ambiguity of theism is strengthened. Let me elaborate very briefly on this proposal—with a view to explaining it only: I make no claim to establish it.

Consider, for instance, the 'evidential' Argument from Evil. It holds that the existence of certain types of evil (such as, to take just one example, the humanly unobserved lingering death of a fawn severely burnt in a forest fire caused by a lightning strike)[24] renders it highly improbable that there exists a God who is both all-powerful and morally perfect. This inference seems to rest, however, on the 'noseeum' assumption[25] that if there were outweighingly valuable higher-order goods that—to use Mackie's term—'absorbed' such evils through having them as a logically necessary precondition, then we should be able to detect them. Yet those with theistic commitments may challenge that assumption: from their perspective, it may be reasonable to hold that infinite God may have morally adequate reasons beyond our ken for permitting natural evils.[26]

On the other side of the debate, consider the teleological argument, for example. This argument depends on taking it that apparently purposive order cannot simply be inherent in the natural order, but must be imposed by the operation of some intelligence—an assumption natural for someone already thinking as a theist, but arguably not compelling for convinced naturalists. Similarly, the cosmological argument from contingency depends on assuming that there has to be some explanation for the highly general fact that there is something rather than nothing—again, an assumption that seems self-evident to a theist but which may be denied by atheistic 'naturalists' for whom it is a sheer brute fact that the Universe came into and persists in existence. It may be, then, that the arguments of natural theology suffer from epistemic circularity, because their premises—including, their hidden premises—could reasonably be rejected by those not already persuaded of the truth of their conclusions.[27] The charge

---

[24] A much-discussed example, due to William L. Rowe, 'The Problem of Evil and Some Varieties of Atheism', *American Philosophical Quarterly*, 16 (1979), 335–41.

[25] This term is due to Stephen J. Wykstra, 'Rowe's Noseeum Arguments from Evil', in Howard-Snyder (ed.), *The Evidential Argument from Evil*, 126–50.

[26] This is the position that has come to be known as 'sceptical theism'. See Paul Draper, 'The Skeptical Theist', in Howard-Snyder (ed.), *The Evidential Argument from Evil*, 175–92.

[27] Compare Stephen T. Davis: 'The premises of a successful theistic proof ... [should] be known to be more plausible than their denials ... by any rational person; and ideally they must be known by the people to whom the rationality of belief in the existence of God is to be demonstrated. If the premises

of epistemic circularity may also, I think, plausibly be levelled against arguments from allegedly miraculous or revelatory historical events,[28] or from personal religious experience. Evidence private to an individual or a community *is* admissible, but, under rational empiricist evidential practice, is widely judged to support belief in God only when *already* interpreted from a theistic point of view, while competing non-theistic (or, 'naturalist') interpretations of the very same evidence seem clearly to be available.

The suggestion, then, is that an examination of attempts at disambiguating between theistic and atheistic/naturalist interpretations of the world might bring to light the fact that there is some systematic, principled reason why such attempts fail. Both theism and naturalism (roughly, the thesis that the world is just as depicted according to our best—or, perhaps rather, our ideally completed—scientific theories) seem able to provide viable overall interpretations of our total evidence. If, furthermore, each side seems to have available resources capable of meeting any new challenge from the other, then it may begin to seem that evidential ambiguity is here somehow necessary. Yet to try actually to establish the truth, let alone the necessary truth, of the evidential ambiguity of theism would be a major and controversial undertaking—and one I shall certainly not attempt.[29] All

of a theistic proof are more plausible than their denials but the relevant people do not know that fact, the rationality of theism will not be demonstrated to them' (*God, Reason, and Theistic Proofs* (Grand Rapids, MI: W. B. Eerdmans Publishers, 1997), 7).

[28] Hume famously argued against the reasonableness of accepting testimonial evidence in favour of supernatural interventionist miracles ('Of Miracles' in his *Enquiry Concerning Human Understanding* ed. P. H. Nidditch, 3rd edn. (Oxford: Clarendon Press, 1975). (For a useful collection of essays on this topic see Richard Swinburne, *Miracles* (London: Collier Macmillan, 1989.) To invoke Hume's rejection of the 'argument from miracles' confidently in the present context would, however, require rehabilitating a version of his argument against recent critics, including, for example, J. Houston, *Reported Miracles: A Critique of Hume* (Cambridge: Cambridge University Press, 1994); David Johnson, *Hume, Holism and Miracles* (Ithaca: Cornell University Press, 1999); and John Earman, *Hume's Abject Failure: The Argument against Miracles* (New York: Oxford University Press, 2000).

[29] Nevertheless, I will remark on two different lines of argument to the effect that the apparent evidential ambiguity of theism is merely apparent.

First, the ingenious suggestion has been made that its (first-order) evidential ambiguity *itself* counts as (second-order) evidence against theism, so that the thesis of evidential ambiguity is self-undermining: see J. L. Schellenberg, *Divine Hiddenness and Human Reason* (Ithaca: Cornell University Press, 1993). But, as Schellenberg notes, the problem of 'divine hiddenness' 'may ... be construed as a special instance of the problem of evil' (6). If it is so construed—I would suggest as a variant on the 'evidential' Argument from Evil—then it will, of course, be open to the same theistic replies. From within the perspective of theism, the hiddenness of God may count as just what is to be expected if the theistic God does indeed exist (as argued, for example, by Paul K. Moser in his exchange with Schellenberg in Michael L. Peterson and Raymond J. VanArragon (eds), *Contemporary Debates in Philosophy of Religion* (Malden, MA: Blackwell, 2004), 30–58).

I shall maintain is that the evidential ambiguity of theism is at least *plausible enough* for it to be important to consider what the implications of its truth would be for reflective believers' concern for the moral justifiability of their continued commitment to theism. It is, indeed, contentious whether or not classical theism is evidentially ambiguous: but it should not be contentious that we need to consider what the implications are if this thesis is true. For, its truth would provide at least one good explanation of the persistent disagreement over classical theism that prevails amongst philosophers of equal integrity and acumen.

I shall proceed, then, on the assumption that our total available evidence *is* ambiguous with respect to the truth of the claim that the God of classical theism exists, at least with respect to rational empiricist evidential practice. Granted that assumption, it follows that reflective theists (those who accept rational empiricist evidential practice, anyway) *cannot* satisfy themselves that their beliefs are evidentially justified. For, if this ambiguity thesis is correct, theistic beliefs are neither self-evident nor incorrigible, nor given in intersubjectively checkable sensory perceptual experience, nor rightly inferable from other evidentially justified beliefs. If epistemic entitlement as certified under this evidential practice is required for the moral probity of living by theistic beliefs, then the upshot is that it is *not* morally justifiable to make theistic faith-commitments. In which case, those inclined to *hold* some form of theism true are morally obliged to ensure that they do not *take* any theistic beliefs to be true in their practical reasoning—and also

Second, some philosophers have maintained that the truth of theism is only *apparently* evidentially ambiguous as a consequence of (a) the need for a person to be in a suitable *affective* state in order to appreciate the true force of the evidence, and (b) the fact that not all persons are in the required affective states. A useful account of the views of Jonathan Edwards and John Henry Newman along these lines is to be found in William J. Wainwright, *Reason and the Heart: A Prolegomenon to a Critique of Passional Reason* (Ithaca: Cornell University Press, 1995). While it is consistent to hold that those who fail to recognize that (specific) theistic beliefs are evidentially justified do so only as a result of sin, or from a failure of 'gratitude and the love of being in general' (Wainwright on Edwards, 51), or through poorly functioning 'noetic faculties' (Wainwright on Newman, 81), such views are not non-question-beggingly supported by the publicly available evidence about the psychological situation of atheists and agnostics. Views of this kind are, I think, better recast as claims that believers have experiences that ought to be admitted as evidence within a broader evidential practice than the rational empiricist one that (arguably) yields the evidential ambiguity of theism. This is, essentially, the approach of Reformed Epistemology, and I shall consider its response to evidential ambiguity in the following chapter. It may alternatively be argued that affectional factors can be admitted neither as *evidence* for the truth of any religious belief, nor as conditions on the possibility of appreciating the true force of the relevant evidence, but nevertheless do play a crucial and morally legitimate role in motivating faith-commitments. I shall be pursuing that Jamesian view from Chapter 5 onwards.

to use indirect means to try to eradicate that inclination, which puts them dispositionally at risk of making a moral error. (Here it is pertinent to remark—parenthetically at least—that although I have been emphasizing, as others often have not, the existence of moral obligations at the second locus of doxastic control (namely, direct control over what we take to be true in our reasoning, and with what weight), I do, of course, entirely accept the much more widely shared view that—where the beliefs concerned may influence morally significant actions—people do have obligations at the first locus of doxastic control (namely, indirect control over formation, retention, and revision of beliefs). Drawing attention to the existence of the second locus of doxastic control makes it clear that those who have failed to meet their obligations at the first locus with respect to a certain belief may have a chance to redeem themselves at the second locus if they recognize their failure and block their tendency to act on the suspect belief. Persons so situated ought also, however, to do what they can to correct their earlier failure by taking steps to eliminate or revise that belief.)

Many philosophers who accept the evidential ambiguity of theism—or, at least, who agree that it is plausible enough for its implications to need to be taken seriously—would want to resist the conclusion that, in view of that evidential ambiguity, theistic faith-commitment cannot be morally justified. They would hope to be able to defend the moral justifiability of taking theistic beliefs to be true (and letting oneself continue to hold them) even if those beliefs cannot be judged adequately evidentially supported under rational empiricist evidential practice. The question now is whether there is any basis for that hope. In the next chapter, then, I shall consider possible responses to the (assumed) truth of the ambiguity thesis from those who seek to show that theistic faith can be ethically viable.

It might thus seem that exploring the implications of the evidential ambiguity thesis for the moral justifiability of theistic faith-commitment could be only of academic interest to philosophers convinced that the truth of theism is either established or excluded by our total available evidence. Such an exploration would, I think, still be worthwhile if that were so—since those who take the evidential ambiguity of theism to be plausible form a large enough critical audience with which to engage.

In fact, however, many philosophers who reject the evidential ambiguity of theism have good reason to be interested in inquiring generally into the moral justifiability of theistic faith-commitments without evidential support. This is true most obviously of those who hold that *generic* theism is evidentially supported, but grant that evidential ambiguity affects every *specific expansion* of generic theism (i.e. who accept that, though Jews, Christians, and Muslims are all evidentially justified in believing that a classical theist God exists, the mutually incompatible claims they make about how God is revealed are beyond non-circular evidential support). It is also, if perhaps less obviously, true of philosophers who think that our total evidence *excludes* classical theism—at least if they wish to go on to maintain that classical theistic commitment is therefore morally unjustified. For, that conclusion depends on holding that commitments made consciously *contrary* to the evidence are morally impermissible. If those philosophers accept—as I think they should—that this claim needs defence and may not simply be dogmatically asserted, they will naturally be drawn into a *general* discussion of the importance of evidential support for morally justifiable faith-commitment. In particular, they will need to consider whether their moral exclusion of classical theism rests on a uniform moral evidentialism or, more narrowly, on the rejection specifically of morally justifiable commitment *contrary to* evidential support. That consideration will be especially important for those rejecters of *classical* theistic commitment who may wish to affirm the moral permissibility of some form of *revisionary* theistic commitment *that goes beyond, but not against,* what may reasonably be established on our total available evidence.

# 4

# Responses to evidential ambiguity: isolationist and Reformed epistemologies

Reflectiveï faith-believers are concerned for the moral justifiability of their practical commitment to the truth of their faith-beliefs. What are the implications, however, if their faith-beliefs are evidentially ambiguous, as may, plausibly enough, be the case with theistic faith-beliefs, as argued in the previous chapter?

If moral evidentialism is correct—if faith-commitments are morally justifiable only if they carry epistemic entitlement, and if that, in turn, requires the beliefs concerned to be evidentially justified—then the evidential ambiguity of theism will entail that theistic faith-commitment is *not* morally permissible. Of course, on those assumptions, practical commitment to the truth of atheism will *also* be morally unjustified, unless an implausibly strong presumption in favour of atheism can be defended.[1] But the parallel plight of reflective atheists will provide but slight comfort to reflective theists who

---

[1] Such a defence would have to maintain that lack of evidence for the truth of theism is *itself* evidence for the truth of atheism. Michael Scriven has subscribed to such a view (*Primary Philosophy* (New York: McGraw-Hill, 1966), 88, 102–7). As Thomas V. Morris has observed, however, lack of confirming evidence for the truth of a claim can be evidence for its falsity only when one is in 'a good epistemic position' with respect to the claim concerned—i.e. only when, had the claim been true, one would have had evidence for its truth. See Thomas V. Morris, 'Agnosticism', *Analysis*, 45 (1985), 222–3. But it may not, without begging the question, be assumed that we are in a good epistemic position with respect to the claim that God exists. Note that Antony Flew's thesis of the presumption of atheism ('The Presumption of Atheism', in id., *The Presumption of Atheism, and Other Philosophical Essays on God, Freedom and Immortality* (London: Elek for Pemberton, 1976), 13–30) falls short of the strong claim required, since the default position he defends is 'negative' atheism, which is merely not believing that God exists. Anthony Kenny provides a useful critique of Flew's view in *What Is Faith? Essays in the Philosophy of Religion* (New York: Oxford University Press, 1992), 58.

accept that, under rational empiricist evidential practice, their faith-beliefs are indeed evidentially ambiguous.[2] Such reflective theists will surely hope that some way of defending their moral probity can be found.

## Two strategies for defending the moral probity of theistic faith-belief in the face of evidential ambiguity

There are two broad strategies available for those who accept the evidential ambiguity of theistic faith-beliefs with respect to rational empiricist evidential practice, yet seek nevertheless to defend the moral justifiability of practical commitment to such beliefs.

The first strategy is to accept moral evidentialism but maintain that the evidential justifiability of theistic belief is not to be measured according to what I have called rational empiricist evidential practice. This strategy maintains that practical commitment to theistic beliefs may carry epistemic entitlement through their being evidentially justified *according to a specifically theistic evidential practice*. This strategy has both an isolationist (or relativist) and a Reformed epistemology variant. In this chapter, I shall consider this first strategy, and will argue that it has limitations that may be corrected only by abandoning it in favour of a second strategy which opens a door to fideism.

That second strategy is to raise doubts about moral evidentialism. Perhaps the ethics of faith-commitment are not uniformly evidentialist? Perhaps it is false that people may be morally justified in practical commitment to their faith-beliefs only if those beliefs are evidentially justified? Arguably, it is intrinsic to theistic (and relevantly similar) faith-beliefs that they have to be taken to be true by faith. Arguably, commitment to faith-propositions requires *doxastic venture*—taking to be true in one's practical reasoning the propositional contents of beliefs one holds while yet recognizing that their

---

[2] Under moral evidentialism, the ambiguity thesis will make greater existential demands on reflective theists than on reflective atheists. For the changes atheists need to make are relatively slight. Living out the suspension of belief in the truth of theist claims is largely equivalent in practice to living out disbelief: refraining from worship, for example, is much the same for those who think it false that God exists as for those who suspend judgement on the question—though agnostics may find socially prudent religious observance less bothersome than convinced atheists do.

truth *lacks* adequate support from one's total available evidence. Recall that moral evidentialism factors into two components: (1) the moral-epistemic link principle—morally justified practical commitment to faith-beliefs must carry epistemic entitlement, and (2) epistemic evidentialism—commitment to faith-beliefs carries epistemic entitlement only if those beliefs are held with evidential justification. It is thus an interesting question whether a defence of the moral justifiability of doxastic venture with respect to faith-beliefs will require rejecting (1) or (2) or both. What is entirely clear is that, if such doxastic venture is ever to be morally justified, the conjunction of (1) and (2) must be rejected.

## Appealing to a special theistic evidential practice/improved epistemologies

I will have more to say about the second strategy and its defence of doxastic venture in the following chapter. My task in this chapter is to consider the first strategy—which will certainly seem more attractive to those who are suspicious of fideism.

The ambiguity thesis holds (as we are assuming) only *relatively to* rational empiricist evidential practice. Theistic faith-commitment might yet conform to moral evidentialism if theistic beliefs were subject to *some other* evidential practice. Rational empiricism, in other words, might be *a bad theory* of the evidential practice appropriate to theistic beliefs. Perhaps, under an epistemology which yields an improved theory of the applicable evidential practice, it turns out that one may be evidentially justified in holding theistic beliefs?

What might those improved epistemologies be? I shall consider proposals of two broad kinds: isolationist epistemology and Reformed epistemology.

## An isolationist epistemology

As its name indicates, this epistemology *epistemically isolates* questions of evidential support for theistic claims from the standards of any wider, generally prevailing, evidential practice. Isolationist epistemology maintains that people's theistic beliefs form a *doxastic framework* within their overall network of beliefs—a framework which, furthermore, carries its own special evidential practice for assessing support for theistic truth-claims. According to an isolationist epistemology of theistic beliefs, there necessarily cannot be any *external* issue of their evidential justifiability, since questions about the extent to which evidence supports their truth make sense only internally to some specifically theistic doxastic framework.[3]

Now, it is true that theistic faith-beliefs do form an identifiable body within a person's overall network of beliefs or 'noetic structure'.[4] Describing that body of beliefs as a 'framework' also seems apt, since certain fundamental principles need to be held true if a person is to have any theistic beliefs at all, and acceptance of these principles is implicated in the generation of further theistic beliefs. To have theistic faith-beliefs, a person must hold it true that some more or less specific kind of theistic God exists, and that certain more or less specific kinds of sources reveal, within limits, God's will and activity. These claims may be described as the 'framing' or 'framework' principles of the person's framework of theistic faith-beliefs.[5] Furthermore, specific theistic framing principles entail that, within the

---

[3] An isolationist epistemology of religious beliefs is widely characterized, following Kai Nielsen, as 'Wittgensteinian fideism', through its association with philosophers influenced by Wittgenstein, such as D. Z. Phillips and Norman Malcolm (Kai Nielsen, 'Wittgensteinian Fideism', *Philosophy*, 42 (1967), 191–209; D. Z. Phillips, *The Concept of Prayer* (London: Routledge and Kegan Paul, 1965); D. Z. Phillips, *Faith and Philosophical Enquiry* (London: Routledge & Kegan Paul, 1970); Norman Malcolm, 'The Groundlessness of Belief', in R. Douglas Geivett and Brendan Sweetman (eds), *Contemporary Perspectives on Religious Epistemology* (New York: Oxford University Press, 1992), first published 1977). Note that the claim that the *meaning* of religious beliefs can be understood only from within the 'form of life' to which they belong ('isolationist semanticism') is not essential to an isolationist epistemology. Indeed, as Gary Gutting observes, to accept isolationist semanticism would undermine the essential functions of religious belief: ' ... if the meaning of religious claims is entirely *sui generis*, then there are no *religious* answers to our basic human questions about suffering, death, love and hope' (*Religious Belief and Religious Skepticism* (Notre Dame, IN: University of Notre Dame Press, 1982), 41). Isolationist semanticism is, however, a caricature not only of Wittgenstein, but also of those influenced by him, such as Phillips. It may also, perhaps, be a caricature to take Phillips to be committed to an isolationist epistemology—yet this view is sufficiently well entrenched as an option in the epistemology of religious belief for it to be worth considering here. For useful discussion, see Richard Amesbury, 'Fideism', in Edward N. Zalta (ed.), *The Stanford Encyclopedia of Philosophy (Summer 2005 Edition)*, <http://plato.stanford.edu/archives/sum2005/entries/fideism/>.

[4] The term is Alvin Plantinga's. See *Warranted Christian Belief*, 83.

[5] Norman Malcolm uses the notion of a framework principle in explicating Wittgenstein's remarks on 'groundless believing' in *On Certainty*, in relation to such examples as 'the principle of the continuity of nature' and 'the assumption that material things do not cease to exist without material cause' (See 'The Groundlessness of Belief', 94.) Compare also Hilary Putnam's use of the term 'framework principles' in the context of the natural sciences to describe principles that 'are employed as auxiliaries to make predictions in an overwhelming number of experiments, without themselves being jeopardized by any possible experimental results'. Putnam gives the physical principle $f = ma$ as an example. See Hilary Putnam, *Mind, Language, and Reality* (Cambridge: Cambridge University Press, 1975), 48–9.

framework, certain beliefs provide evidence for the truth of further beliefs. (For example, certain passages from Paul's Epistle to the Romans count as evidence for the truth of Luther's doctrine of justification by faith alone.) Such inferences will be governed by logical principles applicable to beliefs generally—though special hermeneutic principles will also apply (relating, for example, to discerning 'what the Spirit is saying to the church' through sacred scriptures). In any case, the fact that certain kinds of evidence are admissible only within a theistic doxastic framework is enough to show that its associated evidential practice is, at least in part, distinct from that which applies generally. Theistic faith does, then, involve an identifiable theistic *doxastic practice*, and theistic beliefs form a doxastic framework formed, held, and employed in accordance with that practice.[6]

Isolationist epistemology places a certain interpretation on this—in itself perfectly apt—talk of a theistic doxastic practice and of theistic beliefs as forming a doxastic framework. The key isolationist move is to treat the truth of a theistic doxastic framework's principles as *necessarily* not open to assessment in the light of evidence *from outside* the framework. (Within the framework, of course, their truth is simply presupposed as foundational.) The isolationist insists that a foundational claim such as that God exists and is revealed in Jesus the Christ is not properly treated as an hypothesis open to assessment within rational empiricist evidential practice; rather it is a framing principle of a separate framework of Christian beliefs to which a distinct evidential practice applies. To the evidentialist charge that theists are not epistemically entitled to commit themselves to foundational theistic principles that they are not able to judge evidentially supported, the isolationist will issue the *tu quoque* reply that, by the same token, evidentialists should not be epistemically entitled to rely on the principles of their own frameworks of belief—and they are guilty of double standards

---

[6] I here use the term 'doxastic practice' more in Nicholas Wolterstorff's extended sense than in the sense William Alston originally gave to it. Theistic doxastic practice involves not just 'a constellation of habits of forming beliefs in a certain way on the basis of inputs that consist of sense experiences' (Alston, 'A "Doxastic Practice" Approach to Epistemology', in M. Clay and K. Lehrer (eds), *Knowledge and Skepticism* (Boulder, CO: Westview Press, 1989), 5), but also actions such as 'gathering evidence, appraising the evidence so as to determine probability, etc.' (Wolterstorff, *John Locke and the Ethics of Belief*, xviii), and regulating and judging such actions in the light of accepted norms (the norms of what I have called an 'evidential practice'). My own working definition is as follows: a doxastic practice is a complex of both habituated and voluntary behaviour relating to the formation, revision, and evaluation of beliefs within a given *doxastic framework*, including the assessment of the epistemic merit of beliefs in the light of evidence in accordance with an associated *evidential practice*.

if they assign epistemic blame to theists while assuming their own epistemic virtue.[7]

What reasons may be given, though, for the isolationist's key move? It certainly stands in need of support. For, we may concede the framework structure of theistic beliefs, with foundational framing principles playing a cardinal role, without at all accepting the isolationist claim that the truth of those principles is evidentially insulated from the overall network of beliefs and from wider evidential practice. 'Framework' talk is liable to be heard incautiously as talk of *self-contained* frameworks—but once the metaphor is cashed it is clear that what is meant by acknowledging that theistic beliefs form a framework does not necessarily entail their epistemic isolation. There may be distinctive frameworks of belief within a total noetic structure, but they need not necessarily function as self-contained doxastic islands. The truth of foundational theistic principles does indeed need to be presupposed from within the framework of theistic belief, but that does not imply that those principles are altogether immune from external rational assessment in the light of overall evidence.[8]

Decisive independent support for an isolationist epistemology of theistic belief will be provided, however, if such beliefs require a *non-realist* interpretation, according to which they perform some function *other than* making claims about mind-independent reality. The immunity of foundational theistic framing principles from external evidential assessment would then follow immediately. Let me elaborate.

The contrast between realism and non-realism is, I think, best made at the level of the *utterances* characteristic of a certain kind of discourse—in the present case, theistic religious discourse. Theological realists hold that these utterances express truth-claims about reality as it is independently of any attitudes that anyone has on the matter. Theological non-realists maintain that theistic utterances perform some different function, and they generally

---

[7] Compare Malcolm: 'Religion is a form of life; it is language embedded in action—what Wittgenstein calls a "language game". Science is another. Neither stands in need of justification, the one no more than the other' ('The Groundlessness of Belief', 100).

[8] Compare Kai Nielsen: 'Wittgensteinians such as Malcolm are making a dogmatic, groundless claim—a claim that is hardly a framework-belief in any established language game—when they assert, as Malcolm actually does, that "within a language game there is justification and lack of justification, evidence and proof, mistakes and groundless opinion" but that "one cannot properly apply these terms to the language game itself"' (Kai Nielsen, *God, Scepticism, and Modernity* (Ottawa: University of Ottawa Press, 1989), 131; the encapsulated reference is to Norman Malcolm, *Thought and Knowledge: Essays* (Ithaca, NY: Cornell University Press, 1977), 208).

agree that the *ultimate* function of theological utterances is *expressive* and/or *hortatory*. Such utterances ultimately serve to express the fundamental values of a historical faith community and tradition, and to encourage solidarity in honouring those values. For non-realists, the core theistic belief that God exists, properly understood, functions ultimately as the expression of a certain kind of commitment to values, rather than as a purported description of how things are independently of what we ourselves believe.

The most plausible form of theological non-realism accepts, however, that theological utterances perform their expressive and hortatory function by *describing* states of affairs and events (e.g. God's existence, the Incarnation, etc.). But it maintains that these descriptions can hold true only of a psychosocially constructed 'reality'—in other words, an essentially *fictional* or mythic realm that serves a symbolic function as a vehicle for expressing and encouraging commitment to the community's core values.[9] Theological non-realism is thus typically *cognitivist* in that it accepts that theistic religious utterances have truth-values, even though the truth-makers for such utterances belong to a fictional realm rather than to mind-independent reality.[10]

So, for theological non-realists, it is not quite the case that, as B. R. Tilghman has put it, 'the concept of God and the concept of evidence don't go together'.[11] Given its retention of cognitivism about theological utterances, non-realism holds it to be quite coherent to speak of evidential support for a theological claim's truth, and of the degree of evidential justification enjoyed by a theistic belief. But the question of evidential justification for theistic beliefs can only be, for the theological non-realist, the *internal* question whether their truth is supported by evidence recognized as such *within* an established theistic evidential practice. Tilghman's remark needs revision: for the non-realist, the concept of God and the concept of *external* evidence don't go together. On the non-realist view, there is simply no coherent notion of the truth of a theistic belief beyond its truth-in-context, relative

---

[9] Recall Cupitt's description of God as 'the mythical embodiment of all one is concerned with in the spiritual life' (see Chapter 3, *n.* 2).

[10] Compare Richard Braithwaite's view that a religious assertion is 'the assertion of an intention to carry out a certain behaviour policy, subsumable under a sufficiently general principle to be a moral one, together with the implicit or explicit *statement, but not the assertion*, of certain stories' ('An Empiricist's View of the Nature of Religious Belief', in Basil Mitchell (ed.), *The Philosophy of Religion* (Oxford: Oxford University Press, 1971), 89, (my emphasis).

[11] Benjamin R. Tilghman, *An Introduction to the Philosophy of Religion*, (Oxford: Blackwell, 1994), 225.

to the mythic fictional 'God-world'. If non-realism is correct, then, the only possible epistemology for theistic belief is an isolationist epistemology.

That principled basis for adopting an isolationist epistemology of theistic belief is—obviously—not available to realists, who must resist the truth-relativism of the non-realist view. It might thus seem *ad hoc* for a theological realist to maintain that theistic beliefs belong to an epistemically isolated doxastic framework. *Prima facie*, if theistic beliefs refer just as much to mind-independent reality as perceptual and scientific beliefs do, theistic beliefs must surely fall within the very same evidential practice that applies to the latter?

Fortunately, there is no need here to pursue the question whether there could nevertheless be a good realist reason for adopting an isolationist epistemology of theistic belief, nor to enter the debate between theological realists and non-realists. For, I shall now argue that isolationist epistemology, however motivated, has limited worth in meeting reflective theists' concern for the justifiability of their faith-commitments. Reflective theists, I shall maintain, could not satisfy themselves that their faith-commitments are morally justifiable by judging their beliefs to be evidentially justified in accordance with a purely isolationist account of such justification.

Under isolationist epistemology issues of evidential justifiability are exhausted internally to the framework of theistic belief. Reflective theists will be able to assure themselves that they are evidentially justified in holding particular theistic beliefs by checking that their truth is supported by evidence *that counts as such from within* the framing principles and norms of the relevant theistic evidential practice (a Christian may, for example, be satisfied that scripture and tradition certify the truth of Christ's Resurrection). But, under isolationist epistemology, that method cannot apply without circularity *to the theistic framework's framing principles themselves.* There is no possibility of *first* satisfying oneself from a neutral position that one would be evidentially justified in holding those principles, and *only then* committing oneself to the framework. Under isolationist epistemology, one has in practice either to adopt or not adopt the framework without even the possibility of prior evidential guidance as to the epistemic justifiability of its principles.

The resources of isolationist epistemology, then, cannot provide an answer to *external* questions about the justifiability of commitment to the truth of the principles of the theistic doxastic framework. But such an external question may indeed arise—and, while that question cannot for the isolationist be a question of evidential justifiability, it *may* be the question of *moral* justifiability with which, as I have argued, reflective theists are anyway at root concerned. So, an isolationist *epistemology* does not entail an *altogether* isolationist view of the justifiability of active commitment to the truth of theistic faith-beliefs, since an *external moral* question may arise whether to commit oneself to the theistic doxastic framework as a whole. But, under isolationist epistemology, settling that moral question will have to be done without any possibility of an assurance of evidential support for the truth of the relevant framework principles.[12]

The upshot, then, of adopting an isolationist epistemology in response to the ambiguity thesis is to portray reflective theists as needing to decide whether they may (continue to) take the framing principles of a theistic doxastic framework to be true *in a context where they are necessarily in no position to conform to an evidentialist ethic* by judging the truth of those principles to be supported by independent evidence. This approach turns out, then, to *challenge* moral evidentialism, rather than to offer a way of respecting it in the face of evidential ambiguity under empiricist evidential practice.[13] In fact, isolationist epistemology ends up depicting reflective theists as making a doxastic venture beyond any possible evidential support in their practical

[12] It is important to recognize, then, that an external question about the justifiability of taking theistic beliefs to be true arises *not only for realists but also for non-realists*. The *evidential* justifiability of theistic beliefs can only be an internal matter on a non-realist view—but the question of the *moral* justifiability of adopting the whole framework of theistic doxastic practice remains as, necessarily, an external question. Non-realists tend to fail to recognize the possibility and importance of any external issue as to the justifiability of theistic commitment (the 'this language game is played' syndrome). Realists, on the other hand, readily recognize the justifiability of theistic commitment as an external issue—but they tend to suppose that it is purely epistemic, failing to see that it is ultimately a moral issue.

Imran Aijaz has pointed out (personal communication) that an isolationist who was also a meta-ethical Divine Command theorist (holding that the truth-makers for moral truth are God's commands) would reject external justifiability questions *altogether* by claiming that all moral questions are able to be settled only from within the theistic doxastic framework. Divine Command meta-ethics are, of course, controversial. Even so, the question whether to commit oneself *in practice* to the principles of a theistic doxastic framework (which would, on the view under consideration, incorporate *all* substantive moral principles), will still have to be faced by a reflective theist—and venturing such commitment would then not only necessarily have to proceed without evidential guidance (which is my present main point), but also without any moral guidance. I shall return to the issue of how faith-commitments to claims about what sort of a world this is are related to moral commitments in Chapter 7.

[13] This finding confirms a point already made at the start of Chapter 3. If we adopt theological non-realism—which provides a principled basis for an isolationist epistemology of theistic belief—we lose our grounds for supposing that commitment to theistic beliefs can be morally justified only if it carries epistemic entitlement (i.e. for supposing that the moral-epistemic link principle and, *a fortiori*, moral evidentialism hold true).

commitment to foundational theistic faith-beliefs. Under isolationist epis-temology, then, if such commitment may be morally permissible, moral evidentialism cannot apply uniformly to commitment to faith-propositions: it must sometimes be morally justifiable to make such a commitment with-out being evidentially justified in doing so. The isolationist way of trying to carry out the first strategy ('find an "improved" epistemology more favourable to theistic belief') thus points towards the need to pursue the second, fideist, strategy—namely, to defend the moral permissibility of taking framework principles to be true *without* being able to judge their truth to be supported by one's evidence.

## Reformed epistemology

The first strategy for responding to the presumed evidential ambiguity of theism, it will be recalled, is to accept moral evidentialism but argue that its requirements may be met by theistic belief once it becomes clear that what I have called rational empiricist evidential practice is *not* the evidential practice properly applicable to theistic belief. A different approach to this strategy—different from, and, one might hope, more successful than, the isolationist approach just considered—might be thought to be offered by Reformed epistemology.

The key move of Reformed epistemology is to propose that cer-tain foundational theistic beliefs are *properly basic* beliefs.[14] Reformed epistemologists may concede (*pace* the natural theologians) that core theistic beliefs cannot have their truth established *by inference* from that of other beliefs generally accepted as evidentially justified. They resist concluding, however, that theistic beliefs cannot therefore be evidentially justified. For they maintain that some theistic beliefs may be evidential-ly justified because their truth is (I shall say) *basically, non-inferentially, evident.*

Reformed epistemology thus maintains, in effect, that the correct theory of the evidential practice applicable to theistic belief is *an expansion* of rational empiricist evidential practice that admits as properly basic certain

---

[14] Alvin Plantinga introduces this term in 'Is Belief in God Properly Basic?' in Geivett and Sweetman (eds), *Contemporary Perspectives on Religious Epistemology*, 133–41. This paper was originally published in *Noûs*, 25 (1981), 41–51.

foundational theistic beliefs *in addition to* the foundational logical and mathematical and sensory perceptual beliefs that can count as properly basic for empiricist evidential practice.[15] Reformed epistemology thus shares with isolationist epistemology the fact that it appeals to a *specifically theistic* evidential practice. However, whereas isolationist epistemology locates that special evidential practice in a *separate* theistic doxastic framework whose principles are epistemically insulated from the network of beliefs as a whole, Reformed epistemology preserves the notion of a single evidential practice, but argues that theists may properly take it to admit a class of basically evident theologically laden truths—truths directly revealed in experience—inadmissible under the rational empiricist theory of evidential practice.

Can Reformed epistemology play the role here envisaged for it? Can it be used to show that reflective theists may meet the requirement of moral evidentialism—that is, the requirement to take to be true in practical reasoning only what it is evidentially justified to hold to be true? (Reformed epistemologists themselves would not put the question of the success of their theory in quite this way, since they do not construe evidentialism morally nor even explicitly recognize it as governing active takings-to-be-true-in-reasoning as well as static holdings-true. Nevertheless, Reformed epistemology does affirm that theists do conform to a suitably expanded evidentialism, and the way to test that claim in the dialectical context I have developed is by considering the question just asked.)

Moral evidentialism holds that, to answer their, ultimately moral, *de jure* question, reflective theists need to be satisfied of their epistemic entitlement to take theistic beliefs to be true. And to be satisfied of

---

[15] It was a mistake to express the thesis of Reformed epistemology as the claim that 'it is entirely right, rational, reasonable, and proper to believe in God without any evidence or argument at all', as Plantinga did in his 1983 paper 'Reason and Belief in God' (in Plantinga and Wolterstorff (eds), *Faith and Rationality*, 17). This mistake is well brought to light by Norman Kretzmann in 'Evidence against Anti-Evidentialism', in Kelly James Clark (ed.), *Our Knowledge of God: Essays on Natural and Philosophical Theology* (Dordrecht: Kluwer Academic Publishers, 1992, 17–38). There is room, however, for an improved understanding of Reformed epistemology as resisting *only the narrow kind of evidentialism* that *requires* 'inferential' evidence for justifiably held theistic belief. At the same time, Reformed epistemology, properly understood, affirms *another, broader, kind of evidentialism*—one that admits that it may be evidentially justified to hold some beliefs on the grounds of their being *basically* evident—and claims that theistic belief meets the requirements of *the right kind of* evidentialism, namely the broader kind. As already noted (Chapter 3, *n*. 13), the importance of distinguishing narrow and broad notions of evidential support is helpfully articulated by Stephen J. Wykstra in 'On Behalf of the Evidentialist: a Reply to Wolterstorff'.

that they need to check that those beliefs are evidentially justified. That requires them to be satisfied that their evidence supports the truth of their beliefs, according to the norms of *the right* evidential practice. According to Reformed epistemology, the right evidential practice admits certain foundational theistic beliefs as *basically* evident. To be satisfied of their epistemic entitlement to take such beliefs to be true, however, reflective theists will obviously have to be satisfied of the truth of this last claim. For it is one thing to recognize that there is (or could be) an evidential practice that takes certain theistic beliefs as basically evident, and it is another to satisfy oneself that one may *rightly* commit oneself to such a practice. There could, in principle, be indefinitely many such practices, each taking different kinds of beliefs to be properly basic. To persist with the established bizarre example,[16] someone could *claim* that the belief that the Great Pumpkin returns to the pumpkin patch every Halloween may properly be held as a basic belief, but that claim seems quite unjustified: an evidential practice that licensed such a belief as basically evident would not be legitimate. (Rather more serious examples do, of course, come to mind: the basic faith-beliefs of a suicide bomber, for example, or of nationalists who believe they are specially favoured by God.)

What reason, then, do reflective theists have for taking an evidential practice licensing certain theistic beliefs as basically evident to be legitimately applicable to them? Indeed, can any such reason be found that would not generate a parallel reason for a putative reflective follower of the 'Pumpkinist' cult of Charles Schulz's *Peanuts* cartoons?

Reformed epistemologists have tried two kinds of answers to this pressing question. First, they have explored the extent to which the doxastic practice that takes the truth of some theistic beliefs to be basically evident in experience may be afforded the same status as doxastic practices that are so entrenched that they could not be supposed in practice to be anything other than epistemically legitimate.[17] For example, our sensory perceptual doxastic practice takes perceptual beliefs as basically evident (in the absence of recognized 'overriders', such as conditions known to create illusions, etc.)—and it carries with it an evidential practice that regards

---

[16] See Plantinga, 'Is Belief in God Properly Basic?', 139, and Plantinga, 'Reason and Belief in God', 74.

[17] This is William Alston's approach. See *Perceiving God: The Epistemology of Religious Experience* (Ithaca, NY: Cornell University Press, 1991), ch. 4.

holding such beliefs as, non-inferentially, evidentially justified. But are we epistemically entitled to adopt that empiricist evidential practice? If an affirmative answer requires external evidence which shows that practice to be epistemically legitimate, then, as the history of scepticism indicates, it is highly unlikely that an affirmative answer will be forthcoming. (When we search for such evidence we find no inconsistency in thinking to ourselves: I *might* have a creator to whose deceptive mischief I am subject; I *might* be a brain in a vat. Furthermore, evidence that tells against these claims seems to be admissible only if they are already assumed false.) Yet our inability to provide an external evidential justification for the legitimacy of sensory perceptual doxastic practice does not have the remotest tendency to undermine our practical commitment to it. Furthermore, we do not entertain for a moment that idea that we might not be wholly within our epistemic rights in taking our unoverridden basic perceptual beliefs to be true in our practical reasoning.[18] Is it not, then, simply 'epistemological imperialism' to hold that a doxastic practice that takes certain theistic beliefs as properly basic must be undermined by the absence of external evidence for the truth of those beliefs?[19]

This 'parity' response fails, however. True, external evidence for the epistemic legitimacy of sensory perceptual doxastic practice is not available. A doxastic practice that allows certain theistic beliefs as basically evident in experience may thus be on a par with sensory perceptual doxastic practice in that respect. Furthermore, both sensory perceptual doxastic practice and theistic doxastic practice are established in a way in which Pumpkinist doxastic practice is not established—though, recalling the more serious examples, intolerant exclusivist religions have doxastic practices which surely do count as established. But, short of madness, it would be psychologically impossible not to be committed to sensory perceptual doxastic practice, whereas not committing oneself to theistic doxastic practice is entirely psychologically feasible. When we function properly, we are simply not able generally to refrain from taking our unoverridden basic perceptual beliefs to be true in our practical reasoning; nothing of the sort is true for basic theistic beliefs, at least for the vast majority of those who hold them.

---

[18] Empiricist evidential practice will implicitly specify conditions that override perceptual beliefs: the question of how to articulate these conditions adequately is a major topic in the philosophy of perception.

[19] The term 'epistemological imperialism' is Alston's (*Perceiving God*, 199).

Doubts about *the propositional-attitude-focused issue* of the epistemic status of perceptual beliefs are certainly real, however: even though we cannot generally do otherwise than take them to be true, they *might* be caused in such a way as to lack all epistemic worth (e.g. by a mischievously deceiving creator). Descartes was right, however, to describe these doubts as *hyperbolical*, because they do not give rise to doubts about *the agency-focused issue of our epistemic entitlement to act on such beliefs*.[20] Sane humans simply do not have the capacity not to take such beliefs to be true—even when their philosophical consciousness has been raised to the degree necessary for them to acknowledge the reality of doubts about the epistemic status of those beliefs. We are by nature deeply habituated (even 'hardwired') generally to take our unoverridden basic perceptual beliefs to be true—something for which an explanation might be sought in evolutionary psychology.[21] There can therefore be no real issue as to whether we are generally within our epistemic rights in acting on what our perceptual experience causes us to believe. (Indeed, one has only to articulate that question to be struck by how impossible it would be to take it seriously: 'You might just as well ask whether we are within our property rights when we take in oxygen at each breath.') We are epistemically entitled in general to take our unoverridden basic perceptual beliefs to be true, because we have no real capacity to do otherwise ('ought implies can'). The *de jure* question about basic perceptual belief thus gets answered affirmatively only, so to speak, *by default*. The mere coherence of Cartesian hyperbolical doubt is enough, however, to undermine any attempt to argue from our epistemic entitlement to act on our unoverridden basic perceptual beliefs to the conclusion that those beliefs definitely do possess genuine epistemic worth.

[20] The importance of distinguishing between epistemic entitlement in the agency-focused sense and epistemic justification in the propositional-attitude-focused sense as explained in Chapter 3 is here most salient. If that distinction is ignored, it is easy to suppose that the coherence of Cartesian doubts must impugn our epistemic entitlement to act on perceptual—and, for that matter, mathematical and logical—beliefs.

[21] As already noted in Chapter 2, when it comes to basic perceptual beliefs, our tendency to take to be true in our practical reasoning what we hold to be true may be so deeply habituated that, in many cases, we cannot resist it, and certainly could not *wholly* go against it. Sometimes, of course, we can resist acting on basic perceptual beliefs formed under circumstances we recognize as illusory. So, presumably, with some actually unoverridden basic perceptual beliefs, we could set our minds to the task of trying to ignore them in practice (i.e. trying to behave as if they had been overridden). My present point, however, is that it is not a psychological possibility for a sane person to do this with respect to his or her entire category of basic perceptual beliefs, or even any sizeable subcategory of such beliefs.

There is no real possibility of *our treating them* otherwise, but that does not establish that they *actually* do possess epistemic justification.[22] Our inability to assure ourselves that basic perceptual beliefs do have epistemic worth is, however, scary only in a purely theoretical or 'academic' way: it cannot generate a genuine fear about our actual practice, nor give us any sense that we are taking a risky venture in acting on our basic perceptual beliefs. Accordingly, we are epistemically entitled to follow an evidential practice that accepts unoverridden sensory perceptual beliefs as basically evident, even though no *ultimate* guarantee of the epistemic legitimacy of such a practice is forthcoming.

When it comes to a theistic doxastic practice, with its special evidential practice, the situation is importantly different, however. There *is* a real issue about our epistemic—and, as I have been at pains to point out, our moral—entitlement to act on any theistic beliefs at all. Humans are *not* hardwired to act on theistic—or any religious—beliefs. Manifestly, one can remain sane and altogether refrain from taking any theistic or religious claims to be true. It is true, of course, that religious beliefs—in the sense of beliefs about supernatural agency of various kinds—are remarkably ubiquitous. Recent work in evolutionary psychology and anthropology suggests that our tendency to form religious representations can be understood as a 'spandrel'—a side-effect of evolved capacities for forming beliefs about agents (prey, predators, conspecifics) in our ancestral environment.[23] But that work also shows how ambivalence about religious beliefs is part of our evolved human nature—a feature that fits with the obvious fact that our evolved tendencies to believe in supernatural agencies do not have to be acted upon. Commitment to a theistic doxastic practice, then, is by no means psychologically unavoidable. Accordingly, there *is* an issue as to whether such commitment may

---

[22] I am not suggesting, then, that hyperbolical sceptical doubts about the epistemic status of perceptual beliefs (or mathematical or logical beliefs, for that matter) can be *answered* by appeal to the psychological unavoidability, for sane humans, of practical commitment in general to the truth of such beliefs. Rather, I am drawing attention to something I take to be incontestable: sane humans are unavoidably immersed in certain doxastic practices that essentially involve generally taking certain kinds of truth as basically evident. There can thus be no issue as to whether sane humans are epistemically entitled to take those basic beliefs to be true in their practical reasoning. Their doing so is in accordance with the proper exercise of their epistemic capacities, for those capacities cannot in general be exercised otherwise.

[23] See Pascal Boyer, *Religion Explained: The Evolutionary Origins of Religious Thought* (New York: Basic Books, 2001) and Scott Atran, *In Gods We Trust: The Evolutionary Landscape of Religion*, Evolution and Cognition (New York: Oxford University Press, 2002).

carry epistemic and moral entitlement. And that issue cannot be settled by appealing to the established status of theistic doxastic practice, since that status is historically and psychologically contingent, by contrast with the established status of sensory perceptual doxastic practice, which is a matter of universal psychological necessity. Given the ambiguity thesis, then, to commit oneself in one's actions and way of life to a particular theistic doxastic practice requires *a real, epistemically and morally significant psychological venture* beyond what one is able to establish on the basis of evidence—whereas only a psychologically hardwired and thus purely technical 'venture' lies at the root of commitment to sensory perceptual doxastic practice (or mathematical and logical doxastic practice, for that matter).

The parity argument, then, proves unsatisfactory—and for reasons that point the way towards recognizing that commitment to a theistic doxastic practice requires doxastic venture. There is, however, a second Reformed epistemologist approach to answering the Great Pumpkin objection—a second way of trying to defend the epistemic propriety of commitment to a doxastic practice that allows certain theistic beliefs as basically evident without at the same time indiscriminately admitting indefinitely many absurd or pernicious actual or possible doxastic practices.

The key to this second approach is an appeal to an externalist epistemology—that is, appeal to the claim that a person's beliefs can have epistemic worth in virtue of the way in which they are caused, independently of any support for their truth from evidence accessible to the believer. Alvin Plantinga's Reformed epistemology offers the most fully worked out version of this approach in his theory of 'warrant'. Plantinga uses 'warrant' as a technical term for what counts in my terminology as a propositional-attitude-focused notion: Plantingan warrant is a property that may or may not be possessed by a person's state of belief. For a belief to have warrant is for it to have what is needed to convert true belief to knowledge.[24] And Plantinga gives an externalist theory of what warrant is: for Plantinga, a belief has warrant if it is produced by cognitive faculties functioning properly in an appropriate environment according to a design-plan successfully aimed at truth.[25]

---

[24] See the opening sentence of *Warrant: The Current Debate*, 3.    [25] *Warranted Christian Belief*, 156.

Plantinga applies this externalist account of warrant to theistic belief to yield what I shall here call his *central claim*—namely, that 'if theistic belief is *true*, then it seems likely that it *does* have warrant'.[26] This central claim is supported by arguing that, if a theistic God does indeed exist, the cognitive mechanisms which actually produce basic theistic beliefs constitute the means deliberately intended by God to bring about apprehension of his existence.[27] Thus, if theism is true, conditions sufficient for the 'warrantedness' of basic theistic beliefs obtain. (And, it may be added, basic beliefs in the Great Pumpkin will not be warranted because they do not result from a cognitive mechanism designed to yield truths—but rather through mechanisms whose proper functioning is not truth-directed, mechanisms of wish-fulfilment, for instance.)

Does Plantinga's Reformed epistemology enable reflective theists to assure themselves of their conformity to moral evidentialism?[28] Under moral evidentialism, theistic commitment will carry the required epistemic entitlement only if theistic belief is evidentially justified in the sense that it is held on the basis of the support of the believer's evidence. Now, as already remarked (in Chapter 3), support for the truth of theistic belief

---

[26] *Warranted Christian Belief*, 188

[27] Plantinga uses Calvin's term—*sensus divinitatis*—to refer to the mechanism that produces belief in the existence of the God of classical theism. Since Plantinga's concern is to produce a theory of warranted *Christian* belief, he applies his claim also to the cognitive mechanism that produces specifically Christian doctrinal beliefs, namely, 'the internal instigation of the Holy Spirit'. Plantinga calls his model of Christian Faith 'the extended A/C model', after Aquinas and Calvin. See *Warranted Christian Belief*, chs. 6–8.

[28] I emphasize that this is a question that *I* believe needs to be asked, given the views for which I have already argued about the nature of the reflective theist's *de jure* concern: it is not a question that Plantinga would put himself. For, Plantinga identifies the reflective theist's *de jure* concern neither as a moral question, nor even as a question about taking theistic belief to be true in one's practical reasoning. Furthermore, he thinks that if this *de jure* concern is construed deontologically as a question about one's epistemic entitlement to belief it has an obvious answer:

> Can the Christian believer be within her epistemic rights and epistemically responsible in forming belief as she does? Can she be justified even if she doesn't believe on the basis of propositional evidence …? The answer to *this* question is obvious—*too* obvious, in fact for it to be the *de jure* question, at least if that question is to be worthy of serious disagreement and discussion. *Of course* she can be justified…. (*Warranted Christian Belief*, 102)

Yet the believer's forming and holding her basic Christian beliefs will be epistemically justified only if the evidential practice which confers justification on such beliefs is *itself* justified—and that is a matter obviously open to disagreement and worthy of serious discussion. We may grant, of course, that (depending on the circumstances) a Christian believer may be *epistemically inculpable* in forming and holding certain basic Christian beliefs: but, as already observed (see Chapter 3, *nn.* 6 and 12), inculpability does not entail justification. A person might be inculpable in following an unjustified evidential practice.

could in principle come from *indirect* evidence for its possessing epistemic worth—and, hence, from indirect evidence for its possessing Plantingan warrant. I believe, however, that it is clear that reflective theists could not resolve the question of their entitlement to commit themselves practically to the truth of theism just by appeal to Plantinga's theory.

For, let Plantinga's externalist theory of 'warrant' be granted. Let it be granted, also, that he argues soundly for the conclusion that, if a theistic God exists, then those who hold theistic beliefs as basically evident hold beliefs that have warrant.[29] Reflective theists will still fall short of being able correctly to judge their belief supported on their available evidence—for an obvious reason. Plantinga's central claim is *conditional*, whereas an independently justified *categorical* claim is needed to provide reflective theists with evidence for the truth of their belief.[30] Plantinga (we are assuming) shows that theistic belief has warrant *if* it is true. Yet reflective theists need to be able to judge that their belief has warrant *tout court*. And they cannot do that without begging the question. Obviously, from the (conceded) fact that their theistic belief *would have* warrant if it were true, it does not follow that their theistic belief *actually has* warrant. That conclusion will follow, of course, given the premise that core theistic belief is true. And reflective theists do, of course, hold that premise to be true. But, since what is here at issue for reflective theists is whether *they are evidentially justified in holding* that very belief, they would blatantly beg the question if they sought to resolve that issue by means of an argument that simply assumed its truth.[31]

---

[29] These assumptions are here to be granted only for the sake of the argument. They may, in fact, be questioned. The externalist insight that having the right kind of cause can confer some sort of epistemic worth on a belief is surely correct—though whether (granted the belief's truth) this kind of epistemic worth is enough to yield *knowledge* is contestable. And, if God does exist and deliberately plants the belief that he exists in his creatures in order that they may know the truth, then that belief is caused in such a way as to guarantee its truth, and so certainly has *that much* epistemic worth. As Imran Aijaz (personal communication) observes, however, it may not be as obvious as Plantinga supposes that a perfectly loving God would create us with a natural direct awareness of his existence. Plantinga's appeals to what is 'the natural thing to think' about God's purposes (see *Warranted Christian Belief*, 188–9) involve assumptions that are open to dispute. God might have good reason to remain hidden: so it might conceivably be the case that, although non-inferential belief that God exists did arise in some of God's creatures, this was *not* through a mechanism God had planned for that purpose.

[30] The present discussion of this objection closely follows views already published in my 'How to Answer the *De Jure* Question about Christian Belief', co-authored with Imran Aijaz, *International Journal for Philosophy of Religion*, 56 (2004), 109–29.

[31] Anthony Kenny puts this objection thus: '[t]he doubting believer in God cannot reassure himself that his belief is warranted; for only if there is a God is his belief warranted, and that is what he was beginning to doubt' (*What is Faith?* 71).

Plantinga's Reformed epistemology is of no help, then, to a reflective believer seeking to meet the requirements of moral evidentialism—it will not, in other words, serve the purposes of the first strategy for dealing with evidential ambiguity. It by no means follows, however, that Plantinga's Reformed epistemology is *altogether* worthless so far as the predicament of the reflective believer is concerned. For, if Plantinga's central claim is correct, the absence of *inferential* evidential support for the truth of theistic beliefs by itself fails to establish either that those beliefs lack any epistemic worth or that commitment to their truth must be without epistemic entitlement. Plantinga successfully shows how basic beliefs about God grounded in direct experience (believing that one is sensing God's presence, hearing his voice, etc.) *could* have a certain kind of epistemic worth, if theism is true.

So our evangelical Philosophy 101 student from Chapter 1 may fairly think to himself: 'Even though no arguments for the claim that God exists succeed, my finding God's existence basically evident in my experience might yet constitute a belief caused in such a way as to guarantee its truth. I might, in *that* sense, have knowledge that God exists, even if I find God's existence to be *inferentially* evidentially ambiguous.' But if he is concerned ultimately for the moral probity of continuing to live by theistic beliefs, that thought ought not to satisfy him. There is a significant logical gap from 'My belief that God is present to me will have Plantingan warrant if (as I believe) God does indeed exist' to 'I am warranted in taking (= entitled to take) it to be true that God is present to me'. There is a temptation to overlook this gap. There is a temptation to infer from the fact that the ambiguity of the inferential evidence cannot show that my belief that God exists *does not have Plantingan warrant*, plus the fact that my belief *will* be likely to have Plantingan warrant if theism is true, to the categorical conclusion that *I am warranted in taking* (= entitled to take) that belief to be true in my practical reasoning.[32] But that temptation should be resisted: the agency-focused notion of being warranted in one's practical commitment

---

[32] This temptation is exacerbated by Plantinga's choice of 'warrant' as his technical term for the sort of epistemic worth conferred on a belief by the satisfaction of the externalist conditions of his theory. Note that Plantinga reports that he had earlier used the term 'positive epistemic status' and that Ernest Sosa had suggested 'epistemic aptness' (*Warrant: The Current Debate*, 5). Sosa himself develops a distinction between a belief's 'aptness' and its 'justification' in 'Reliabilism and Intellectual Virtue', *Knowledge in Perspective* (Cambridge: Cambridge University Press, 1991), 131–45.

to a belief's truth is distinct from the propositional-attitude-focused notion of Plantingan warrant in holding its propositional content to be true. My belief's being Plantingan-warranted could provide evidence-based warrant (= entitlement) for my action in taking it to be true only if *I have evidence* for the truth of the claim that my holding that belief has Plantingan warrant; and, on Plantinga's theory, I have such evidence only conditionally on the assumption that my belief is indeed true. I am thus caught in a tight epistemic circle.

As already noted, it is quite apt to talk of specifically theistic doxastic practices and of frameworks of theistic belief. Isolationist epistemology puts a certain spin on such talk, by holding that the truth of the framing principles of a theistic doxastic framework is immune to any external assessment. Reformed epistemology, too, puts its own spin on this 'framework' talk: a theist's overall noetic structure includes a framing principle allowing certain theistic beliefs as basically evident in his or her experience—at least under certain conditions implicit in the associated theistic evidential practice. The possibility that such a noetic structure could have epistemic integrity is then established by appeal to externalist epistemology: holding it directly evident in experience that (e.g.) God is present will likely possess epistemic worth if the presupposed belief—that God exists—is indeed true. Basic theistic beliefs are not self-evidently true, though, nor is the experience of their truth as directly evident universal amongst normally functioning human beings.[33] There can thus be a real question whether to commit oneself in practice to the distinctive framing principles that make one's overall noetic structure a theistic one—and it is that question, of course, with which the reflective theist is concerned. If, as we are assuming, the truth of theism lacks the support of our ordinary empirical evidence, then any theistic commitment must be made without being based on the support of evidence—for the evidence that supports theistic beliefs is available only from within the perspective of theistic commitment. Such commitment, then, must require doxastic venture—and if it is to be

---

[33] Note that the fact that many people do not find any theistic beliefs basically evident in their experience does not necessarily show theistic commitment to be epistemically unjustified. For a theistic doxastic framework may have internal resources for explaining the widespread lack of basic theistic belief—for example, as resulting from the effects of sin in blocking the proper operation of the human capacity to 'perceive' the divine directly (though such explanations may, of course, be both philosophically and theologically contestable).

morally justified, then doxastic venture (in cases of this kind) must itself be morally justifiable.

The Reformed epistemologist approach to the first strategy, then, ends up, as the isolationist approach did, pointing the way to the need *to reject* moral evidentialism for the case of theistic commitment. It points the way, that is, to the need to adopt a strategy for responding to the evidential ambiguity of theism that accepts some version of fideism.[34] The externalist insight of Reformed epistemology does indeed usefully show that beliefs to which people commit themselves without evidential support might actually possess a certain kind of epistemic worth. But recognizing that possibility does not obviate the need for a moral defence of doxastic venture. The required moral defence might be assisted, however, by appealing to externalism to indicate how doxastic venture *might* turn out to be a way of grasping truth. (I will take this point up again in Chapter 8.)

It is notable, however, that Reformed epistemologists themselves resist the fideist implications of their position. Plantinga is emphatic:

Faith, according to the [extended A/C] model, is far indeed from being a blind leap; it isn't even remotely like a leap in the dark … [y]ou might as well claim that a memory belief, or the belief that $3 + 1 = 4$ is a leap in the dark.[35]

There is no 'leap', of course, if one is already committed to a theistic doxastic practice licensing certain theistic beliefs as basically evident. And, if it were psychologically impossible to operate outside a theistic doxastic practice—in the same way that it is psychologically impossible to operate outside our sensory perceptual, memory, or arithmetical doxastic practices—then Plantinga would be right: taking basically evident theistic beliefs to be true would not involve any actual venture beyond the evidence. We may not, perhaps, altogether exclude the possibility that for some—fortunate?—people it really is a matter of psychological necessity to find God's presence basically evident. For those people, if such there be,

---

[34] This conclusion concurs with C. Stephen Evans's diagnosis of Reformed epistemology as (in a certain sense) fideist—indeed, Evans argues that fideism is actually implied by the commitment to an externalist epistemology. See *Faith Beyond Reason: A Kierkegaardian Account* (Grand Rapids, MI: W. B. Eerdmans Publishers, 1998), 45–7.

[35] *Warranted Christian Belief*, 263. Plantinga evidently stands by his earlier rejection of the suggestion that Reformed Epistemology is in any, even 'moderate', sense fideist ('Reason and Belief in God' in Plantinga and Wolterstorff (eds), *Faith and Rationality*).

taking it to be true that God exists, loves them, and so forth, will involve no leap, no venture.

Yet human beings generally do not inevitably find the truth of basic theistic beliefs to be simply evident in their experience. Were it otherwise, the attempt to defend epistemic entitlement to act on basic theistic belief would be popularly seen as equally esoteric and risible as the parallel attempt with respect to basic perceptual beliefs. Furthermore, plenty of people who *do* believe in God do not count that belief on a par with basic perceptual or memory or arithmetical beliefs. Many who do have religious experiences in which they are in some sense directly aware of God's presence, God's help, even God's voice, would *not* assimilate that awareness to a basically evident perceptual, memory, or arithmetical belief. They would not do so because, on reflection, they recognize that they are choosing to interpret their experiences in a religious way when that interpretation is not unavoidable for them.[36] Indeed, many would regard their faith as *enabling* them to see the divine presence and loving activity in perfectly ordinary experiences (e.g. the breaking of bread, the binding of wounds)—experiences that could be understood otherwise, albeit, they believe, to their great impoverishment. (Here it might be observed that *all* perceptual experience involves active interpretation by the mind. True: but in the case of basic sensory perceptual beliefs the mind's activity is both subconscious and involuntary; whereas, in the case of basic theistic beliefs we may become conscious that we are placing a religious construal on our experience, that such a construal is not inevitable, and that we have a real capacity not to act upon it.) For reflective theists for whom their basic beliefs are not quasi-perceptual, the question arises as to their entitlement to take those beliefs to be true (and, hence also, all the beliefs of the theistic doxastic framework that depend upon them). This is the situation of the vast majority of theists—indeed, there may be good theological reasons why it should be so, relating to the nature of meritorious faith and the

---

[36] It has been observed that theists frequently do not hold their basic theistic beliefs with the degree of firmness apparently envisaged on Plantinga's model of faith (see Richard Swinburne, 'Plantinga on Warrant', *Religious Studies*, 37 (2001), 203; and Andrew Chignell, 'Epistemology for Saints'[Website], 2002 <http:/www.christianitytoday.com/bc/2002/002/10.20.html>, accessed 2005). My point here is the further one that, even for those theists who do (on occasion, anyway) very firmly believe their basic beliefs, that firmness of belief is not experienced as just like the firmness of belief that arises utterly routinely with (e.g.) perceptual beliefs under normal conditions.

hiddenness of God. Furthermore, reflective theists for whom the *de jure* question is existentially pressing are not bothered merely by a hyperbolical doubt of purely theoretical interest. Under the assumption of the evidential ambiguity of theism, then, it seems that, though God no doubt could have given us a *sensus divinitatis* that was literally akin to a further sensory faculty, in fact—if he exists—he appears to have chosen a more complex cognitive mechanism in which our conscious active concurrence in making practical commitment to an uncompelled religious interpretation of our experience is required.

## Conclusion: the need for a fideist response to ambiguity

The first strategy for responding to the assumed ambiguity of theistic belief with respect to rational empiricist evidential practice seeks to show that with respect to a better theory of the applicable evidential practice, reflective theists may indeed be assured that they are evidentially justified in holding theistic belief. Both isolationist and Reformed epistemology offer variants on this strategy. On examination, however, they both fail for the same basic reason: they cannot answer the reflective theist's *de jure* question about *overall* commitment to a theistic doxastic framework. In making such commitment, theists venture beyond what they can justify on their evidence. So, if they are entitled to make such a commitment, a uniform evidentialist ethics of our actions in taking propositions to be true in practical reasoning must be mistaken. It must sometimes be morally justifiable to take to be true in one's practical reasoning beliefs whose truth one recognizes not to be adequately supported by one's evidence. And, in particular, it must be morally justifiable to make such a doxastic venture with respect to the framing principles of a framework of faith-beliefs of the sort typified in theistic religion. If the evidential ambiguity thesis is correct, theistic faith commitment does indeed require a leap, though whether that leap deserves to be designated—denigrated?—as a blind one is one of the issues we shall need to consider.

Critical examination of the first strategy for responding to the evidential ambiguity thesis, then, points to the need to pursue the second strategy instead. It shows that we need to consider the *fideist* strategy of rejecting moral evidentialism, and so defending as morally—and perhaps even epistemically?—justifiable doxastic venture with respect to framing principles such as those at the foundation of theistic faith-beliefs. I shall begin to consider the prospects for success with this fideist strategy in the next chapter, beginning with the question whether a doxastic venture model of theistic faith-beliefs deserves to be considered even as a coherent possibility.

# 5

# Faith as doxastic venture

There are several possible reactions to the claim that our total available evidence leaves it ambiguous whether we should adopt a theistic or a naturalist/atheistic interpretation of the world. One reaction is to reject this evidential ambiguity thesis (as any more than *prima facie* plausible) by maintaining that our evidence *does* establish the truth of theism, at least to a sufficient degree of probability. Another reaction rejects the ambiguity thesis on the grounds that our evidence establishes *the falsity* of theism, at least to a sufficient degree of probability. A third reaction, however, accepts the evidential ambiguity thesis at least as likely to be true—and it is with this third reaction that I am now concerned.

Indeed, my focus will be on those who not only accept the evidential ambiguity thesis, but also agree with the fideist claim that practical theistic commitment must therefore involve *doxastic venture*—that is, taking faith-beliefs to be true in one's practical reasoning without adequate support from one's total evidence. In the previous chapter, I argued that both Reformed and isolationist epistemologists *ought* to come over to this fideist view (on the grounds that, though they rightly defend the evidential justifiability of theistic belief with respect to specifically theistic evidential practices, they cannot disguise the fact that *overall* commitment to theistic belief—*carrying with it* acceptance of some specifically theistic evidential practice—requires commitment beyond external evidential support). But, whether or not I am joined at this turn by 'reformed' Reformed and isolationist epistemologists, I will now proceed on the assumption that the right response to accepting the evidential ambiguity of theistic belief is indeed to recognize that theistic faith-commitment requires doxastic venture, and can therefore be morally permissible only if, at least under certain conditions, it is morally permissible to make a doxastic venture in favour of faith-propositions of the sort involved in theistic religious belief.

Given the current historical state of the debate over theism, it is hard not to agree that the evidential ambiguity thesis has significant plausibility. One might nevertheless be quite strongly motivated to reject it, however, through fear of the fideist alternative.[1] In this chapter, I shall begin investigating whether or not there is a sound basis for that fear. May we be morally entitled to take faith-propositions to be true in our action while recognizing that their truth lacks evidential support? Can it sometimes be morally right to act on faith-beliefs with a confidence *not* proportioned to our total available evidence? I hope to show that a fideism which gives the affirmative answer to these questions need be neither morally nor epistemically irresponsible: doxastic ventures in religious commitment may be defensible without any wholesale endorsement of cognitive 'leaps in the dark' from wholly non-epistemic motives.

## Agenda for a defence of doxastic venture

What needs to be done if the moral justifiability of doxastic venture in favour of faith-propositions is to be established?

First, a fuller articulation of what doxastic venture is supposed to be needs to be given. And that articulation needs, in particular, to show clearly *how doxastic venture is possible.* Is it really possible to take a faith-belief to be true in one's practical reasoning when one is aware that it lacks adequate evidential support? Maybe the only psychologically possible response to ambiguity is to suspend judgement and act accordingly? This first item on the agenda for a defence of doxastic venture is the business of the present chapter.

Second, granted an understanding of what doxastic venture exactly involves and how it is psychologically possible, it needs to be shown *how doxastic venture in favour of faith-beliefs may be morally permissible.* In

[1] A notable case in point is that of Terence Penelhum, who maintains that philosophers have a clear duty to continue to work hard on the project of 'disambiguation': '...there is one unqualified obligation for all rational beings, whether they have a prior faith or not: to seek the disambiguation of their world' ('Reflections on the Ambiguity of the World', 171). Penelhum rightly observes that disambiguation will have to be achieved in a world which exhibits '*multiple* religious and ideological ambiguity' (170), not merely ambiguity between theistic and naturalist world-views.

the next chapter, I will develop a thesis inspired by William James's famous 'will-to-believe' doctrine that sets out conditions under which doxastic venture is morally permissible. I will show how this thesis may be understood as applying to faith-beliefs of the sort exemplified in theistic religion—and, in particular, to those foundational beliefs that I have described in the previous chapter as framing principles (for example, the belief that an omnipotent and morally perfect Creator exists whose nature and will are revealed in Jesus the Christ). In Chapter 7, I will consider a major line of objection to the Jamesian thesis developed in Chapter 6, and, in response, propose an augmented version of the thesis. Finally, in Chapters 8 and 9, I will consider the case for favouring the version of fideism expressed in my augmented Jamesian thesis over a hard-line evidentialism that rejects all religious believing by faith.

## The nature of theistic faith

My immediate agenda, then, is to arrive at a fuller understanding of the nature of doxastic venture, and, for this purpose, it will be helpful to consider how a doxastic venture model of theistic faith compares and contrasts with alternative models. Strictly speaking, of course, there is no such thing as 'theistic faith': rather there are *specific* theistic *Faiths* (with a capital and in the plural). There are, that is, specific historical traditions of religious faith that share belief in some kind of theistic God. I will confine my discussion here to theistic faith in the Christian tradition. I will therefore leave it open whether a doxastic venture model could be a serious candidate for understanding faith in other theistic religious traditions, except to say that whenever such a tradition countenances acceptance of the evidential ambiguity thesis, the doxastic venture model of faith is likely to be salient.

Christian faith is subject to competing interpretative theories. These result, in part, from differences in explaining how Christian faith can, at one and the same time, be understood both as a gift of God's grace and also as involving an act on the part of the believer.[2] Evidently, Christian faith

---

[2] For Christian faith as linked to action, consider: 'So with faith, if it does not lead to action, it is in itself a lifeless thing' (James 2: 17); 'We call to mind before our God and Father, how your faith has shown itself in action...' (I Thessalonians 1: 3); and Hebrews 11 which gives a long list of First

has both active and passive elements, and models of Christian faith differ according to (*a*) the extent to which they emphasize an active element in faith, and (*b*), how they understand the nature of that active element.

Consider, for a key example, Calvin's model of Christian faith, a major influence on the Reformed epistemology of Alvin Plantinga discussed in the previous chapter. Calvin defines faith as 'a firm and certain knowledge of God's benevolence towards us, founded upon the truth of the freely given promise in Christ, both revealed to our minds and sealed upon our hearts through the Holy Spirit'.[3] For Calvin, then, two components of faith are largely passive—gifts from God to be received by the believer—namely, the cognitive component and the evaluative-affectional component.

The *cognitive* component of faith amounts to the propositions held and taken to be true by the person of faith characteristic of the specific variety of faith concerned—propositions of the kind I have been referring to as 'faith-propositions'. So the cognitive component of Christian faith includes the belief that God exists, that Jesus is saviour, and so on.[4] On Calvin's model, the cognitive component of faith is largely passive—or, perhaps better to say, receptive. The truth of Christian faith-propositions is held, on his model, to be directly revealed by God to the believer, through the operation of the Holy Spirit. The believer need only be open to receiving God's revelation—something by no means trivial, given the impediment of sin, but, nevertheless, not requiring any active venture or self-exerted leap of faith. (As Plantinga's work makes clear, Calvin's counting directly revealed faith-beliefs as knowledge indicates a thoroughly externalist rejection of any essential connexion between the relevant notion of knowledge and the believer's own activity in acquiring or certifying it.)[5]

---

Testament figures who did great deeds 'by faith'. For faith as a gift, consider: 'In virtue of the gift that God in his grace has given me I say to everyone among you: do not be conceited...; but think your way to a sober estimate based on the measure of faith that God has dealt to each of you' (Romans 12: 3); and, '... another, by the same Spirit is granted faith' (I Corinthians 12: 9) (*New English Bible*).

[3] See *Warranted Christian Belief*, especially chs. 8 and 9. This quotation is as quoted in *Warranted Christian Belief*, 244, from John Calvin, *Institutes* III, ii, 7, 551. As Plantinga's discussion makes clear, Calvin's model of faith is a variant of the Thomist and Tridentine model. As already noted in the previous chapter, Plantinga calls his own model of faith the 'A/C' model, with 'A/C' short for 'Aquinas/Calvin'.

[4] It is, of course, moot just what, if anything, constitutes *the* cognitive component of Christian faith. If the existence of significant differences in their cognitive components is definitive of different species of the genus 'Christian faith', many such species of Christian faith will need to be acknowledged.

[5] There are, of course, different conceptions of knowledge. Calvin's—and Plantinga's—conception emphasizes the need for the state of knowing to bear the right kind of relationship to the truth

On the Thomist model, too, the cognitive component of faith is largely receptive—although not to the same degree as Calvin's model would have it. For, the Thomist allows that our own rational exertion can establish both God's existence and the fact that certain truths are historically revealed by God, so that we may assure ourselves by indirect inference that we are evidentially justified in holding Christian faith-beliefs. Aquinas held back, however, from counting faith-beliefs as knowledge, on the grounds that though we may be fully justified in holding them on divine authority, we cannot in principle make our own direct check on their truth.[6]

The *evaluative-affectional* component of faith is the believer's *welcoming* the content of the cognitive component of his or her faith. Scripture says that 'the devils also believe, and shudder' (James 2:19): they possess Christian faith-beliefs, but are repelled by the good God who is revealed, and commit themselves to work against his will. The faithful, by contrast, rejoice in what makes the devils shudder. For Calvin, this capacity too is also a gift of God; believers' love for what is revealed is 'sealed on their hearts' by the Holy Spirit. So the Calvinist model of faith emphasizes receptivity with respect to its evaluative-affectional, as well as its cognitive, component.

There surely are, however, active components in Christian faith—or, at least, in *meritorious* Christian faith. Faith is not just a matter of holding faith-beliefs, and being glad of the truths so held. Faith involves commitment, so *some* kind of *act* is thereby essential to faith.[7] Theoretically, a person could hold Christian faith-beliefs, welcome their truth, and yet—through some kind of weakness of will—do nothing in consequence. To be a person of Christian faith, one has to *do* something in virtue of one's faith-beliefs, namely *commit* oneself to God—and that involves entrusting oneself to

---

known; other conceptions emphasize the need for the knower to have good reason to take what is known to be true; yet other conceptions require as well that the knower understands the truth known. For useful discussion of different conceptions of knowledge see J. L. Mackie, *Problems from Locke* (Oxford: Clarendon Press, 1976), 218–20, and Ernest Sosa's contrast between 'animal' and 'reflective' knowledge ('Knowledge and Intellectual Virtue' in *Knowledge in Perspective: Selected Essays in Epistemology* (Cambridge: Cambridge University Press, 1991), 240).

[6] For useful discussions of the Thomist model of faith see Swinburne, *Faith and Reason*, 105–10, and Kenny, *What Is Faith?* ch. 4. Swinburne notes that Aquinas describes belief as 'faith's inner act' (*Faith and Reason*, 106), but it is not clear whether this description introduces any further active element into the cognitive component of faith. Swinburne is not deterred, anyway, from holding that 'the Thomist view [is] that the man of faith is a man who holds certain beliefs-that' (*Faith and Reason*, 108).

[7] Aquinas distinguishes between faith and meritorious faith, holding that to have faith it is necessary only to believe the truth as revealed by God. Meritorious faith requires a commitment to do the good works that God wills.

God and seeking to do God's will. Any acceptable model of Christian faith thus needs to acknowledge not only that faith has cognitive and evaluative-affectional elements, but also that faith has an element of active commitment to it.[8]

It is thus widely accepted that the active commitment of Christian faith is *in some sense* venturesome and risky. Christians rely on God for their ultimate welfare, and must therefore relinquish the egotistic fantasy of trusting only themselves for directive control over their lives—and that involves genuine risk and real venture. That is common ground: what is contentious is *the nature* of the venture or ventures involved in authentic Christian faith.

## The doxastic venture model

Theists make a practical commitment to the truth that God exists—though always, of course, in the context of commitment to the truth of doctrines specific to their particular variety of 'expanded' theism. (For simplicity, however, I will confine discussion to the core belief of 'generic' theism.) The doxastic venture model of such faith-commitment maintains that it involves *an active venture in practical commitment to the truth of faith-propositions that the believer correctly recognizes not to be adequately supported by his or her evidence.*[9]

According to the doxastic venture model, a theist's practical commitment involves:

(1) taking it to be true (with full weight) that God exists in his or her practical reasoning; and

---

[8] It may be held (by Calvinists, in particular) that it is predestined who will be able to make an active commitment in which they entrust themselves to God and seek to do his will; and so, in a certain sense, that active element of faith also counts as a gift from God to the believer. I will not explore the familiar issues which this view raises, noting only that even on predestinarian assumptions Christian faith does require acts of will on the part of the believer (it is just that those acts of will are *also* predestined by God).

[9] Note that the doxastic venture model is a model of what is involved in 'believing by faith'—that is, of what is involved in a certain kind of cognitive commitment essential to faith. The doxastic venture model may therefore be accepted consistently with the view that faith itself is a virtue (where virtue is a certain sort of disposition of character). For a recent defence of faith as a virtue, see Tim Chappell, 'Why Is Faith a Virtue?' in Charles Taliaferro and Paul J. Griffiths (eds), *Philosophy of Religion: An Anthology* (Malden, MA: Blackwell, 2003), 546–52.

(2) doing so while holding that God exists (i.e. while having the belief that God exists); while yet

(3) recognizing, correctly in accordance with the relevant norms, that it is *not* the case that his or her total available evidence adequately supports the truth that God exists.

Several features of this model require further elaboration and comment:

The reference to the 'relevant norms' in clause (3) is to the norms of the applicable evidential practice. Note that doxastic venturers judge the truth on which they act not to be evidentially well supported in accordance with the norms of an evidential practice *they themselves at least implicitly accept as applicable*. Doxastic venture is thus a matter of commitment in the face of intellectual doubt. (The contrast with Reformed epistemology is worth emphasizing once again. Reformed epistemology in effect proposes a rival, *specifically theistic*, theory of applicable evidential practice under which—trivially enough—the ambiguity dissolves and, with it, any occasion for doxastic venture. But, as argued in the previous chapter, the reflective theist's question is ultimately about entitlement to practical commitment to the framework of theistic belief *as a whole*, and so must be asked *from outside* any specifically theistic evidential practice and in a context where empiricist evidential practice is generally assumed to apply—by reflective theists themselves as much as by anyone else.)[10]

Note that clause (3) requires the doxastic venturer to *recognize* that the truth of his belief is not sufficiently supported by his evidence—that is, the venturing involved in doxastic venture is *conscious* venturing. So someone whose faith-belief *in fact* lacked evidential justification (i.e. whose belief was held other than on the basis of adequate evidential support for its truth), but who did not realize this because he or she simply made no judgement at all as to evidential support, would not count as making a doxastic venture in taking that faith-belief to be true. Obviously, there is room for the

---

[10] It is, of course, possible that what counts as doxastic venture with respect to one particular theory of correct evidential practice counts as acting in accordance with evidentially supported belief with respect to a different theory. Under an extreme rationalist foundationalist theory of evidential practice, for instance, acting on any causal beliefs (as Hume showed) amounts to doxastic venture; but causal beliefs may count as evidentially justified under a more liberal empiricist theory of correct evidential practice. As explained in Chapter 3, I am proceeding on the assumption that the truth of theism is evidentially ambiguous with respect to a secure enough consensus theory of the applicable evidential practice. That assumption is, contentious: it is plausible enough, however, for it to be important to consider how commitment to theistic faith-beliefs could be ethically acceptable if it is indeed true.

concept of *unconscious* doxastic venture as applied to such a case: but since the focus of this inquiry is on *reflective* faith-believers—and, by this stage, on reflective faith-believers who consciously accept the evidential ambiguity of their faith-beliefs—it will pose no problem to restrict attention to the justifiability of conscious doxastic venture.

Note, too, that clause (3) also requires doxastic venturers' judgements about lack of evidential support for their faith-beliefs to be *correct*. So, reflective faith-believers who *incorrectly* judge that their beliefs lack support and then commit themselves to their truth will not *in fact* be making doxastic ventures. And those who *incorrectly* judge the truth of their beliefs *to be* evidentially well supported, will in fact venture beyond their evidence in taking them to be true, contrary to their conscious understanding of their situation. Once again, a focus on the perspective of *reflective* faith-believers cuts through these complications: what reflective believers want to know is whether they can be morally justified in taking to be true faith-beliefs that, *according to their own best judgement*, actually do lack adequate support from their total available evidence under the applicable norms. Of course, they cannot exclude the possibility that their best judgement is mistaken—and they may be mistaken in different ways (applying the wrong norms, applying the right norms wrongly, etc.). But the issue is whether, with a correct judgement of lack of evidential support for faith-beliefs *taken to be fixed*, practical commitment to their truth might yet be morally justified. Hence the inclusion of a 'correctness' requirement in clause (3).

The doxastic venture model contrasts with prominent models of theistic faith recently described by Paul Helm as *evidential proportion* models.[11] According to evidential proportion models, the cognitive component of faith conforms to the—assumedly uniform—requirement to proportion one's degree of belief to one's evidence. The Calvinist model of faith, the Thomist model of faith (or, at least, of *meritorious* faith), and Alvin Plantinga's 'A/C' model of faith all purport to be evidential proportion models of faith. These models of faith might also be described as *purely fiducial venture* models, since they locate the venture of faith just in believers' trusting themselves to God, and not in any way in their holding or taking it to be true that the trustworthy God exists. Doxastic venture models of faith, by contrast, claim that the venture of faith *also* involves practical commitment to the truth

---

[11] Helm, *Faith with Reason*, 21.

of faith-propositions without evidential support. It is doubtful, however, whether doxastic venture models are aptly described, following Helm's terminology, as *evidential deficiency* models which understand faith 'as making up for gaps in the evidence for the religious claims believed by adopting a degree of certitude not warranted by the evidence'.[12] Doxastic venture does not 'make up for' what the evidence fails to supply—namely, some doubt-removing epistemic certification—rather, it *embraces* the evidential deficiency, and makes a commitment without epistemic guarantee. (This point will be reinforced later in the chapter, when I shall consider how doxastic venture is possible, and clearly differentiate it from any direct or indirect self-inducing of belief.)

An example of a doxastic venture model is Kierkegaard's definition of faith as 'an objective uncertainty held fast in an appropriation process of the most passionate inwardness'.[13] Another example is Paul Tillich's account of faith as 'the state of being ultimately concerned', which involves taking it to be true that God, 'success', 'the nation'—or whatever the object may be—'demands total surrender' and 'promises total fulfilment even if all other claims have to be subjected to it or rejected in its name'. But what is taken to be an 'object of ultimate concern' might in fact be a 'false ultimate', and there can be no rational means of excluding this possibility. 'Doubt is [thus] a necessary element' in such faith, because what is accepted as true cannot be rationally certified on the evidence.[14,15]

Evidential proportion models obviously cannot accommodate acceptance of the evidential ambiguity of theistic faith-beliefs—for the only way to

[12] *Ibid.*

[13] See Søren Kierkegaard, *Concluding Unscientific Postscript*, trans. David F. Swenson and Walter Lowrie (Princeton: Princeton University Press, 1968), 180. Note that the quoted phrase is offered first as a definition of 'subjective' truth, but shortly after it becomes clear that truth as thus defined 'is an equivalent expression for faith'.

[14] Paul Tillich, *Dynamics of Faith* (New York: HarperCollins, 1957; 2001 edn), 1 and 21. Note that Tillich rejects any understanding of faith 'as a type of *knowledge* which has a low degree of evidence but is supported by religious authority' (38, my emphasis). That is not to deny, however, that faith requires commitment beyond evidential support. What Tillich is excluding is the idea that, in the absence of evidential support, *something else* can supply an epistemic guarantee for the truth-claim to which practical commitment is made 'by faith'.

[15] Despite his emphasizing religious experience over the believing of faith-propositions, John Hick's account of faith as 'the interpretive element in religious experience' involving 'the exercise of cognitive freedom' is arguably best interpreted as a doxastic venture model of faith. (See his *Faith and Knowledge*, 2nd edn (Ithaca, NY: Cornell University Press, 1966), Part II, and *An Interpretation of Religion*, ch. 10.) For, Hick's account of faith is based on accepting the evidential ambiguity of theism (as already noted (Chapter 3, *n.* 23)), and he allows that theistic experience involves 'the positive *judgement* ... that in this situation or event or place or person God is present' (*An Interpretation of Religion*, 160, my emphasis).

proportion one's belief to the evidence if the ambiguity thesis is true is to suspend judgement or (perhaps) give the hypothesis that God exists an intermediate degree of partial belief. But that latter course—taking God's existence to be as likely as not—is clearly not consistent with having authentic theistic faith. Authentic faith requires *full* pragmatic commitment—as clause (1) of the doxastic venture model indicates: theistic doxastic venture involves giving the truth that God exists *full weight* in one's practical reasoning. What this means is that the weight given to the truth that God exists is not some intermediate degree of partial belief, but the kind of weight that naturally goes along with straightforwardly *believing that it is true* that God exists.[16] Often people of faith also *feel* confident in making that commitment—they not only give faith-propositions full weight in practical reasoning, they also *actually believe* them to be true. Taking a proposition p to be true with full weight in practical reasoning and actually holding p to be true can, however, come apart, as is made clear, for example, by cases in which people act confidently, though experimentally, on an assumption, and cases of pretending to believe.[17] So clause (2) is not redundant: indeed, some philosophers have argued for a *sub-doxastic venture* model of faith which fits clauses (1) and (3) but not clause (2)—that is, for the view that people may have authentic theistic faith if they act with full pragmatic commitment beyond their evidence while believing no more than that theistic faith-propositions have a non-negligible probability of being true.[18]

---

[16] As already noted (Chapter 2, *n*. 13), there are well-known problems with identifying believing with a certain high degree of partial belief, either 1 itself or a degree of belief over a threshold near enough to 1 (see Kaplan, *Decision Theory as Philosophy*, for discussion). I am here assuming, however, that these problems do not undermine the coherence of understanding a person's taking p to be true in reasoning as involving giving p's truth full weight, in the sense of the kind of weight that naturally follows upon (non-partial) belief that p is true.

[17] See my earlier discussion in Chapter 2. In earlier work, I used a notion of 'believing acceptance' of a proposition's truth in one's practical reasoning which ran these two features together (see my 'Faith as Doxastic Venture', *Religious Studies*, 38 (2002), 474). It is important to recognize that, though both features are involved in a fully doxastic venture model of faith, they are indeed distinct.

[18] A sub-doxastic model of faith is proposed by Richard Swinburne (though not, of course, under that name):

...a man S has faith if he *acts on the assumption* that there is a God who has the properties which Christians ascribe to him and has provided for men the means of salvation and the prospect of glory, and that he will do for S what he knows that S needs or wants—so long as S has good purposes. (*Faith and Reason*, 116, my emphasis)

Swinburne has recently restated this (as he calls it) 'pragmatist' model of faith in 'Plantinga on Warrant', 211. Compare also Louis Pojman's defence of the view that faith is a matter of hope rather than belief ('Faith without Belief?' *Faith and Philosophy*, 3 (1986), 157–76; and, 'Faith, Doubt and Belief, or Does

A sub-doxastic venture model of faith would be the only rival to evidential proportion models if *fully* doxastic venture under evidential ambiguity proved to be impossible. But fully doxastic venture is *not* impossible, either conceptually or psychologically, as I shall now proceed to show.

## The psychological possibility of doxastic venture

Some philosophers might dismiss the doxastic venture model on the grounds that it mistakenly treats beliefs as if they were under direct voluntary control. But, as I have argued in Chapter 2, the idea that faith may involve some kind of cognitive venture beyond the evidence is undoubtedly coherent, since acting on faith-beliefs has a directly voluntary component—namely, *taking their propositional contents to be true in practical reasoning.*[19] It is thus undoubtedly *conceptually* possible for agents to take to be true, in their practical reasoning, faith-propositions whose truth they themselves judge to lack evidential support. Whether such practical commitment in the face of intellectual doubt is really *psychologically* possible is, however, another matter—especially when (as the doxastic venture model affirms in clause (2)) the venture is supposedly accompanied by *genuine belief* in the truth of what is *at the same time* rationally judged to lack

Faith Entail Belief?' in Richard M. Gale and Alexander R. Pruss (eds), *The Existence of God* (Aldershot, Hants, Burlington, VT: Ashgate/Dartmouth, 2003), 1–15).

Andrei Buckareff has recently argued that *only* sub-doxastic venture can be admitted (Andrei Buckareff, 'Can Faith Be a Doxastic Venture?' *Religious Studies*, 41 (2005), 435–45), and notes Joshua Golding as another proponent of this view (Joshua L. Golding, 'Toward a Pragmatic Conception of Religious Faith', *Faith and Philosophy*, 7 (1990), 486–503 and id., *Rationality and Religious Theism*). I will have more to say about the merits of a sub-doxastic venture model at the end of the present chapter.

[19] Authentic faith needs to be freely chosen—a requirement that is explicit in the traditional Thomist account of faith. For someone such as Swinburne who takes the view that we can exercise freedom over our beliefs only indirectly by the choices we make over the processes of inquiry that form them (that is, who recognizes only what I referred to in Chapter 2 as the *first* locus of doxastic control), the only way to accommodate this freedom requirement is to conclude that meritorious Thomist faith 'has to result from religious inquiry of some sort' (Swinburne, *Faith and Reason*, 109). That conclusion is uncomfortably elitist. Once one acknowledges the *second* locus of direct doxastic control, however, it is easy to see how the Thomist can vindicate faith's freedom. It is *up to agents themselves* whether they do or do not take faith-propositions to be true in their reasoning. Of course, for the Thomist, taking those propositions to be true will not require any venture beyond the evidence, since, according to the Thomist, believers may correctly judge the truth of their faith-propositions to be well supported by the evidence (though they do have to venture beyond any ability of their own *directly to verify* 'revealed' truths or to *understand why* they are true). Believers nevertheless retain a free choice whether to make the practical commitment that fits their judgement of the weight of the evidence or to act (with the devils) in defiance of that judgement.

evidential support. I turn now to consider, then, how doxastic venture can be psychologically possible.

## A Jamesian account

The main influence on the position I shall develop in answer to this preliminary question—as, indeed, to my main question about the moral permissibility of doxastic venture with respect to faith-beliefs—is William James's lecture, 'The Will to Believe'. In that lecture, James describes himself as aiming to provide:

a justification *of* faith, a defence of our right to adopt a believing attitude in religious matters in spite of the fact that our merely logical intellect may not have been coerced.[20]

My aim is to develop an account of the possibility and moral permissibility (under certain conditions) of doxastic venture in favour of faith-beliefs of the kind exemplified by theistic faith-beliefs. As should already be clear, though venturing in the absence of intellectual coercion by the force of one's evidence is indeed involved, doxastic venture on my account is *not* well described as a matter of 'adopting a believing attitude' as James here puts it. On my account, doxastic venturing involves *taking to be true with full weight in one's practical reasoning* a proposition whose truth one recognizes not to have adequate evidential support. (Thus, in this respect—and others—the account I am here developing is *not* intended as a scholarly interpretation of James's own view. As Richard Gale has recently argued, though James's 'will-to-believe' thesis is 'his most distinctive and influential doctrine', it is difficult to give a clearly consistent formulation of it in the light of all that James wrote about it.[21] My account is 'Jamesian', then, only in the sense that it is James-inspired.)

[20]    *The Will to Believe*, 1–2.

[21]    Richard M. Gale, *The Divided Self of William James* (Cambridge: Cambridge University Press, 1999), 93. Gale's ch. 4 brings to light a number of tensions in James's will-to-believe doctrine, and argues for a 'reconstructed' version of it in defence of the view that the doctrine is 'one of the great contributions to the history of philosophy' that retains 'great importance and resiliency' (116). The Jamesian thesis I shall here develop is quite different from Gale's own reconstructed version of James's will-to-believe doctrine.

## 'Passionally' caused beliefs

To return, then, to the question of how doxastic venture can be psychologically possible. We do have direct control over what we take to be true—and with what weight—in our practical reasoning. And so we have the ability, in particular, to take proposition p to be true in our practical reasoning even though we judge ourselves not to have adequate evidential support for holding p true. That capacity, however, is not enough to secure a capacity for fully doxastic venture. As such, exercising that capacity amounts just to *acting on the assumption* that p, and, of course, acting on the assumption that p need not be accompanied by *believing* that p. What is needed for fully doxastic venture with respect to the faith-proposition that p is taking p to be true with full weight in practical reasoning while *having the attitude that p is true*. In fully doxastic venture one does act on the assumption that p; but, more than that, one gives that assumption the full weight appropriate to holding it true that p; and, more than that again, one actually does *believe* that p.

But how could a person have the attitude that proposition p is true, while also recognizing that it is not the case that p's truth is supported by the total available evidence? One can indeed take to be true in practical reasoning a proposition whose truth one recognizes not to be evidentially well supported: but that recognition will surely undermine any possibility of doing so *believingly*—that is, while actually having the belief that p is true? As noted in Chapter 2, the attitude of holding true is essentially *responsive*: one cannot adopt it directly at will (though intentionally acquiring it indirectly may sometimes be feasible). One typical, and functionally central, cause of the attitude of belief is rational consideration (often undeliberate and sometimes subconscious) of evidence which indicates the truth of the proposition concerned. In cases of doxastic venture, however, believers are aware of *the lack* of evidential support for the proposition they both hold true and take to be true in their practical reasoning. In the absence of awareness of evidential support, what could possibly cause their believing attitude?

James gives an answer to this question in 'The Will to Believe'. In a key formulation of his essay's central thesis, James says:

Our passional nature not only lawfully may, but must, decide an option between propositions, whenever it is a genuine option that cannot by its nature be decided on intellectual grounds ... [22]

James's notion of 'our passional nature' 'deciding an option' indicates how doxastic venture can indeed be psychologically possible. The responsive attitude of holding a proposition true may be elicited by causes *other than* the believer's recognition, as such, of evidence for the belief's truth under the evidential practice assumed to be applicable (which, in the limiting case of a belief which that practice counts as properly basic, amounts simply to finding its truth basically evident in experience). We may follow James in describing such *non-evidential* causes of beliefs as *passional*—though it is important to emphasize the proviso that the term 'passional' must here be interpreted broadly enough to include *all* types of causes of belief that do not consist in providing the believer with grounds (relative to the assumed correct evidential practice) for holding the proposition believed to be true.[23]

A wide variety of possible passional causes of beliefs needs to be acknowledged. Emotions may give rise to beliefs—and not just strong emotions such as anger, fear, or admiration, but also milder emotional attitudes, such as approval and disapproval. Wishes and desires, too, can generate beliefs—the phenomenon of wishful thinking. And a belief can sometimes issue directly from the evaluative belief that the proposition concerned ought to be true or that it would be good if it were true (though, on some accounts of evaluative beliefs this reduces to a category already mentioned—namely, a belief caused by the quiet emotion of approval). In addition, people's affections and affiliations can be causes of their beliefs—and this is particularly salient with respect to religious faith-beliefs, which often are caused by people's immersion in or encounter

[22] *The Will to Believe*, 11.
[23] Note that reference to the assumed correct evidential practice is essential here. It is not inconceivable that beliefs which count as passionally, non-evidentially, caused relative to one theory of correct evidential practice might count as evidentially caused relative to another. The contrast between the passional and the rational—or, in the present context, between passional and evidential causes of belief—may be to some degree theory-laden and contestable. On the need to understand the notion of a passional cause of belief broadly, note that James sometimes speaks of an 'interest' determining belief (see, for example, 'The Sentiment of Rationality', in id., *The Will to Believe and Other Essays in Popular Philosophy, and Human Immortality* (New York: Dover, 1956), 89).

with specific cultural and religious traditions.[24] It is true, of course, that lack of evidential support for a proposition's truth does *tend*, once we become aware of it, to undermine any inclination we may have had to hold the proposition true—and that general tendency is no doubt central to proper cognitive functioning. To take that tendency for a universal psychological law, however, would be a rationalist fantasy—plausibly itself an example of passionally believing that things are as one thinks they ought to be! To consciously believe that p, for some proposition p, is indeed to *find oneself with* the attitude towards p that it is true; but to find oneself with the attitude towards p that it is true is only typically but *not necessarily* to find p's truth *evident or evidentially supported*. To believe is, indeed, to *believe true*; it is not necessarily to *believe evident*.[25]

Doxastic venture is psychologically possible, then, because the responsive attitude of holding a proposition true can have a non-evidential, passional, cause. But a further condition is also necessary: those passional causes have to be able *to sustain* belief *even though the believer recognizes that the truth of the proposition believed lacks adequate evidential support*. Indeed, for doxastic venture to be possible, it must be possible for the passional cause of the relevant belief *to motivate* the believer to venture to take it to be true in his or her practical reasoning despite recognizing its lack of evidential support. Passional *causes* for holding a proposition true, that is, have to

---

[24] Compare James's own list of 'non-evidential' factors shaping our tendencies to believe: 'fear and hope, prejudice and passion, imitation and partisanship, the circumpressure of our caste and set' (*The Will to Believe*, 9). (Being caused to believe through the 'circumpressure' of one's group is, of course, to be carefully distinguished from being caused to believe by inference from the fact that the proposition concerned is widely held to be true within one's group.) For a recent discussion of the significance of emotions for religious beliefs see Mark Wynn, *Emotional Experience and Religious Understanding: Integrating Perception Conception and Feeling* (Cambridge: Cambridge University Press, 2005).

[25] My claims here conflict with Jonathan Adler's view that it is intrinsic to the concept of belief that one literally cannot believe any proposition for whose truth one recognizes oneself to have insufficient evidence (Adler, *Belief's Own Ethics*: see especially ch. 1). Adler's arguments deserve a more thorough critique than I can attempt here. Suffice it to observe, however, first, that Adler does recognize that his thesis faces certain 'recalcitrant cases' (see *Belief's Own Ethics*, 33–4), and, second, that the modest Jamesian version of fideism for which I shall be arguing restricts permissible doxastic venture with respect to faith-propositions to options that *could not in principle* be decided on the evidence. There are thus prospects for conceding Adler's central claim, but in a non-absolutist spirit. That is, one might allow that, in general, 'one's believing that p is proper (i.e. in accord with the concept of belief) if and only if one's evidence establishes that p is true' (*Belief's Own Ethics*, 51), while maintaining that an exception must yet be made for the special case where the proposition p functions in such a way that its truth or falsity could not in principle be established evidentially. In Chapter 6, I will take up the question how any proposition might possibly function in such a way.

be able to become passional *motivations* for the mental action of taking the proposition to be true with full weight in practical reasoning. Only if all these conditions are contingently met will the psychic resources be available for a person to make a doxastic venture.

To illustrate. Imagine someone who is passionally caused to hold it true that God exists—say, through being formed or moved by encounter with a theistic religious tradition. Suppose also that she comes to think that God's existence is not established on the evidence—perhaps, indeed, that it could not be so established. Provided it is contingently the case that the passional cause of her belief can motivate her to commit herself to its truth in her practical reasoning despite her recognition of its lack of evidential support, she has the psychic resources to make, *if she chooses*, a doxastic venture in favour of God's existence. To make that venture she takes the proposition that God exists to be true in her practical reasoning, letting herself do so with the commitment that goes with holding that content true, this attitude being sustained by passional motivation.

Note that this Jamesian account of how doxastic venture is possible will accommodate both the active and the passive or gifted aspects of Christian faith remarked on earlier. The idea that faith is a gift is sustained by a crucial feature of the account, namely that doxastic venture is possible only for those who have the psychic resources to be motivated to take the belief concerned to be true—resources which have to be passional since evidence-based intellectual resources for evincing belief are (by definition) lacking. Whether any particular person passionally believes is a contingent matter—and a contingent matter, furthermore, beyond the person's own direct control. On a Christian understanding of faith as doxastic venture, if one does contingently possess the needed passional motivation to take the great truths of the Gospel to be true in one's way of life, then that is ultimately only by the grace of God.[26] Having the gift of effective passional motivation is not, however, sufficient for doxastic venture: the believer must also act with this motivation. The act of doxastic venture, however, should emphatically not be thought of as an unmotivated wilful leap: it is, rather, a motivated choice to take to be true what one holds true through

---

[26] And there is, of course, a question how it could be that an omnibenevolent and omnipotent God should fail to supply to all the grace needed to make the venture of faith. If the evidential ambiguity of theistic belief is correct—as we are currently assuming—then there will need to be some consistent way of explaining the absence of such universal psychic resources from within a theistic perspective.

causes that one recognizes oneself to be non-evidential. As emphasized in Chapter 2, there is a natural habituated flow from holding a proposition true to taking it to be true in practical reasoning—and doxastic venturers *let themselves go with that flow* even though they recognize that what they hold true lacks adequate evidential support and even though they could block the flow if they so chose.

It is clear, then, that on the present account, *doxastic venture does not amount to any kind of self-inducing of belief*, whether direct or indirect. When one judges that a certain proposition's truth is not well supported by one's evidence, one cannot simply decide to believe it nonetheless, however much one might desire to do so for non-epistemic reasons (e.g. because believing it is expected to have good consequences). One might, of course, proceed on the assumption of the proposition's truth. It is possible, that is, to decide to give a proposition's truth full weight in one's practical reasoning despite the recognition that its truth lacks evidential support; but deciding *to believe it* is impossible—arguably, for conceptual, and not merely for psychological, reasons (as already noted in Chapter 2).

I suspect that the whole idea of doxastic venture is regularly dismissed out of hand by many philosophers because they assume that all 'doxastic venture' could mean would be the impossible basic intentional action of directly forming a belief while recognizing that its truth lacked evidential support. I have here shown, however, that 'doxastic venture' can mean something quite different and entirely psychologically possible. Doxastic venture does not and could not involve directly making oneself believe in the absence of persuasive evidence. Rather, it *presupposes* that one *already* believes—and that one does so *from passional causes*. Just *holding* a proposition true without evidential support is not in itself any kind of venture (it cannot be, since holding a proposition true is not an action). The venture consists in freely taking the proposition to be true in one's practical reasoning, thereby *letting the passional cause of one's holding it true become one's motivation for practical commitment to its truth*.[27] Our inability

---

[27] On the question whether this is a fair interpretation of James's own position in 'The Will to Believe', Robert J. Vanden Burgt writes that 'James is defending the right to believe, and he is not talking about a faith brought about through any sheer act of willing. ... [What he is talking about is] a belief toward which we are inclined by the deeper forces of our being, and the question becomes whether we should refrain from such belief because of its objective uncertainty' (*The Religious Philosophy of William James* (Chicago: Nelson-Hall, 1981), 69). I am indebted to Imran Aijaz for drawing my attention to Vanden Burgt's work.

7

directly to satisfy a desire to believe a particular proposition to be true does show that something other than one's own will has to be the cause of one's holding a proposition true. But evidential causes are not the only such possible causes—and when someone does hold a proposition true from non-evidential causes, that person is then in a position to choose to make a doxastic venture.

The present account of doxastic venture thus differs significantly from interpretations of James's will-to-believe thesis as a doctrine about the permissibility of *indirectly* inducing in oneself beliefs unsupported by evidence whose possession one expects to have good consequences.[28] *Indirect* self-inducing of belief is not, of course, conceptually impossible in the way that *direct* self-inducing of belief is. Furthermore, as noted in Chapter 2, it is sometimes psychologically possible for people to cause themselves to form a certain determinate belief—though special conditions may need to be satisfied, such as conditions enabling self-deception about how the belief was acquired. So, people who judge that the truth of proposition p is not supported by their evidence, and who nevertheless desire to believe that p, might then act with the intention of acquiring that belief. One possible action-plan for such people would be to try to get themselves to view the evidence differently, so that they would come to hold that p's truth *was* evidentially well supported, and their belief that p would then be produced in the regular, evidence-influenced, manner. A different possible action-plan is to try to get the desired belief produced through non-evidential causes. Just such an action-plan is recommended by Pascal to those not persuaded of God's existence by the evidence yet convinced by his 'Wager' argument: 'Go, then, and take holy water, and have masses said; belief will come and stupefy your scruples,—*Cela vous fera croire et vous abêtira*'.[29] This kind of self-manipulation may well strike us as untoward;[30]

---

[28] Richard Gale's reconstructed account of James's doctrine adopts such an interpretation (see *The Divided Self of William James*, ch. 4), and he thus attributes to James a 'pragmatist' or consequentialist justification of his doctrine. In his *Faith, Skepticism, and Evidence*, Stephen T. Davis offers reasons for rejecting this interpretation, at least so far as James's position in 'The Will to Believe' is concerned (132–5). I shall not pursue this scholarly issue, however. It suffices to emphasize that my own Jamesian fideism differs from Gale's, and that defending it along consequentialist lines is unlikely to prove successful (an issue I shall take up again in Chapter 8).

[29] James's report of Pascal's advice, *The Will to Believe*, 6

[30] The sense that that there is something untoward about this kind of self-manipulation may be related to the idea that the presence of passional causes for theistic faith-beliefs is in God's gift, and one should not try to induce a state that is properly bestowed by divine grace. (The fact that the

yet there is no denying that it may, under some circumstances anyway, be entirely psychologically feasible. Engaging in such self-manipulation is not doxastic venturing, however. Intentionally inducing passional causes for a certain belief in order to satisfy an essentially non-epistemic desire to have that belief (such as, e.g. the desire to reap advantages believed to flow from it) does *not* amount to doxastic venture on my present account. On my present account, as I must again emphasize, there can be occasion for doxastic venture only if there is *already* a passionally caused tendency to hold the proposition concerned to be true.[31]

That concludes, then, my account of what doxastic venture is and how it is possible. Once it is recognized that beliefs can have non-evidential causes, there is no need to think that an evidential deficiency view of faith could only involve *sub*-doxastic venture—that is, that to venture beyond evidential support could only be to act on the assumption of the truth of faith-beliefs without actually believing them. Where the belief concerned has a passional cause, *fully* doxastic venture is possible, in which the venturer not only takes a faith-proposition to be true beyond the evidence with full weight in practical reasoning, but also actually holds it to be true.

There is no need to insist, however, that authentic faith *essentially* involves fully doxastic rather than sub-doxastic venture. Authentic faith does essentially require a preparedness to take faith-propositions to be true *with full weight* in one's practical reasoning. But if people *can* be so prepared without actually believing the truth of the faith-propositions on which they act, then it ought to be conceded that they may indeed be making an authentic venture in faith.[32] For, certainly, it is *practical* rather than *merely felt* conviction which is at the heart of this venture model of faith:

---

attempt to induce belief is motivated by self-interest does not seem by itself quite enough to explain our reservations.) Compare James's comment: 'We feel that a faith in masses and holy water adopted wilfully after such a mechanical calculation would lack the inner soul of faith's reality; and if we were ourselves in the place of the Deity, we should probably take particular pleasure in cutting off believers of this pattern from their infinite reward' (*The Will to Believe*, 6).

[31] If Pascal's mechanism for acquiring non-evidentially caused belief in God works in a particular case, then a doxastic venture will eventually be implicated—but only at the point at which belief in God has successfully been acquired passionally. At that point, acting on the passionally acquired belief will involve doxastic venture. My point is just that actions taken in an attempt to passionally induce belief are not *themselves* to be identified as doxastic ventures; attempts to self-induce belief can at best bring about *the occasion for* doxastic venture.

[32] 'Lord, I believe; help thou mine unbelief' (Mark 9: 24) could then be rendered coherent by reading 'I believe' to mean 'I commit myself with full weight', and 'mine unbelief' to mean 'without actually having the attitude that the proposition to which I commit myself is true'.

it is *the act* of taking a faith-proposition to be true while recognizing its lack of evidential support that is the venture. (Taking faith-propositions to be true with merely an intermediate degree of partial belief would thus not count as authentic faith under a doxastic venture model. And further conditions may also be required: for example, full commitment to a faith-proposition's truth will not suffice for authentic faith if it is undertaken in a purely experimental spirit, or as an exercise in pretending to believe. It is important, however, to note that full practical commitment to a proposition's truth does not entail *dogmatic* commitment to it, and is consistent with a certain kind of open-mindedness which may arguably be a desideratum of a morally permissible venture in faith.)[33]

But how might people be motivated to take it to be true with full weight in their reasoning (e.g.) that God exists without actually believing the truth of that proposition? Those who suffer 'the dark night of the soul' continue heroically to commit themselves in practice to God's existence without experiencing God's presence or goodness—but do they perform the (even more heroic?) feat of doing so even though they no longer believe it true that there is a God? It is hard to know: and, if they do, what motivates them? According to Swinburne, the reason why a person of faith acts on the assumption that there is a God is that ' … unless there is[,] that which is most worthwhile is not to be had'. Swinburne continues:

He prays for his brethren, not necessarily because he *believes* there is a God who hears his prayers, but because only if there is can the world be set to right. He lives the good life, not necessarily because he *believes* that God will reward him, but because only if there is a God who will reward him can he find the deep long-term well-being for which he seeks.[34]

Full commitment to a faith-proposition's truth may be motivated even in the absence of actual belief, then, by the belief that it would be good—supremely good, perhaps the only way the supreme good could be realized—if that faith-proposition were true. It is thus necessary to concede that *fully* doxastic venture is *not essential* to authentic theistic faith—though it is important to recognize that a sub-doxastic venture is still a venture that practically commits to the *truth* of what is recognized not to be evidentially established. Only clause (2) of the doxastic venture model as stated above proves non-essential, then: clauses (1) and (3) remain.

---

[33] I revisit this issue in Chapter 6.      [34] *Faith and Reason*, 117.

Those who suppose that the fact that agents judge that God's existence lacks evidential support *just entails* their not believing that God exists will, of course, be obliged to allow only a sub-doxastic venture model of believing by faith. But that supposition, as I have suggested, arises from a rationalist fantasy about how beliefs are caused in the real world. Once freed of that rationalist fantasy through acknowledging that certain of our beliefs can have non-evidential causes, we may accept that the venture of theistic faith can be, and quite typically is, fully doxastic.

Supporters of a model of faith that will accommodate evidential ambiguity are not *driven*, then, to a purely sub-doxastic venture model. Nevertheless, authentic faith might indeed *sometimes* be sub-doxastic. That concession is, however, a relatively minor matter. The really important issue is whether decisive venturing beyond the evidence in what one takes to be true in one's practical reasoning (whether or not it occurs in the presence of actual belief) is something to which a person may be morally or indeed epistemically entitled—and, if so, under what conditions. I shall develop a Jamesian answer to this question in the next chapter.

# 6

# Believing by faith: a Jamesian position

Reflective theists' concern for the justifiability of their faith-beliefs is ultimately, I have argued, about whether they are *morally* entitled to take those beliefs to be true in their actions and way of life. Moral entitlement in turn seems to require epistemic entitlement—granted a realist interpretation of faith-beliefs, anyway. If epistemic entitlement to take a faith-belief to be true is assumed to require that the believer hold it on the basis of evidence that adequately supports its truth (or, in other words, to require that the belief, and the believer insofar as he or she holds the belief, be 'evidentially justified'), then *moral evidentialism* follows: practical commitment to a faith-proposition's truth can be morally justified only if one is evidentially justified in holding it true. With respect to a prevailing rational empiricist theory of correct evidential practice, however, theistic belief may be evidentially ambiguous: arguably, our total available evidence is viably interpretable both on a theistic and on a non-theistic view of the world.

The evidential ambiguity of theism is, of course, contested. It is plausible enough, however, for the question of the moral status of theistic commitment under evidential ambiguity to be important. If evidential ambiguity is accepted, morally justifiable theistic commitment *rests on the possibility of morally justifiable doxastic (or sub-doxastic) venture in favour of beliefs of that kind*—so I have argued, anyway (in Chapter 4). In Chapter 5, I have explained the nature of ventures of this kind, and shown how they are possible only when the beliefs concerned have non–evidential causes. The question now is whether such ventures can ever be permissible—and, if so, under what conditions.

Here, then, is the issue. Assuming the evidential ambiguity of theism, ought people to refrain from commitment to the truth of theistic faith-propositions, perhaps on W. K. Clifford's sweeping grounds that 'it is wrong, always, everywhere, and for anyone, to believe anything upon insufficient evidence'? Or do people have a perfect moral right to commit themselves beyond their evidence to the truth of faith-beliefs if they so choose—and have the necessary psychic resources? William James thought that people do have a right to make such commitments. In this chapter, I will develop a James-inspired thesis for the moral permissibility, under specific conditions, of doxastic ventures *with respect to faith-beliefs of the kind exemplified by theistic faith-beliefs*. The emphasized qualification is important: it will not be enough to show (what is anyway apparent) that the absolutist moral evidentialism expressed in the famous quote from Clifford cannot be correct. It may not be controversial that moral evidentialism must admit *certain kinds of* exceptions—what the defence of fideism requires, however, is to show that moral evidentialism admits of exceptions permitting doxastic venture *in the kind of case* exemplified by commitment to theistic religious belief in an acknowledged context of evidential ambiguity.

## An initial hypothesis for a Jamesian thesis on permissible doxastic venture

Without doubt it is usually wrong to act on a belief when one recognizes that one has insufficient evidence for its truth. The general importance of giving serious regard in practical reasoning to the extent of one's evidential support for the relevant propositions must be acknowledged: doxastic venture can be defended, then, only against the background of a general acceptance of evidentialism. The hypothesis I shall here propose maintains that stance: if doxastic venture is to be permissible at all, it will be so only under significant constraints that pick out legitimate exceptions to the general presumption in favour of evidentialism.

What, then, might the constraints on doxastic venture be? James gives an answer in section IV of 'The Will to Believe'. He says that letting ourselves resolve an option for belief through 'passional' motivation is permissible 'whenever it is *a genuine option* that *cannot by its nature be decided on intellectual grounds*' (my emphasis). I shall take this as a suitable starting point, then, for an attempt to develop a thesis on the jointly sufficient and severally necessary conditions for permissible doxastic venture that will apply to the kind of case exemplified by commitment to theistic belief under acknowledged evidential ambiguity. (Let me reiterate that my interest here is in using Jamesian resources to develop a fideist thesis that deserves to be accepted as true, and not in achieving a scholarly account of James's own position.)

Consider, then, the following initial Jamesian hypothesis for a thesis on permissible doxastic venture:

> ($J_i$)   It is morally permissible for people to take a proposition p to be true with full weight in their practical reasoning while correctly judging that it is not the case that p's truth is adequately supported by their total available evidence, if and only if:
> (i) the question whether p presents itself to them as a 'genuine option'; and
> (ii) the question whether p 'cannot by its nature be decided on intellectual grounds'.

Note that the notion of 'full weight' is used here in the sense introduced in the previous chapter: to take a proposition p to be true with full weight is to employ p in one's practical reasoning, giving its truth the kind of weight that naturally goes along with straightforwardly—non-partially—believing that p is true.

It will be possible for people to act as described on the left-hand side of the equivalence stated in ($J_i$) only if they have some passional motivation for practical commitment to p's truth despite their recognizing its lack of evidential support. (As indicated in Chapter 5, 'passional' motivation is 'non-evidential' motivation—that is, any motivation *other than* the motivation that comes from finding a proposition's truth to be evident, or inferable, deductively or otherwise, from other truths found to be evident.) A standard passional motivation for commitment to a truth recognized as lacking evidential support is an already held passionally caused *belief* that p is true, and ventures thus motivated will be fully doxastic. As conceded at the conclusion of the previous chapter, however, passional motivation for taking a faith-proposition to be true with full weight might sometimes obtain in the absence of any actual belief that p is true—and ($J_i$) equally affirms the moral permissibility, under its stated conditions, of such sub-doxastic ventures. What is controversial about ($J_i$), however, is its permission of the venture—whether fully doxastic or not—of taking a proposition to be true with full weight without adequate evidential support, and it is on that issue that I shall focus discussion.

## The notion of a 'genuine option'

How are the constraints ($J_i$) places on permissible doxastic venture to be understood? The fideism ($J_i$) articulates accepts a presumption in favour of moral evidentialism. It therefore limits permissible doxastic venture to circumstances where, *for some clearly principled reason*, an exception needs to be made to the evidentialist maxim. ($J_i$)'s conditions may be understood as seeking to express in general terms what such a principled reason would have to be.

($J_i$)'s first condition is that a morally permissible doxastic venture has to resolve a 'genuine option'. The point of this first condition is to restrict permissible doxastic venture to choices that are both important and unavoidable: only then could it possibly be justifiable to go against the moral evidentialist presumption. James's notion of a genuine option captures this condition well—on the following understanding of what is meant. (What follows is thus intended as *specifying* the notion needed for the present account, rather than simply as an accurate interpretation of James's own notion.)[1]

An option is, on James's own definition, 'a decision between two hypotheses' on a given issue.[2] James defines a *genuine* option as one that is *living, forced*, and *momentous*. Each of these features—and therefore, too, the overall feature of the 'genuineness' of an option—is a *contextual* feature. Merely knowing the content of an option is insufficient to determine whether it is genuine; its genuineness depends on certain properties of the situation in which the person who faces it is placed.

For an option to be *living* for a given person, the hypotheses for choice have to be 'live', in the sense that each has, in James's words, some 'appeal

---

[1] I do in fact believe that my account *does* accurately reflect James: but it is not necessary for present purposes to defend this claim.

[2] *The Will to Believe*, 3.

as a real possibility to [the person] to whom it is proposed'.[3] The choice
thus has to make sense to, and have point for, the person concerned.
Living options are *momentous* for people when it matters significantly
which hypothesis they adopt—where what they take to be true affects
significant actions of theirs or, more broadly, what kind of lives they
lead or persons they become. Furthermore, a momentous option must
present an opportunity in some sense unique and unrepeatable, so that it
matters *here and now* which hypothesis the person adopts.[4] (Some important
options may be of a type likely to recur in a person's life—perhaps
many times. That does not block their momentousness if it will make
a significant difference *from the moment of choice on* which hypothesis the
person adopts.)

On the notion of a *forced* option James says this:

> If I say 'Either love me or hate me' … your option is avoidable. You may remain
> indifferent to me, neither loving nor hating … But if I say 'Either accept this truth
> or go without it', I put you on a forced option, for there is no standing place
> outside of the alternative. Every dilemma based on a complete logical disjunction,
> with no possibility of not choosing, is an option of this forced kind.[5]

Forced options occur in practical reasoning, then, only when we have
to decide *whether or not* to take a given proposition, p, to be true. The
question whether to take p to be true presents itself as forced for people just
when *what matters in their situation is the choice between taking p to be true and
not taking p to be true*. The forcedness or unforcedness of an option is thus, as
already indicated, a contextual feature. To vary James's analogy—using an
institutional variant on 'loving or hating'—I may have an option whether
to support or contest a colleague's bid for promotion. My option will not
be forced if I can remain neutral. But if the Dean asks me whether I will
or will not support the promotion, my option is then forced. Once the
context shifts so that the option becomes forced, positively opposing the
promotion and merely abstaining from supporting it—which are *otherwise*

---

[3]  *The Will to Believe*, 2.

[4]  William J. Wainwright's summary of James's notion of a genuine option (*Reason and the Heart*,
86–7) may not, I think, quite get to grips with the 'uniqueness' aspect of what James means by a
'momentous option'. The 'uniqueness and irreversibility' of an option is actually *not* 'important only
because [these features] sometimes contribute to the significance of our choices', as Wainwright suggests
(see 87, *n.* 4), but rather arises from the fact that it matters significantly which option is chosen *from the
point of choice onwards*.

[5]  *The Will to Believe*, 3.

significantly distinct, given that they involve importantly different attitudes on my part—become *in practice* equivalent: they both amount to not giving support.

We may thus appreciate, by analogy, how options relating to taking propositions to be true in our practical reasoning may be forced. A proposition (as, for example, the claim that Jesus is my personal saviour) will present a forced option to me just in case what matters to me is whether I do or do not commit myself in practice to its truth, with there being for me no salient practical difference between not doing so while suspending judgement on the question and not doing so while 'positively' disbelieving it. (Evangelical Christians do in fact understand this choice as forced—and, indeed, also as momentous—for anyone who properly understands it. Though the life I lead if I suspend belief may differ somewhat from the life I lead if I disbelieve, the cases are the same insofar as in neither do I 'accept Christ into my life'.)[6,7]

Clause (i) of my James-inspired thesis ($J_i$), then, confines permissible doxastic venture with respect to a given proposition p to contexts in which what matters—and matters significantly for how they live from the time

---

[6] Evangelical Christians understand accepting that Jesus is one's personal saviour as necessary for salvation—but does the forced option whether or not to take the Evangelical claim to be true have the *uniqueness* required for momentousness (and hence for genuineness)? That may not seem obvious: whatever choice I make now, surely the same choice can be re-presented to me later? If I do not take Christ to be my saviour, I may yet—perhaps on my death bed—face the same option and decide differently. And if I do now accept Christ, a test of my faith may come the very next day. Yet, reversible as the present decision may be, what I decide *now* determines what style of life I lead until I may face the option again—and who knows when 'the Lord may come'? Death beds do not unfailingly announce themselves as such. So an Evangelical Christian understanding of the option to believe in Christ as saviour is not only forced but also momentous in Jamesian terms.

[7] Stephen T. Davis suggests that 'if an option is forced—we must decide—it does not matter whether it is also live or momentous' (*Faith, Skepticism, and Evidence*, 122), and accordingly rests his defence of James's 'right to believe' doctrine on the significance of its being restricted to forced options. While I agree that the forcedness of a genuine option is dialectically to the fore in constraining permissible doxastic venture, I do not agree that liveness and momentousness 'do not matter'. To go back to James's own example: your choice either to love me or hate me—which is unforced—may often be of little importance: we may be so little connected that it really does not matter to your life what you think of me and you will probably remain indifferent. But if that choice presents itself as forced, so that the issue for you is whether you do or do not love me (or for that matter, do or do not hate me), must that not be because what you think about me does have real significance for you—and must it not be important here and now to resolve the issue? Thus, while the notion of an option's being forced is clearly *logically* distinct from the notion of its being momentous, in fact *psychologically* it may be true that options present themselves to people as forced only when they are momentous. If, however, there are options that are *merely* forced (and not momentous, or not even live), there will be no point in contesting the presumption that they be decided in accordance with the evidentialist principle.

of decision onwards—is whether people do or do not take p to be true with full weight in their practical reasoning (so that the difference between not taking p to be true while holding p to be false and not doing so while neither holding p true nor holding p false does not, in the context, make any practically significant difference).

## A 'degrees of belief' challenge

It may be questioned, however, whether it makes sense to suppose that decisions about what to take to be true in practical reasoning could ever present forced options in the above sense. Some options for action are indeed forced—voting for or against a proposal is a good example: but can there be an analogue of this *when it comes specifically to mental actions that consist in employing propositions in practical reasoning*? As already noted, the evidentialist position has often been put in Hume's terms: 'the wise man *proportions* his belief to the evidence'.[8] This presupposes that people are able differentially to *weight* their practical commitment to the truth of propositions. Bayesian epistemology idealizes this capacity using the notion of *degrees of partial belief* (or *credences*) determined by subjective judgements of the probability of the relevant proposition's truth—and the Humean principle prescribes that those judgements should assign whatever degree of probability is indicated by the evidence. Decision theory then explains how people's credences may be taken into account, along with estimates of the utility of potential outcomes, in their practical reasoning.[9] It may seem, then, that decisions about what to take to be true in practical reasoning *never* present themselves as forced, since all we ever have to decide is the degree of partial belief to afford the relevant propositions. Arguably, we are never forced to decide whether or not to take a proposition p to be true: arguably, practical commitment requires weighting p's truth as probable to some degree, not an all or nothing choice whether or not to afford p's truth full weight. This suggests that condition (i) of thesis

---

[8] Hume, *Enquiry Concerning Human Understanding*, 110.

[9] For a useful survey discussion of the theoretical context in which the notion of degrees of belief (or degrees of confidence) is central, see William Talbott, 'Bayesian Epistemology', in Edward N. Zalta (ed.), *The Stanford Encyclopedia of Philosophy (Fall 2001 Edition)*, <http://plato.stanford.edu/archives/-fall2001/entries/epistemology-bayesian/>.

(J$_i$) has the effect of ensuring that it necessarily lacks application to any real case.[10]

There is, then, a 'degrees of belief' challenge to thesis (J$_i$). This challenge will have to be met by proponents of (J$_i$) who think that it *does* have real application—and, in particular, to the case of evidentially ambiguous faith-propositions such as we are currently assuming are involved in theistic religion. To meet this challenge it will need to be shown how it is possible to be presented with a forced option whether or not to take such propositions to be true with full weight in practical reasoning. I think this 'degrees of belief' challenge can be met, as might already be suggested by the Evangelical Christian example used above. Forced options *do* arise when we need to choose whether or not to commit ourselves to framing principles of the sort already identified in Chapter 4—principles that mark the cardinal presuppositions of, and the entry point into, a whole doxastic framework. Before elaborating on this point, however, it is necessary to comment on (J$_i$)'s second condition.

## Evidentially undecidable forced options

Doxastic venture is justifiable, then, according to thesis (J$_i$), only when it settles practical commitment on a question that presents a genuine option. The further necessary condition stated in (J$_i$)—condition (ii)—is that the genuine option concerned must be one that, in James's words, 'by its nature cannot be decided on intellectual grounds'. The broad intention of this condition is clear: options that *can* be decided by rational assessment of one's evidence fall under the moral evidentialist imperative. Doxastic venture could possibly be permissible only when the option concerned is undecidable on the evidence. But how is this undecidability condition to be understood?

What does it mean to say that an option whether to take proposition p to be true or not 'cannot by its nature be decided on intellectual grounds'?

[10] Compare Bertand Russell's claim that James's 'will to believe' doctrine ignores the notion of probability (*History of Western Philosophy* (London: Allen & Unwin, 1946), 843). Note that those who, objecting to the notion that believing that p can come in degrees, prefer rather to speak of believing that a certain level of probability attaches to p's truth will readily be able to reformulate the present challenge using their preferred locution.

Well, to decide on intellectual grounds would be to decide in accordance with one's judgement of how the total available evidence bears on the question whether p—in other words, to 'let the evidence decide'. So an option which could not be decided on intellectual grounds would be one where 'the evidence could not decide'. What precisely would it mean, though, for a decision about what to take to be true in one's practical reasoning to be unable to be settled on the evidence? And how could such a circumstance arise?

Whatever the state of one's evidence on the question whether p, that evidence will determine (under the norms of the applicable evidential practice) a rational attitude towards the proposition that p. In *that* sense, it could never happen that 'the evidence could not decide'. Of course, the evidence might not clearly support either p's truth or p's falsity (the evidence might show neither that it is significantly more probable than not that p is true nor that it is significantly more probable than not that p is false). In such cases, however, the evidence determines suspension of belief (or suspension of judgement) as the rational attitude to take towards p—and, if one admits the notion of partial belief, it will determine a particular intermediate degree of partial belief (or, at least, partial belief within a particular range of degrees of partial belief) corresponding to the extent to which the evidence renders it probable that p is true.

We are here concerned, however, not just with propositional attitudes but with *taking propositions to be true in one's practical reasoning*—and, as I argued in Chapter 2, such takings-to-be-true are mental actions in which agents exercise their own control and about which they can (sometimes) make real choices.[11] Accordingly, judging the bearing of one's evidence on the question whether p and on that basis forming a corresponding attitude towards p is one thing, and deciding what to take to be true on the question whether p in relevant practical reasoning is another. And it is *those* decisions—decisions about practical commitment to p's truth—that may sometimes be unable to be settled on the evidence alone.

---

[11] The qualification arises from a point already made: with many beliefs (e.g. perceptual beliefs) the disposition to take them to be true in one's reasoning is so deeply habituated—even hardwired—that we do not have any real choice about the matter. In other cases, however, such as in the examples given in Chapter 2, we clearly do have a choice about whether to take to be true in practical reasoning what we hold to be true—and, of course, we are able to take propositions to be true without having the attitude that they are true, as the cases of acting on a hypothesis for experimental purposes and of pretending to believe clearly illustrate.

That claim may be contested, however. Indeed, it looks to be false as soon as we admit the notion of partial belief. For, people may commit to p's truth with a degree of partial belief proportioned to their evidence even when that evidence shows neither that p's truth nor that p's falsity is significantly more probable than not—and that weighting may then be taken into account in practical, decision-theoretic reasoning. So, lack of a clear direction on the evidence as to p's truth or falsity does not entail that our use of the proposition p in our reasoning cannot be sensitive to the bearing our evidence has on its truth. Arguably, *whatever* the bearing of the evidence on the question whether p, our practical commitment can match it by carrying a suitably proportioned weighting. Arguably, then, there can be no cases where 'the evidence does not decide': in every case, we may follow the policy of letting our decision about what we take to be true (and with what weight) simply mirror our judgement of the bearing of the relevant evidence. In which case, all such decisions *can* be made on intellectual grounds, and, contrary to what $(J_i)$ envisages, there will never be occasion for letting passional inclinations settle our practical commitment to the truth of any propositions.

To be understood properly, however, $(J_i)$'s 'evidential undecidability' condition (ii) should be seen as additional to condition (i)—the requirement that the option settled by doxastic venture be 'genuine', and, in particular, *forced*. Now, I have already noted that there is a 'degrees of belief' challenge to the view that options for practical commitment ever genuinely present as forced. Later in this chapter, I will meet that challenge by showing that some options presented by faith-propositions could indeed be forced—that is, that sometimes what matters is whether people do or do not commit themselves with full weight to the truth of the faith-proposition concerned. For the moment, let me issue a promissory note to that effect, and follow through the implications for the present discussion of $(J_i)$'s evidential undecidability condition. For, I think it can be shown that, *if* an option presented by a faith-proposition is indeed forced, then good sense can be made of the possibility that such an option could not be settled *purely* on the basis of an intellectual judgement of the bearing of the relevant evidence.

If one has to make the forced decision whether or not to take it to be true that p, and one judges (let us assume, correctly) that one's evidence neither supports p's truth nor p's falsity, it is not feasible to make the decision by following a policy of *simply mirroring* one's evidential judgement. Obviously, if one decided to commit to p's truth under such circumstances, one would be going beyond, though not against, what the evidence indicates, and could not thus rightly claim to be *merely* letting one's choice be settled by one's judgement of the evidence. Less obviously perhaps—but just as surely—the alternative decision not to commit to p's truth also cannot rightly be described as resulting *purely* from one's evidential judgement, though it is certainly consistent with that judgement. For, the only way one could simply mirror in one's practical commitment the judgement that the evidence supports neither p's truth nor p's falsity, would be to take p to be true with some intermediate degree of partial belief—but, *assuming that the option is forced*, that outcome is excluded since, under a forced option, not taking p to be true is *in practice* equivalent to taking p to be false. (Suppose, for example, that a person faces a forced option whether to take it to be true that Jesus Christ is his personal saviour. If he judges that the evidence indicates neither the truth nor the falsity of that claim, and he then decides not to take it to be true that Jesus is his saviour, he will *in practice* be going beyond, though not against, what his evidence indicates because he will be placing himself practically in exactly the same position as someone who judges the evidence to indicate the falsity of the Evangelical claim, though his *attitude* towards that claim will of course differ.)

But, surely, someone will say, choosing to take p to be true *is* ruled out by evidence which neither supports p's truth nor p's falsity, since the right attitude to match such evidence is to suspend judgement and the only choice consistent with that attitude is *not* to take p to be true. (If, to continue our example, one finds that the evidence leaves it open whether Jesus may or may not be the saviour, then the only way one can 'follow the evidence' is not to take the Evangelical claim to be true.)[12] This response seems commonsensical, yet it masks a seductive error. Certainly, *if one takes*

---

[12] Compare Richard Feldman: 'If the religious option is the choice between believing that God exists and not believing that God exists, and evidence concerning the existence of God is counterbalanced, then the option *is* intellectually decidable. ... Since ... the evidence is counterbalanced, the intellect *can* decide the case. It decides in favour of not believing (by suspending judgement)' ('Clifford's Principle and James's Options', *Social Epistemology*, 20 (2006), 23–4). (Note that to say that evidence concerning a proposition is 'counterbalanced' is to say that it 'equally supports the proposition and its negation'.) Along similar lines, Jonathan Adler has objected that 'James knows that the choice between believing and disbelieving is not an excluded middle. Yet the crux of his argument is that it should be so treated. But you cannot alter a logical truth to harmonize with a practical end' (Adler, *Belief's Own Ethics*, 120).

*evidentialism to apply*, then lack of evidence clearly supporting either p's truth or p's falsity in the context of a forced option will *in conjunction with that normative commitment* dictate that one should *not* commit to p's truth. But it would be mistaken to present that decision as something entailed by a policy of letting oneself be guided by intellectual assessment of the evidence *alone*. Such a decision can result only given some normative stance stronger than the principle that one should simply mirror in one's decisions about what to take to be true the attitudes that are rational given one's judgement of the evidence. And that normative stance might not need to be evidentialism. An alternative to evidentialism *could* be applicable to some forced options—as, indeed, (J₁) proposes—and then the outcome in response to open evidence will be different.

This point is so important that it could do with reinforcing. In the case of a forced option whether or not to take p to be true in one's practical reasoning, the resolution of that option may be based on a judgement of the state of the evidence alone only if either (*a*) the evidence is judged to support p's truth—in which case, the decision is to take p to be true, or (*b*) the evidence is judged to support p's falsity—in which case, the decision is not to take p to be true. However, if (*c*) the evidence neither supports p's truth nor p's falsity, then either taking p to be true or not doing so would be consistent with intellectual assessment of the evidence, and the decision must be determined by some further assumption about *what one ought to do* in such a situation of open evidence. But it is a matter for debate what that assumption should be: in particular, it is possible to contest the assumption that following the evidence in such a situation requires not taking the relevant proposition to be true, an assumption which follows, of course, from the evidentialist principle that it is permissible to take p to be true only if p's truth is evidentially well supported. (Some philosophers may regard it as obvious that the only practical course consistent with open evidence on the question whether p is not taking p to be true because they hold the view that one could not—psychologically or even conceptually—be motivated to take p to be true other than by recognizing evidence supporting it. That view is mistaken, however, as I argued in Chapter 5: one may be passionally, non-evidentially, motivated to take a proposition to be true, and that motivation can sometimes sustain commitment to p's truth despite the recognition of its lack of adequate evidential support.)

The effect of $(J_i)$'s condition (ii), then, is to restrict morally permissible doxastic venture with respect to a proposition, p, to cases where the genuine option whether or not to take p to be true is *evidentially undecidable* in the sense that the person facing the option is not able to settle it *purely* by following a correct judgement either that p's truth or p's falsity is significantly more probable than not given his or her total available evidence. In fact, condition (ii) imposes the stronger requirement that a genuine option permissibly resolved through doxastic venture be such that it 'cannot *by its nature* be decided on intellectual grounds': the option has to be, in some sense, *essentially* evidentially undecidable. According to $(J_i)$, then, the general presumption in favour of moral evidentialism as applied to our choices about what we take to be true in our reasoning may not be defeated just because it merely *happens* to be the case that a person's evidence does not settle the question of the truth of the relevant proposition—it may be defeated only if, somehow as a matter of principle, no evidential support for its truth *could* be forthcoming.[13]

The 'degrees of belief' challenge to $(J_i)$ still remains, however. On a 'degrees of belief' view, forced options with respect to what one takes to be true in practical reasoning cannot arise, since the state of the evidence, whatever it is, may be reflected in the weight attached to the relevant proposition's truth. On that view, the evidence always will decide, since it will always determine *some* appropriate weight for p's truth to be afforded in relevant practical reasoning. This view thus questions the very possibility of forced evidentially undecidable options at the level of choices about what we take to be true in practical reasoning. That challenge will have to be met. $(J_i)$ will necessarily lack application unless it can be shown that there can be forced options where what matters is whether or not one takes a faith-proposition to be true, and that those options can sometimes be evidentially undecidable—and, indeed, essentially so—in the sense outlined.

Before I explain how this challenge may be met, however, let me draw out an important implication of the fact that an evidential undecidability condition features in $(J_i)$ at all.

---

[13] Note that the evidential undecidability condition I am here proposing is much stronger than the condition that many commentators attribute to James in 'The Will to Believe'. Compare, for example, William J. Wainwright, who takes James to be requiring only that 'the evidence should not clearly or conclusively point in one direction or the other' (*Reason and the Heart*, 89).

## Permissible doxastic venture: supra- not counter-evidential

It might be thought that an evidential undecidability condition on permissible doxastic venture is redundant since the fact that it obtains would seem to follow directly from the very meaning of doxastic venture. It might be thought, that is, that where an option *can* be settled on the evidence, there *conceptually* could not be any such thing as passionally motivated doxastic venture. But that thought is not correct.

The opportunity for doxastic venture with respect to proposition p *is* conceptually pre-empted, of course, if one's intellectual assessment of the evidence confirms p's truth—even if one should already happen to hold that p through purely passional causes. But it is not conceptually impossible for people to take a proposition to be true *contrary to* their judgement of what the evidence indicates. It is conceptually possible for people to judge correctly that their evidence justifies holding *that not-p*, and yet, in their practical reasoning, give full weight to the claim *that p*. For this to be psychologically possible in a particular case, some motivation for such *counter-evidential* commitment must, unusually, be present and be sufficient to counter the motivational force of the person's assessment of the evidence. But such unusual psychological conditions sometimes do obtain. Psychic mechanisms, akin to those involved in self-deception, may so compartmentalize an evidence-based judgement from a non-evidential motive for practical commitment that they may co-exist while giving contrary indications.

Counter-evidential doxastic—or, at least, sub-doxastic—venture seems to be possible, then, and the question therefore arises as to its permissibility. Furthermore, a *possible* view of virtuous Christian faith, in particular, is that it requires the 'knight of faith' to commit himself to Christian doctrines *contrary to* his own rational assessment of their evidential justification. I shall call this view *counter-evidential fideism*.[14] Counter-evidential fideism is,

---

[14] Tertullian and Kierkegaard are usually cited as Christian proponents of counter-evidential fideism—though *credo quia absurdum est* is wrongly attributed to Tertullian (what he said was *credibile est, quia ineptum est* (Tertullian, *De Carne Christi*, trans. Ernest Evans (London: S.P.C.K., 1956), 5.4). It also seems doubtful that Kierkegaard's fideism was counter-evidential (see C. Stephen Evans, *Faith Beyond Reason: A Kierkegaardian Account*; and Christopher Insole, 'Kierkegaard: A Reasonable Fideist?' *Heythrop Journal*, 39 (1998), 363–78). I suspect that the claim that Christian faith involves embracing contradictions is best interpreted, not as referring to logical contradictions, but rather as a way of pointing out that true Christian faith requires believers to reverse their 'natural' assumptions about the

however, widely regarded as suspect. And so one way of objecting to a doxastic venture model of (meritorious) faith is on the grounds that accepting it would entail condoning counter-evidential fideism. That objection assumes, however, that any position which permitted doxastic venture with respect to faith-propositions would be committed to allowing that non-evidential, passional, influences may properly, in such cases, *simply override* the deliverances of our rational capacities for assessing the force of evidence. The effect of (J$_i$)'s condition (ii), however, is to repudiate any such assumption. Condition (ii) restricts virtuous doxastic venture to options that (essentially) cannot be resolved purely by an assessment of the evidence. Condition (ii) thus renders impermissible all counter-evidential doxastic ventures. Where a genuine option *can* be decided on the evidence, then, even if doxastic venture motivated by a passional tendency to believe contrary to that intellectual judgement is in the circumstances a real psychological possibility, no such venture can be morally permissible—or so (J$_i$) implies.

Condition (ii) might seem too strong: may we not imagine cases where people who have the psychic resources to make a certain counter-evidential doxastic venture would be morally obliged to do so? (Consider, for a classic example, the alpinist whose sole chance of saving himself is passionally to commit himself to taking it to be true that he can make a dangerous jump which he realizes on the evidence he would be most unlikely to make safely.)[15] Nevertheless, so far as it applies to doxastic venture in favour of theistic faith-propositions, condition (ii) of the Jamesian thesis (J$_i$) has what will widely be regarded as the merit of giving no comfort to counter-evidential fideists. Thesis (J$_i$) affirms moral evidentialism as applying to all genuine options that people *can* resolve on their total available evidence: in such cases, according to (J$_i$), it is indeed our ethical

divine. So it is not clear that anyone has seriously held the extreme counter-evidential fideist view that Christian faith requires one to take the incoherent to be true. Biblical literalists, however, would seem to be committed to counter-evidential fideism, since the accounts of creation in Genesis are, taken literally, plainly excluded by our total empirical evidence. Unwillingness even in conservative theological quarters to accept counter-evidential fideism is well illustrated, however, by the emergence of 'young earth creationism' amongst Biblical literalists—that is, by the attempt to put the six-day creation story forward as a serious scientific theory.

[15] Richard Gale refers to James's use of this kind of example (*The Divided Self of William James*, 112). (Gale has corrected the reference there given [personal communication]: it should be to William James, *Essays in Philosophy* (Cambridge, MA: Harvard University Press, 1978), 332.) As I argue in Chapter 7, however, I am unpersuaded by this particular kind of case, though I do accept that morally justifiable cases of practical commitment to truth-claims contrary to one's correct judgement of the evidence must be possible.

duty to take to be true only what the evidence shows to be true, irrespective of where our passional inclinations may lie.

($J_i$) affirms as permissible, then, only what may be called *supra-evidential* doxastic venture—or, to use a term of James's, 'overbelief'.[16] ($J_i$) sanctions taking to be true, through passional motivation, only what *goes beyond*, *yet is still consistent with*, what one finds to be rationally supported on the evidence. According to ($J_i$), it is only when a genuine option cannot be resolved on the evidence that we have the right to let ourselves resolve it in practice through passional motivation. As I have noted, this aspect of ($J_i$) seems, taken generally, to be too strong: but, when it comes to theistic religious faith-commitment *et sim.*, it yields the clear—and generally welcome—verdict that judging on a rational assessment of argument and evidence that a belief is false (let alone, absurd) and then going right ahead with practical commitment to its truth is morally beyond the pale. Thesis ($J_i$) is thus an expression of what may be referred to as *supra-evidential fideism.*[17]

## How theistic religion could present essentially evidentially undecidable genuine options: the notion of a highest-order framing principle

So much, then, for an account of the meaning of the conditions that thesis ($J_i$) imposes on permissible doxastic venture. My task now is to consider

[16] James does not use this term in 'The Will to Believe' but he does employ it elsewhere—e.g. in *Pragmatism*, where he speaks of 'the various overbeliefs of men, their several faith-ventures'. See William James, *Pragmatism* (Cambridge, MA: Harvard University Press, 1975), 144.

[17] The view that only supra-evidential and not counter-evidential believing by faith can be morally permissible is clearly James's view in 'The Will to Believe'. Whether that was James's actual overall view has been disputed, however. Richard Gale has argued that for James 'the only justification for believing is pragmatic, based on maximizing desire-satisfaction, with epistemic considerations entering only in a rule-instrumental manner as useful guiding principles' (*The Divided Self of William James*, 95). Gale thus takes James to be equally willing to endorse both counter-evidential and supra-evidential believing by faith when the relevant consequentialist conditions are met. (Note that a consequentialist interpretation of James's 'will to believe' doctrine is also adopted by Jeff Jordan, in 'Pragmatic Arguments and Belief'.) I will consider the possibility of a consequentialist justification of doxastic venture in favour of faith-propositions in Chapter 8. In Gale's view, what he calls the 'dualist account of belief-justification' in 'The Will to Believe' is to be explained as a matter of James conceding as much to his scientifically minded audience as he can, in order to make his doctrine as palatable to them as possible. The view that passional commitment to truth-claims is permissible only when evidence is necessarily unavailable is, then, on Gale's view, merely a debating concession on James's part. It is not to my present purpose to try to decide whether Gale is correct about this: I simply observe here that this feature of ($J_i$)—drawn as it is from a key claim made by James in 'The Will to Believe'—has the potential advantage of securing a moderate fideism that rejects the widely repudiated counter-evidential variety.

the challenge that ($J_i$) has no application: that is, the allegation that there could not be any genuine—and, in particular, forced—options that are also essentially evidentially undecidable. Recall that this 'degrees of belief' challenge maintains that, for any given proposition p, whatever the state of the relevant evidence, it will always be possible to assign p's truth a probability in proportion to the weight of the evidence, so no one could ever be forced to decide for or against *full* practical commitment to a proposition's truth in a situation where 'the evidence could not decide'.

Since my aim is to show that thesis ($J_i$) may apply to doxastic venture with respect to faith-propositions (such as those that constitute the cognitive component of theistic faith), a pertinent reply to the 'degrees of belief' challenge will need to indicate how the question whether to make a practical commitment to the truth of such a faith-proposition could indeed present a live, momentous, and forced option that was also essentially evidentially undecidable.[18] This possibility may be shown, I think, by means of an argument that builds on the fact (already noted in discussing isolationist and Reformed epistemology in Chapter 4) that theistic faith-beliefs form a doxastic framework that presupposes the truth of certain framing principles. The cognitive component of any traditional theistic faith constitutes a framework of beliefs that depend on framing principles that claim the existence of a classical theistic God, whose nature, will, and activity is revealed in certain historical events and sacred writings, and will also include (as noted in Chapter 4) an implicit claim that a certain evidential practice applies within the framework. Unless people are committed to some theistic framing principles of this kind, they will not have any theistic *faith*-beliefs at all.[19]

These observations should not be controversial, although the use that some philosophers have made of the notion of a doxastic framework has often been highly contestable. The whole idea of doxastic frameworks requires cautious handling. In particular, as already emphasized in Chapter

---

[18] I shall not, therefore, attempt a *general* account of how essentially evidentially undecidable genuine options can arise, but will provide only *one* account of how *faith-propositions* could present such an option. Evidence relevant to a proposition could be necessarily unavailable for a number of different reasons other than the one which I am about to outline: whether any of those different reasons could apply to the case of faith-propositions is an issue I shall consider later (in Chapter 8).

[19] As already noted in Chapter 2, people might have *purely metaphysical*, 'thin', theistic beliefs that lack reference to any historical revelation of God's nature and will. The present claim is to be understood as applying only to theistic beliefs held in the context of an actual theistic religious faith.

4, recognizing that a person's theistic faith-beliefs form a framework that depends on distinctive framing principles is *not necessarily* to take the isolationist view of that framework as wholly epistemically self-contained. All that is entailed is recognition of a certain feature of the cognitive architecture of the person's overall noetic structure (i.e. the whole structure of his or her beliefs, and the norms and associated practices associated with holding, retaining, revising, and acting on beliefs). For an identifiable doxastic framework to be a feature of a person's overall noetic structure is for the person to have a related set of beliefs that all presuppose the truth of a specific set of framing principles. Beliefs within a particular framework may, however, have important epistemic and logical relationships with beliefs elsewhere in the overall noetic structure—and this includes the framework's framing principles. Any connotation that a doxastic framework *must* form an epistemically autonomous compartment in the person's overall noetic structure should therefore be blocked. Operating within a given doxastic framework need not at all entail operating in a separate context to which all other doxastic commitments are irrelevant.

How may we build, then, on this notion of a doxastic framework in order to show how faith-propositions could present options that are genuine (and, in particular, forced) and also essentially evidentially undecidable—that is, options of the kind specified by thesis ($J_i$) as necessary and sufficient for morally permissible doxastic venture with respect to such propositions? We may do so, I maintain, by arguing that *the choice whether or not to commit to the truth of the framing principles of a whole doxastic framework of faith-beliefs could present just such a genuine and essentially evidentially undecidable option.*

The first step in the argument is to note that framing principles generate options that are inevitably forced. With respect to any given framing principle, one either commits oneself to it, and to operating within the doxastic framework that depends on it, or one does not. To suspend judgement on taking a framing principle to be true in one's practical reasoning is necessarily not to commit oneself to taking it to be true, and hence in practice to stand outside the particular doxastic framework that depends on it. One either 'buys into' the framework by commitment to its principles or one does not. The celebrated 'game' analogy is indeed apt here, provided it is recognized just as an analogy: either one is 'playing the game' or one is not. Of course, one may commit oneself in practice to the truth of a framework's framing principles with a wide variety of attitudes to their truth: one need not necessarily actually believe that the principles are true (such commitment can be, as already acknowledged, sub-doxastic). There is nothing forced about what attitude one holds to their truth: what is forced is whether one does or does not take them to be true in practice, and that is the kind of option with which we are concerned (held attitudes are not, directly, matters for option, anyway). In particular, then, the choice whether or not to take to be true the framing principles of a given theistic religious tradition is a forced choice, and one that, in a given context, may also be living and momentous.

The second step of the argument seeks to show that a forced choice whether or not to make practical commitment to the truth of framing principles could also be essentially evidentially undecidable—and that this applies, in particular, to the case of the specific framing principles of a theistic religious tradition. Our present discussion is within the scope of the assumption that the belief that a classical theistic God exists—a core component of every particular set of theistic religious framing principles—is evidentially ambiguous. Insofar as this assumption is plausible at all, it is, I think, also plausible that the ambiguity is not merely contingent—at least from within the natural historical order.[20] For, if one is persuaded with respect to the wide range of suggested evidence in favour of holding that God exists that the very same evidence can reasonably be interpreted as consistent with naturalist atheism, and persuaded also that the wide range of suggested evidence against holding that God exists can reasonably be interpreted as consistent with theism, then one may properly conclude that, probably, there is some reason *in principle* why each of these incompatible *Gestalts* seems equally sustainable in the light of the overall evidence. The evidential ambiguity of theism is, of course, contestable: but arguably it is not as contestable to maintain that if the evidential ambiguity thesis is true, it is likely to be non-contingently so. If one is prepared to agree that human history until now has not managed to resolve the question of God's

[20] I thus set aside the possibility that classical theism may be open to post-mortem eschatological verification. Those who envisage such a possibility may perhaps be too sanguine, however, in imagining experiences after death that would decisively establish God's existence. Suppose we *do* find that 'when we've been there ten thousand years bright shining as the sun, we've no less days to sing God's praise than when we first begun', would that really suffice to establish the existence of an all-powerful and morally perfect Creator? Would we know then that we were indeed in heaven, and not in hell? See Bernard Williams, 'The Makropulos Case: Reflections on the Tedium of Immortality' in *Problems of the Self*, 82–100. Compare, however, John Hick, 'Eschatological Verification Reconsidered', *Religious Studies*, 13 (1977), 189–202.

existence, then surely one should also agree that it is more likely than not that this question *necessarily* cannot be resolved on the evidence?

Not obviously so: some philosophers think that disambiguation *could* be achieved by future inquiry despite what they accept as the record of historical failure.[21] Such philosophers will obviously regard the present evidential ambiguity of theism as a contingent feature—deeply and puzzling so, perhaps, but contingent nonetheless. Despite such dissenting voices, however, surely it is clear that the evidential ambiguity of classical theism at least *could* be—indeed, could *well* be—necessary, and that a forced option to commit to some specific classical theistic position *could* therefore be essentially evidentially undecidable? This claim will not be fully persuasive, however, unless a plausible explanation can be given of *how* this could be so.

It seems clear that the truth of a framing principle would be essentially evidentially undecidable—and, indeed, persistently so—if that framing principle were 'highest-order'. If we consider noetic architecture *in abstracto*, we see that commitment to the truth of *some* framing principles could be nested in the sense of being rationally secured within the scope of commitment to the truth of wider framing principles. On pain of an infinite regress, however, this means of securing their truth cannot apply to *all* framing principles—and those to which it cannot apply we may describe as *highest-order framing principles*. No doubt any claim to the effect that a given framing principle is indeed highest-order will be fallible—but insofar as one may reasonably hold a given framing principle to be highest-order, one may thereby reasonably hold its truth to be essentially evidentially undecidable—and, indeed, persistently so (i.e. the necessary lack of evidence is not a temporary feature).

Returning now to the concrete case of the framing principles of a specific classical theist doxastic framework: some philosophers (Swinburne and Penelhum, for example) implicitly deny that those framing principles are highest-order.[22] Philosophers who take the evidential ambiguity of theism to be necessary may be characterized, by contrast, as implicitly holding that

---

[21] I have already cited Terence Penelhum as a prominent case in point (Ch. 4).

[22] In Swinburne's case, this denial is based on the conviction that the truth of theistic framing principles may be shown to be secured without circularity on the basis of wider principles; Penelhum's denial, however, is a matter only of a continuing faith that disambiguation with respect to such principles must be possible, either one way or the other.

classical theist framing principles *are* of highest-order. This view underlies both isolationist and Reformed epistemologies of religious belief—with isolationism interpreting these highest-order framing principles as giving rise to an epistemically autonomous doxastic framework (typically understood in a non-realist way), and Reformed epistemology interpreting them under realism as belonging to the set of highest-order framing principles that characterize a whole, integrated, noetic structure.[23]

The view that theistic framing principles are of highest order may also be held by supra-evidential fideists—and, indeed, it provides them with a response to the 'degrees of belief' challenge by showing how thesis ($J_i$) could have application, and application to theistic faith-propositions in particular. The beliefs that form the cognitive component of a specific theistic religious faith constitute a doxastic framework. If the framing principles of that framework are of highest-order, then the question whether to take those framing principles to be true presents an option which is forced and persistently essentially evidentially undecidable, and which may, in a given context, also be living and momentous. Thesis ($J_i$), then, does have application, at least in the case of options for commitment presented by the highest-order framing principles of a whole doxastic framework.

Let me reinforce this conclusion. When a highest-order framing principle, p, presents itself as a genuine option, its truth is persistently essentially evidentially undecidable. In such a case, we must either venture necessarily without evidential support by taking p to be true or else keep within the limits of what can be supported on our evidence by refraining from so doing. Taking p to be true with some intermediate degree of belief (a default credence of 0.5, say) is not a viable *via media*. For, in the first place, there is a conceptual problem about assigning any credences at all in a situation where *as a matter of principle* there is a persistent absence of evidence. A credence of 0.5 is the rational response to a judgement that *there is* evidence, but evidence that is mixed in a way that indicates the proposition concerned to be as likely to be true as not. Assigning a default credence of 0.5 may also sometimes be a rational response to an absence of evidence, in a situation where that assignment is open to correction by

---

[23] Compare also John Hick, who takes religious faith to involve commitment to propositions 'stating a total interpretation'. Hick provides a useful defence of the view that 'the concept of probability is not applicable to comprehensive world-views' which is relevant to the reply to the 'degrees of belief' challenge I am here developing. See Hick's *Faith and Knowledge*, ch. 7, 154.

expected future evidence. But assigning credence of 0.5 is never a rational response to a *necessarily persistent* absence of evidence. Furthermore, where p is the content of a highest-order framing principle, the option whether or not to take p to be true necessarily amounts to the forced choice between buying into a whole doxastic framework or not buying into it. There is no room for any half measure. Either one is practically committed to the framework's principles or one is not. Either one takes them to be true with full weight or one does not. (That is not to say, of course, that one may not take them to be true without actually believing them to be true: but that is a matter of one's held attitude, and what is at issue here is what one takes to be true in one's practical reasoning. With framing principles generally, one must either take them to be true or not.)

To put the matter in terms of a concrete case, consider the option whether or not to take it to be true that God exists and is revealed in Jesus the Christ. Ordinarily that would be regarded as a factual claim assessable in the light of relevant evidence. If this claim is taken to be subject to evidential ambiguity, however—and, indeed, not merely as a matter of contingency—it will then be understood to function quite differently from any ordinary factual claim. A truth-claim that could not in principle have its truth decided on the basis of evidence is a special kind of claim. It is a claim whose truth is a cardinal presupposition of a whole framework of beliefs—in this case, Christian beliefs. It is a claim that functions as a framing principle for a Christian doxastic framework.[24] It is a claim that presents one with the forced choice whether to take it to be true or not: one either buys into a Christian way of understanding how things are and ought to be or one does not. Though one may commit oneself to Christian framing principles with a variety of different *attitudes* as to their truth, and though one's commitment may have varying degrees of stability or staying power, at any given point of decision the truth of those principles must either be accepted in one's practical reasoning with full weight or not. Taking those principles to be true necessarily requires venturing beyond what can be supported on one's evidence—and that venture may be either fully doxastic (when accompanied by actual belief in their truth) or sub-doxastic (when not so accompanied). Thesis (Jᵢ) asserts that such ventures

---

[24] There are, of course, many such possible frameworks, arising from more or less subtle differences in the content of their framing principles—with respect to what sources count as authoritative, what hermeneutic methods apply, etc.

may be morally justifiable—provided that the forced options they present to the venturer are important enough. 'God exists and is revealed in Jesus', functioning as a highest-order framing principle, may (for some people) be just such a case in point.

I submit, then, that there can be no doubt that thesis $(J_i)$ can have application, at least to foundational faith-propositions that are highest-order framing principles. For, such principles present options which have to be both forced and essentially evidentially undecidable.[25] But it is, of course, a further question whether thesis $(J_i)$ should be accepted as correct.

Before I proceed to consider that further question, a parenthetical point needs to be made. During the foregoing it will have been easy to hear the lingering ghost of logical positivism maintaining that essentially evidentially undecidable highest-order framing principles cannot be factually meaningful, but must have some other, non-assertoric, function. Now it is true that the position just articulated *does* share with logical positivism the view that a claim such as 'God exists and is revealed in Jesus' does not function as an ordinary factual claim. And there is a temptation to use analogies that suggest the logical positivist's non-cognitivist conclusion—for instance, by drawing parallels between framing principles and the rules of a game. Yet, though there is something important to be learnt from such analogies—provided one keeps actively in mind that every analogy contains elements of disanalogy—there is no need, short of sheer positivist dogma, to accept that Christian framing principles *et sim.* lack truth-values. No doubt *some* framing principles do require a non-cognitivist construal: to commit to some framing principles may be to commit to accepting certain rules or conventions, or to endorsing certain evaluative attitudes. But there is no need to insist that all highest-order framing principles *must* receive such a construal: some such principles may be genuinely assertoric. As already remarked, even theological non-realists, under the only plausible version of their view, concede cognitivism with respect to theistic claims: for non-realists, commitment to theistic framing principles is commitment to their truth, albeit truth within a fictional realm socially constructed to express, and encourage adherence to, a privileged set of values. Theological realists, of course, take Christian framing principles to make assertions about

---

[25] An impressive defence of the claim that it is just such *weltanschaulich* principles that James himself intended to be the subject of his 'will to believe' doctrine is to be found in Robert J. O'Connell, *William James on the Courage to Believe* 2nd edn (New York: Fordham University Press, 1997).

mind-independent reality, a view which they will maintain even as they accept that those framing principles are of highest-order and their truth essentially unable to be decided on the basis of evidence.

## Restricting thesis (J$_i$) to faith-propositions: thesis (J)

Now that an answer has been given to the challenge that thesis (J$_i$) can have no application, it is high time to proceed to consider whether thesis (J$_i$) should be accepted as true.

It is plain enough—and widely agreed—that an absolutist, Cliffordian, evidentialist ethic is mistaken. It is patently *not* wrong, *always, everywhere, and for anyone*, to take to be true in practical reasoning propositions whose truth is insufficiently supported by the evidence. The moral evidentialist principle that one should take propositions to be true in one's practical reasoning only with a weight proportioned to one's judgement of their degree of evidential support holds only *prima facie*, and may be overridden in certain kinds of cases. For example: venturing to take a proposition true without the support of one's evidence for the purposes of experiment is obviously often entirely permissible. We may also readily imagine cases where it is morally obligatory to act as if you firmly believed what you know to be false: a fugitive's life, for example, may depend on your pretending to believe that he is not in the hiding place where you know he is sheltering. There are also cases where it seems clearly morally permissible to make a fully doxastic venture to take a proposition true without sufficient support from one's evidence. In personal relations, for example, we often need to trust others beyond any evidence of their trustworthiness that could be available at the outset: to lack willingness to make ventures of this kind would be churlish and a great handicap in building good relationships.

My present inquiry, however, is specifically focused on the moral permissibility of doxastic venture *in favour of faith-propositions of the general kind involved in theistic faith*, and it is far from clear that this may be extrapolated from the (pretty much uncontroversial) permissibility of doxastic venture in cases like those just cited. I will, however, return later (in Chapter 8) to consider whether something might be made of such extrapolative arguments—whether believing by faith that God exists and is revealed in Jesus (for example) might turn out to be relevantly similar to morally admirable cases of (for example) believing by faith at the outset of a significant interpersonal interaction that another person will prove trustworthy.

As already briefly noted, however, it is also plain enough that thesis (J$_i$) is too strong as a general thesis providing necessary and sufficient conditions for permissibly taking propositions to be true without sufficient evidential support. Experimentally taking proposition p to be true beyond one's evidence does not seem to be permissible only when the 'genuineness' conditions are met, nor need it be required that evidence supporting p is *essentially* unavailable (indeed, to the contrary, the whole point of taking p true in practice for the purposes of experiment is *to generate* relevant evidence). Even if we set aside experimental ventures beyond the evidence as a special case, however, (J$_i$)'s conditions still seem too strong. As already observed, condition (ii) excludes all counter-evidential ventures as impermissible, yet surely we can imagine circumstances in which an overriding moral imperative licences taking p to be true contrary to one's evidence (assuming, of course, that one has the psychic resources to achieve this feat).

Since my interest is in defending the moral permissibility of doxastic ventures *in favour of faith-propositions of the kind exemplified in theistic faith*, it will be perfectly convenient to restrict thesis (J$_i$) so that it becomes a claim *solely about such cases*. There is no need (so far as the present project is concerned) to provide a completely general set of necessary and sufficient conditions for morally permissible doxastic or sub-doxastic venture. So the fact that (J$_i$), as it stands, does not seem quite fitted for *that* task is no embarrassment. Besides, as my discussion of how (J$_i$)'s condition of *essential* evidential undecidability could be met has indicated, (J$_i$) anyway seems specifically suited to the case of foundational faith-propositions that serve as highest-order framing principles for a whole framework of faith-beliefs. Options presented by such highest-order framing principles are, as we have seen, *persistently* essentially evidentially undecidable. If religious commitment of the sort exemplified in theistic religions does indeed rest on commitment to the truth of such propositions, then the need for supra-evidential venture is *intrinsic* to it, and the condition of evidential ambiguity ineliminable.[26] A common fideist view that such religious faith

---

[26] As already noted in Chapter 3, commitment to the truth of certain historical claims is typically essential to any actual 'expanded' theistic religious commitment: clearly, the truth *of such historical*

*would not be what it is* if evidential support for its cognitive commitments were forthcoming is thus sustained.

So, let me now restate my thesis in this restricted form as a thesis about the moral permissibility of what may be called *faith-ventures*—doxastic (or sub-doxastic) ventures with respect to faith-propositions of the kind involved in theistic religious (and relevantly similar) forms of faith. I will call this more specific thesis 'thesis (J)'.

(J)   Where p is a faith-proposition of the kind exemplified in the context of theistic religious faith, it is morally permissible for people to take p to be true with full weight in their practical reasoning while correctly judging that it is not the case that p's truth is adequately supported by their total available evidence ('to make a faith-venture in favour of p') if and only if:

 (i)  the question whether p presents itself to them as a genuine option; and

 (ii) the question whether p is essentially evidentially undecidable.

(Note that, given my account of how faith-propositions could be evidentially undecidable, thesis (J) is effectively equivalent to the claim that it is morally permissible for people to commit themselves in practice to any highest-order framing principle that presents them with a genuine option. Faith-propositions that are derived within a specific theistic doxastic framework—for example, within an orthodox Christian doxastic framework, the proposition that Christ ascended into heaven and is seated at the right hand of the Father—are held on the basis of evidence in accordance with the evidential practice applicable to such propositions under the framework's framing principles. Those principles themselves—including, for example, the claim that doctrinal truth is revealed in certain canonical ways through the Church—if they are indeed highest-order framing principles, can be taken to be true only through supra-evidential venture, since they necessarily have no, non-circular, evidential support.)

Given thesis (J), those who are concerned about whether they are morally justified (or would be morally justified) in some particular faith-venture will need to satisfy themselves that both the 'genuineness' condition and

---

*claims* is not in principle beyond evidential determination. What arguably is essentially evidentially undecidable, however, is understanding the claimed historical facts as revelatory of the actions and will of a classical theistic God.

the 'essential evidential undecidability' condition are met in their own case. To the extent that, on their best judgement of the matter, they are satisfied on this point, they will reasonably take their particular faith-ventures to be morally justifiable.

It should be noted, however, that a person's best judgement as to the satisfaction of the conditions required by (J) for morally permissible faith-venture might, in fact, be mistaken. (Depending on the circumstances, the mistake may or may not be culpable. Note, however, that an agent's not being morally blameworthy does not entail that what the agent does is not morally wrong. Thus, someone who inculpably misjudges the permissibility of her faith-venture is morally entitled to make it only in the sense that she is to be held blameless for the error, not in the sense that her venture actually is morally permitted.) For individual reflective theists, the possibility that they might reasonably but mistakenly judge (J)'s conditions to be met in their own case serves as a limit to their inquiry into the moral permissibility of their faith-ventures—a limit that properly blocks any pretension to be able to complete it finally and infallibly. Because confidence in the moral permissibility of faith-ventures rests on fallible judgements, they should be made in a manner open to the possibility that later developments may bring those judgements into question, and require modification or even withdrawal of the faith-commitments concerned. Those who care about the moral justifiability of their faith-ventures, then, need to make them in a spirit that is non-dogmatic and open-minded. It does not follow, however, that their faith-ventures may only be 'tentative'—indeed, whether they are fully doxastic or sub-doxastic, they are characterized by full practical commitment.[27] Full,

---

[27] Thus, although I am sympathetic to Robert McKim's case for the view that those who acknowledge evidential ambiguity in matters religious should adopt what he calls the 'Critical Stance', I have reservations about accepting McKim's view that such a stance includes a 'T-principle' permitting no more than tentative belief. (See *Religious Ambiguity and Religious Diversity*, 154–84.) Similarly, Stephen T. Davis's reconstruction of James's 'right to believe' doctrine strikes me as poorly worded given that Davis, too, describes permissible faith-ventures as 'tentative':

'Where a person is faced with a forced option between two mutually exclusive hypotheses and where a decision between the two hypotheses cannot be made on the basis of evidence, with full epistemological justification he can choose between the hypotheses on some basis other than evidence and can tentatively (i.e. with his mind still open) accept the hypothesis chosen and act as if it were true.' (*Faith, Skepticism, and Evidence*, 171)

Davis's formulation also appears to differ from my (J) in being a thesis about the 'full epistemological justification' of doxastic venture—although Davis later (182) builds the notion of moral permissibility

non-tentative, commitment through passionally motivated supra-evidential venture neither need nor should amount to irreversible, non-revisable, or dogmatic commitment, however.

It is important to note that (J) is a permissibility thesis, not a thesis positing any ethical obligation. (J) leaves it open whether or not those who are passionally motivated to commit themselves to the truth of faith-propositions under conditions (i) and (ii) would do wrong if they were *not* to venture to make that commitment. (Conceivably, however, in order to argue for (J) as against the rival position that upholds moral evidentialism even when conditions (i) and (ii) are met, it will be necessary to make the stronger claim that people *ought* to follow their passional promptings when faced with religious or similar genuine options.)[28]

It also important to note that accepting thesis (J) is likely to lead to *a moral pluralism about faith-ventures*. For, (J)'s conditions may well be met by people with different and mutually incompatible passionally caused faith-beliefs. It is likely that reflective *Christians*, for example, will be able to conclude that their faith-ventures meet (J)'s requirement only under conditions where they must acknowledge that (e.g.) reflective *Muslims* may also reasonably draw the parallel conclusion with respect to their incompatible theistic faith-ventures. There is thus further reason for faith-ventures to be made in a non-doctrinaire spirit. Also, certain implications may result for the content of the faith-propositions one may justifiably accept—in particular, any doctrines as to the *moral* exclusivity of one's own religious tradition would seem to be ruled out. I shall return to this point in Chapter 9.

The question now is this: should we accept thesis (J)? Or should we reject it, and uphold moral evidentialism *as applying to options presented by foundational faith-propositions* (even if we admit—as undoubtedly we should—that moral evidentialism does not apply absolutely)?

---

into his account of 'epistemological justification'. I shall take up again the question whether proponents of (J) should hold that doxastic venture under the stated conditions can carry epistemic as well as moral entitlement in the following chapter.

[28] In his introduction to the Harvard edition of *The Will to Believe and Other Essays in Popular Philosophy* (Cambridge, MA: Harvard University Press, 1979), Peter Madden suggests that James himself offers both a 'weak and a strong version of his will to believe doctrine—that we have a right to believe either alternative in question and that, because of certain features of our passional nature, we should believe one alternative rather than other.' (Cited in Wainwright, *Reason and the Heart*, 94, n. 12) I shall return to this issue in Chapter 9.

Before I tackle this question directly (as I shall in Chapter 8), I want first to face up to a common line of objection to thesis (J) closely related to the point just made about its pluralist implications. The objection is that thesis (J) is altogether too liberal, condoning faith-ventures that seem intuitively morally untoward. Chapter 7 is devoted to considering how to reply to this 'too liberal' objection.

# 7

# Integrationist values: limiting permissible doxastic venture

The fideist ethics of faith-commitment proposed in the previous chapter is open to the objection that it is too liberal. According to thesis (J), if an option presented by a faith-proposition is 'genuine' (in effect, unavoidable and existentially significant) and also essentially undecidable on the evidence, that suffices for it to be permissible to settle it through passional motivation. By that criterion, however, forms of faith-commitment subject to wide moral condemnation will count as morally permissible. In this chapter, I shall consider two different ways of articulating this 'too liberal' objection. I shall argue that it may be met by interpreting proponents of (J) as committed to 'integrationist' values. Some augmentation to (J)'s conditions will accordingly be entailed.

## Can counter-evidential fideism be non-arbitrarily excluded?

The first form of the 'too liberal' objection maintains that there is no non-arbitrary way to admit doxastic venture in favour of faith-beliefs without opening the door to *counter*-evidential faith-ventures: hence, if, as is widely assumed, such ventures should be resisted, no faith-ventures should be allowed at all. In other words, the objection goes, anyone who thinks there is good reason to reject the type of fideism that lauds commitment to faith-beliefs contrary to one's evidence must therefore also reject thesis (J).

Now, thesis (J) does of course explicitly exclude counter-evidential faith-ventures. According to (J), only *supra*-evidential faith-ventures may be acceptable. For, (J) permits venture in favour of faith-propositions only when they are essentially evidentially undecidable—yet counter-evidential venture is a matter of practical commitment to the truth of propositions whose truth is evidentially excluded, hence (to labour the point somewhat) evidentially decided, and hence not evidentially undecidable. So (J) would not, for example, permit a scientist convinced that her evidence supports the truth of Darwinian evolutionary theory to make a faith-venture in favour of the existence of the God of the Biblical literalists, who created the world in six days. That hypothesis is excluded by the scientist's available evidence under the norms of an evidential practice to which she is committed, and so, according to (J), she may not take it to be true by a venture of faith, even if she should be passionally so inclined.

The current objection recognizes this feature of thesis (J), but argues that its restricting permissible faith-commitments to the supra-evidential case is essentially arbitrary. The objection may be put as a challenge: why should it be acceptable to set epistemic concern aside *only so far and no farther*? If it can be permissible to commit oneself to foundational faith-propositions *beyond* adequate evidential support, why may it not also be permissible to commit oneself *independently* of the state of the evidence, and, hence, in directions against what the evidence shows? Better to use evidentialist caution, the objector concludes, and consistently constrain one's commitments according to one's evidence.

How may this challenge be met? For an answer, I shall first consider what reasons there are for judging it impermissible to take faith-propositions to be true through counter-evidential venture. I shall then consider whether these reasons also imply that believing by faith *beyond but not against* one's evidence will always be wrong.

The obvious way to justify rejecting counter-evidential fideism would be to show counter-evidential commitment to be universally wrong. That quick route seems unavailable, however. As already mentioned in the previous chapter, an absolutist prohibition on counter-evidential venture looks to be unwarranted, since an obligation to commit oneself to truth-claims only according to the strength of one's evidence might on occasion be overridden by more pressing moral obligations.

That possibility is easy enough to prove by appeal to contrived examples in which some external agency intervenes to attach an overwhelming advantage to a counter-evidential doxastic venture. The Martians capture me and convince me that they will destroy the world unless I forthwith take it to be true that p in my practical reasoning, for some proposition p such that I rightly judge my evidence to exclude p's truth. I will not be able *actually to believe* that p forthwith, but I may be able to commit myself in practice immediately and fully to p's truth, and, if so, it is certainly morally permissible—indeed, morally obligatory—for me to do so. This will, then, be a case of morally acceptable *sub-doxastic* counter-evidential venture. To upgrade this to a *fully* doxastic case of counter-evidential venture, the Martians would have to attach the advantage to my taking p to be true while also *actually believing* that p: they would need some kind of 'doxascope' to be able to tell whether or not genuine belief was present; and I would have to have recourse to hypnosis or some kind of pill I could take that would reliably and promptly induce the belief that p in me.[1]

Uncontrived examples of alleged ethical suspension of the epistemic are widely mentioned, however—though they are not always convincing. Consider, for instance, the case of the alpinist mentioned in the previous chapter. Here it is a psychologically necessary condition for success in leaping the chasm that the alpinist should believe, not just that he *might*, but that he *definitely will* succeed. If he has the psychic resources to maintain this belief despite recognizing that its truth is contrary to the weight of his evidence, then he is surely justified in doing so—for his only chance of survival may depend on his attempting the leap with this belief. I doubt that a doxastic venture is involved here, however: all the alpinist has to *take to be true* in his practical reasoning is the *evidentially justified* claim that he has no chance of surviving unless he attempts the leap. Given his desire to survive, he accordingly forms the intention to attempt the leap—and if he is able *to hold it true* as he carries out that intention that his attempt will definitely succeed, so much the better. But holdings-true, of course, are not actions but propositional-attitude states, and, though they may have passional causes (as the alpinist's belief in his success here has a passional cause), *their obtaining* cannot count as a venture. The most we may conclude, I think, is that the alpinist would be morally justified

---

[1] Whether there really are any psychologically feasible methods of reliably and promptly inducing a particular belief is, I think, quite doubtful—and it is doubtful, too, whether the kind of particular belief-detecting machinery the Martians would require is even conceptually possible. Note, however, that Richard Gale appeals to the possibility of 'a belief-in-p-inducing pill' in order to illustrate his belief-consequentialist interpretation of James's 'will-to-believe' doctrine. See *The Divided Self of William James*, 93.

in *not* taking steps to try to eradicate his counter-evidential belief that he will succeed, since his possessing it is obviously a great boon. But that does not fit the description of a counter-evidential doxastic venture, which must involve taking a proposition to be true in one's reasoning against the acknowledged weight of one's evidence. In any case, I suspect that the right applied psychology of success in such cases is to focus clearly in one's imagination on the idea of succeeding in the daunting task with which one is confronted, excluding any notion of failure. Actually believing that one will succeed, though it might assist that feat of imagination, does not seem necessary for it.

Another commonly proposed example of apparently justified counter-evidential doxastic venture is taking it to be true that a partner or friend remains faithful in the face of even strong evidence of betrayal. Obligations of loyalty may—it is argued—override epistemic obligations, on occasion requiring that one takes to be true in action what is contrary to one's rational assessment of the evidence. Yet cases of this type do not always present clear examples of morally justifiable counter-evidential doxastic venture. For, in most such cases, there seems no reason not to understand them in terms of *coincident* epistemic and moral virtues, namely the virtue of tenacious adherence to what is well established by past experience in the face even of quite strong new apparent counter-evidence. Though the new evidence is pretty damning, I can weigh against it all the evidence I have of my partner's past faithfulness, with the result that the balance of all the evidence available to me supports my refusing to take it to be true that he has betrayed me. At some point, however, as the damning evidence mounts, such tenacity will shade into foolhardiness—and, then, surely, I will no longer be either morally or evidentially justified in continuing to refuse to take his betrayal to be true? A moral justification for counter-evidential venture in such a case might arise, however, if acting in accordance with what the damning evidence shows would have sufficiently bad consequences—a really messy divorce, for example.[2]

---

[2] Compare John Heil's example (discussed in Conee and Feldman, *Evidentialism: Essays in Epistemology*, 91) of Sally who has a *prudential* obligation to refrain from believing her husband to be unfaithful in order to avoid a divorce even though, given her evidence, her *epistemic* obligation is to believe the contrary. To upgrade Sally's prudential obligation to a moral one, however, divorce would have to be, in the circumstances, a sufficiently bad outcome. Note also that, for counter-evidential doxastic venture, the obligation will, of course, attach to what Sally takes to be true in her practical reasoning and not to her doxastic attitude itself.

So I think it is necessary to concede that counter-evidential doxastic venture *could* under exceptional circumstances be morally permissible—if only on the grounds that the consequences of refraining from it might, in more or less contrived circumstances, be sufficiently serious. The case against counter-evidential fideism, then, cannot simply be that counter-evidential doxastic venture is *always* impermissible. A case might yet be made, however, specifically against the permissibility of counter-evidentially taking to be true *faith-propositions of the sort involved in theistic faith*. What might that case be? And can it be made to target *counter-evidential* believing by faith solely, leaving intact the *supra-evidential fideist* position that (J) affirms?

## A coherence requirement and integrationist values

A good way to generate grounds for rejecting counter-evidential fideism is to proceed by *reductio* and consider the implications of *affirming* that meritorious theistic faith *does* involve counter-evidential doxastic venture, and then reflect on why one might find those implications unwelcome.

Suppose, then, just for the sake of this *reductio*, that commitment to Christian faith-beliefs is a matter of doxastic venture contrary to the evidence. If counter-evidential fideism counts such commitment as permissible, will it not have to do the same for commitment to *any* doxastic framework of faith-beliefs the truth of whose principles is excluded by one's evidence? But, surely, that implication is thoroughly problematic? There is no limit to the crazy and dangerous religious beliefs that have their truth ruled out by our total available evidence! Perhaps, taking a leaf out of James's book, the would-be counter-evidential fideist will require that the evidentially excluded hypothesis present a 'genuine' option—one that is living, forced, and momentous for the person concerned. But it would be rashly over-optimistic to suppose that this requirement will narrow the field satisfactorily. This is, indeed, a big problem for counter-evidential fideism... but there is, of course, *a parallel* big problem for its supra-evidential fideist cousin, and hence for thesis (J)! Whether we simply allow ventures *beyond* rational assessment of the available evidence, or whether we go the whole fideist hog and allow them to be made *contrary to* such assessment, it seems inevitable that, even with the Jamesian 'genuine option' constraint, we will end up condoning thoroughly objectionable doxastic ventures. I shall return to this 'big problem' later in the chapter.

For now, let me mention a problematic implication of accepting counter-evidential fideism that, unlike this one, obviously does distinguish it from supra-evidential fideism and so offers prospects for accepting the latter while non-arbitrarily rejecting the former.

Counter-evidential fideism holds that it sometimes permissible for people to commit themselves to a doxastic framework the truth of whose framing principles they recognize to be excluded by their evidence, according to norms they *otherwise* generally accept. If commitment to foundational Christian truth-claims (for example) is counter-evidential, then those who make that commitment must *also* be committed to some wider evidential practice according to which those claims are to be judged false. They must thus accept that *their overall commitments to what they take to be true do not need to be mutually logically coherent.* Supra-evidential fideism, by contrast, has no such implication: those who commit themselves beyond (but not against) the weight of their evidence obviously can and do accept a condition of logical coherence as applying to their overall network of beliefs. One may therefore reject counter-evidential fideism on the grounds that it fails to respect the basic epistemic requirement for overall coherence amongst one's beliefs, without thereby impugning supra-evidential fideist views as well.

This observation may, at first blush, seem to meet the objection that there is something arbitrary about permitting supra-evidential doxastic venture while rejecting its counter-evidential counterpart. That impression, however, may fail to appreciate the objection's full force. We may justifiably reject counter-evidential fideism on the grounds that it permits agents not to respect a requirement for overall coherence amongst the truths on which they are prepared to act only if such a coherence requirement ought indeed to be met. Now, that requirement would usually be assumed to need no defence, since it is fundamental to the epistemic concern to gain truth and avoid error. In the present context, however, if we are to defend supra-evidential fideism while non-arbitrarily rejecting counter-evidential fideism, more explanation is needed. We need to explain why overall logical coherence amongst one's beliefs is required in a way that leaves it open that it *could* be permissible *not* to respect *further* rational requirements on overall networks of belief that are more substantive than the bare logical coherence requirement but that also seem clearly motivated by epistemic concern. Arguably, one such requirement is the evidentialist requirement not to commit oneself to the truth of propositions without the support of one's evidence (where, of course, 'evidence' is intended in the broad sense indicated in Chapter 3 — that is, to include truths that count as *basically* evident according to the norms of the applicable evidential practice).

Can we provide the required explanation? Ultimately, I think, the only way to do this is to provide a positive defence of thesis (J) as a claim, not only about moral, but also about *epistemic* entitlement to doxastic venture with respect to faith-propositions. Let me elaborate.

It is pertinent to observe that to permit counter-evidential doxastic venture is to allow *fragmentation* of one's overall network of beliefs. It is to allow some doxastic framework belonging to that overall noetic structure to be *epistemically insulated*, with its own *sui generis* evidential practice and norms. If, for example, a person commits herself counter-evidentially to literalist Biblical Christianity, then, necessarily, no developments in her beliefs on scientific cosmology (say) will ever impinge on developments in her Christian beliefs. What she takes to be true in the one framework will essentially lack any bearing on what she takes to be true in the other. When it comes to her scientific beliefs she will seek to respect the norms of scientific evidential practice; her Christian beliefs, however, will be assessed according to a distinct set of norms, including, for example, the norm that whatever the Bible states is to be accepted as true.[3]

Now, there is an ethical perspective from which compartmentalization of this isolating kind is unwelcome. This is the perspective of those who adopt *integrationist values*. Broadly speaking, integrationists value connecting things so that they can influence each other rather than separating them into isolated spheres or bailiwicks. An integrationist would think, for example, that individual flourishing is to be promoted holistically, rather than by merely summing separate and unrelated efforts to ensure good physical health, good mental health, good moral and spiritual health, and so forth. Another example: in dealing with complex institutions, integrationists will maintain that their constituent agencies should not be run as separate empires, but brought into dynamic relationship and creative tension with one another. And so on.

Applying integrationist values to our overall networks of belief (*integrationist doxastic values*) will thus lead to rejecting anything that can result in

---

[3] The fact that the norms governing her religious beliefs are distinct from those governing her scientific beliefs does not, of course, preclude there being significant overlap between them—indeed, many particular norms (e.g. norms governing deductive inference) will belong to both sets.

the epistemic insulation of an entire doxastic framework from a person's noetic structure as a whole. The integrationist ideal is that a person's noetic structure should be, overall, coherent: though incoherence amongst one's beliefs may sometimes have to be lived with, those committed to integrationist doxastic values will never accept that they are evidentially justified in holding beliefs that turn out to be mutually logically inconsistent. Doxastic integrationists do not deny that specific doxastic frameworks and framing principles may properly be distinguished with a person's overall noetic structure. In particular, they allow that there are theistic doxastic frameworks within which distinct evidential practices apply. What they reject is just the notion that it could be justifiable to commit oneself to the framing principles of any such distinctive doxastic frameworks while recognizing that the truth of those principles fails to cohere with doxastic commitments external to those frameworks.[4]

Integrationist doxastic values will thus exclude counter-evidential fideism—that is, counter-evidential venture in favour of the framing principles of a whole doxastic framework of faith-beliefs. Doxastic integrationism has no need to be absolutist, however. Indeed, the integrationist will need to accept that counter-evidential venture may be permissible in exceptional cases (such as in the contrived 'Martians' case canvassed earlier), where there is no risk that the irrational venture will undergird commitment to a whole framework of epistemically insulated beliefs.

Now, integrationist doxastic values do seem attractive, and might commend themselves from a variety of normative theoretical positions. Yet excluding counter-evidential fideism on grounds of commitment to integrationist doxastic values would have more force if some further grounds for that commitment could be given (beyond the attractiveness of integrationist values generally). After all, committed counter-evidential fideists may complain that doxastic integration is unattractively totalitarian, and will be able

---

[4] Endorsing integrationist doxastic values may at first appear to conflict with empirical evidence in cognitive science for the 'modularity of mind'. It is arguable, however, that modularity relates to beliefs, however, only with respect to the way in which *basic* beliefs are produced by cognitive mechanisms. Arguably, once cognitive processes result in content-bearing states at the level of beliefs they do not remain in informationally encapsulated modules: indeed, to the contrary, the role of beliefs seems to belong to central processing that seeks to integrate the deliverances of modules such as perceptual modules. (Compare Jerry Fodor, '... the idea of a really massively ... modular cognitive architecture is pretty close to incoherent. Mechanisms that operate as modules presuppose mechanisms that don't' (*The Mind Doesn't Work That Way: The Scope and Limits of Computational Psychology* (Cambridge, MA: MIT Press, 2000), 71).

to argue that, since their position and that of the integrationist *mutually* exclude one another, they may, with equal justice, reject integrationist doxastic values on grounds of commitment to counter-evidential fideism.

A principled basis for commitment to integrationist doxastic values is to be found in realism—the claim that faith-beliefs are about reality, and *there is but one reality*. (This assumption that 'reality is one' is a crucial, though sometimes unremarked, element in realism logically additional to the defining realist claim that the truth-makers for beliefs are mind-independent features of reality.) Given realism's commitment to one reality, it immediately follows that any other of one's beliefs may in principle have a bearing on one's faith-beliefs. Realism about faith-beliefs thus supports integrationist doxastic values in their exclusion of counter-evidential fideism.

Integrationist doxastic values may thus be rejected, then, by those who affirm a non-realist account of faith-beliefs. As observed in Chapter 5, if a non-realist interpretation of a given doxastic framework is correct (a fiction-alist interpretation of Christian belief, for instance, as referring to a socially constructed mythic reality symbolic of value commitments), then that framework will necessarily be epistemically isolated. Non-realism entails an isolationist epistemology that insulates a framework's beliefs, since, under non-realism, it simply *makes no sense* to assess those beliefs from any external perspective. (Under isolationist epistemology, a *sui generis* doxastic frame-work will 'cohere' with other such frameworks only in the trivial sense that commitment to it may be combined with any other such commitments.)

So there can be an *isolationist fideism* that will, of course, be reject-ed by those committed to integrationist doxastic values along with its counter-evidential fideist cousin (with which it is, effectively, functionally equivalent).[5] A case for rejecting isolationist fideism will not, however, be able to be made along the lines suggested above for rejecting its counter-evidentialist cousin, since the appeal to realism will beg the question unless some further, independent, defence of realism can be provided. And it

---

[5] A doxastic framework gets to be equally epistemically *sui generis* whether commitment to it is permissible even though it *cannot in principle be rationally supported* from an external perspective (isolationist fideism) or whether commitment to it is permissible even though it *is in fact rationally excluded* from an external perspective (counter-evidential fideism). Isolationist fideism may then be the position that counter-evidential fideists graduate to when they recognize realist integrationist objections to their position, and notice that they can get a functionally equivalent position just by abandoning realism about faith-beliefs.

would be a bold assumption indeed to suppose that such a defence will be forthcoming—the state of the debate over realism with respect to theistic faith-beliefs, let alone more generally, might well suggest that the choice between realism and non-realism may *itself* be an essentially evidentially undecidable genuine option—or meta-option. So, when it comes to the dismissal of isolationist fideism, advocates of integrationist doxastic values will most probably have to rest their argument purely on a broad integrationist preference. (Though they might bolster their case at least rhetorically by observing the irony in views that insulate religious beliefs from evaluation in the light of the evidence of other beliefs, given that the etymologically salient, 'binding together' function of religion ought surely to promote rather than resist overall doxastic integration.)[6]

It may well not be possible, then, to establish in a non-question-begging way that integrationist doxastic values *ought* to be adopted: indeed, it seems likely that the choice for or against them is a fundamental value option closely related to the choice for or against realism. Realists, however, clearly can appeal to integrationist doxastic values, and so put paid to counter-evidential fideism—and if that stance also leaves open the possibility that supra-evidential doxastic ventures in favour of faith-beliefs may sometimes be permissible, then a satisfactory answer may be given to the 'arbitrariness' objection currently under consideration.

But *does* (realist) commitment to integrationist doxastic values leave supra-evidential fideism open? Why would it not be an offence against integrationist doxastic values to countenance commitment to a doxastic framework whose framing principles lack external evidential support—even if it may not be *as* serious an offence as condoning such commitment contrary to the evidence? The question remains: how far should realist epistemic concern take us? How tightly integrated ought our overall network of beliefs to be, if we are to do our best to grasp truth and avoid error?

---

[6] Etymologically, 'religion' carries the sense of that which binds (Latin, *religere*, to bind). While this may connote the social, often authoritarian, role of religion, a happier—and, I suspect, fundamental—connotation is the role of religion in making sense of the whole of human existence in the world, in 'tying it all together' and overcoming the temptation to live compartmentalized lives. Compare Paul J. Griffiths: 'If you offer an account of things that seems to you comprehensive (to embrace all other accounts that you give), of central importance to your life, and not capable of being surpassed or subsumed by other accounts, then you offer a religious account of things' ('Religious Identity: Introduction', in Charles Taliaferro and Paul J. Griffiths (eds), *Philosophy of Religion: An Anthology* (Malden, MA: Blackwell, 2003), 4).

Evidentialists are, of course, committed to integrationist doxastic values, and their answer to the question of how tight that integration should be is given by the principle of epistemic evidentialism. That principle affirms that our practical commitment to the truth of a proposition carries epistemic entitlement only if it is made solely in accordance with our correct judgements of evidential support—and if there are occasional exceptions to this principle they certainly do not include supra-, let alone counter-evidential commitment to the framing principles of a whole doxastic framework (as is involved in commitment to, for example, theistic faith-beliefs). The only way to resist this answer—as, of course, it must be resisted if thesis (J) is to be defended—is to provide positive support for the claim that people may commit themselves *with epistemic entitlement* beyond the support of their evidence to the truth of such framing principles.

This clears up, then, an issue about the defence of thesis (J) so far left unsettled. (J) affirms the moral permissibility of commitment beyond the evidence to (foundational) faith-beliefs, and it must therefore deny moral evidentialism (the principle that it is morally permissible to commit oneself only in accordance with one's correct judgement of evidential support). But moral evidentialism, it will be recalled, may be factored into (1) the moral-epistemic link principle (for commitment to be morally justifiable it must carry epistemic entitlement) and (2) the principle of epistemic evidentialism (for commitment to carry epistemic entitlement the proposition committed to must be held with evidential justification). And the issue so far left unsettled is the question whether the denial of moral evidentialism to which the proponent of (J) is committed requires denying (1), the moral-epistemic link principle, or (2), epistemic evidentialism (or, possibly, both). It now becomes clear, however, that supra-evidential fideist proponents of (J), who adopt realist integrationist doxastic values in excluding counter-evidential fideism, need to retain (1) and deny (2). They need to insist, that is, that supra-evidential fideist commitments *may* be made with epistemic entitlement—that is, that such commitments may be made consistently with the right exercise of the epistemic capacities of those who make them. For, proponents of (J) need to reply to the objection that any preparedness to commit without the benefit of a judgement of adequate evidential support involves abandoning the integrationist doxastic values motivated by realism: they need to make a direct reply to the allegation that such ventures involve a wholesale suspension of epistemic concern that leaves supra-evidential and counter-evidential fideism in the same (leaky) boat.

Proponents of thesis (J), then, are not arguing for the ethical suspension of the epistemic with respect to commitment to foundational faith-beliefs. To the contrary, they hold that such faith-commitments must remain within the ambit of broad realist epistemic concern—of concern that one's beliefs about how things are should as far as possible grasp truth and eschew falsehood. While it may occasionally be morally justifiable to make practical commitments that do not carry epistemic entitlement, when commitment to framing principles is at issue—and, therefore, to whole doxastic frameworks—epistemic entitlement is essential if such commitments are to be morally justified. 'Reason', in its epistemic, evidence-assessing, function, may indeed need 'to make room for faith', but not by allowing itself to be simply displaced by it.[7] Under realist integrationist doxastic values, epistemic entitlement in making such faith-commitments requires that their truth not be evidentially excluded under the applicable evidential practice. But epistemic entitlement *may* attach to supra-evidential ventures in favour of framing principles foundational to a whole framework of faith-beliefs. Taking such principles to be true by faith need not require us to abandon or override the proper exercise of our epistemic capacities, nor need it fail to respect integrationist doxastic values.

There *is* a perspective, then, from which it is *not* arbitrary to countenance supra-evidential but reject counter-evidential doxastic venture in favour of faith-beliefs—namely, the perspective of the realist committed to integrationist doxastic values. That perspective affirms thesis (J). That perspective agrees with the evidentialists that, to be morally permissible, practical commitments to faith-beliefs must carry epistemic entitlement in the sense that they are made through the right exercise of our epistemic capacities. Where it differs from evidentialism is in holding that ventures beyond the support of one's evidence can sometimes meet that requirement: that, provided the option concerned is 'genuine', one may *with epistemic entitlement* venture

---

[7] In Christian evangelical circles, counter-rationalist fideism enjoys a certain popularity, due, I suspect, to its being perceived as the only antidote to an idolatrous over-reliance on human reason in matters of religious belief. But it is not the only antidote, as thesis (J) makes clear. According to (J), supra-evidential faith-commitments are not solely determined 'by reason', since their truth is not established by a rational assessment of the evidence, yet they may nevertheless be made without overriding the proper exercise of epistemic rationality.

to take foundational faith-beliefs to be true when their truth is essentially unable to be decided on the evidence.

Whether this supra-evidentialist position ought to be accepted or rejected in favour of moral evidentialism with respect to faith-beliefs is, of course, a further question—the question that I shall take up in the next chapter. But first I must tackle the 'big problem' faced by proponents of thesis (J) identified earlier: is it not clear that intuitively unacceptable faith-commitments will be able to meet (J)'s conditions?

## Moral integration of faith-commitments

Earlier in this chapter I identified a 'big problem' for proponents of thesis (J): it seems inevitable that, even with the 'genuine option' constraint in place, (J) will condone thoroughly objectionable doxastic ventures. (J) seems, that is, to be *morally* too liberal. For example, in a particular historical context, it may be a living, momentous, and forced option for a person whether or not to make a faith-commitment to the existence of the Nazi gods; furthermore, the question whether the Nazi gods exist may be evidentially undecidable because it functions as a highest-order framing principle for the religious doxastic framework that, according to some commentators, constituted the heart of Nazism.[8] As it currently stands, (J) would admit a passionally motivated commitment to the principles of Nazi religion under such circumstances as morally permissible—yet surely it could not be so. (J) thus stands refuted by counter-example.

The obvious response for proponents of (J) is to consider some further qualification to the conditions it places on morally permissible venture in favour of faith-beliefs. One option may be to constrain acceptable passional, non-evidential, motivations for such ventures—and that approach might also commend itself as a way of dealing with another objection that is in the offing, namely that to permit doxastic venture is to permit commitments with less than morally admirable motivations, such as fear, wishful thinking, or conformity to peer pressure.[9] There do seem to be different possible

[8] For a thorough defence of the status of Nazism as a religion, see Michael Burleigh, *The Third Reich: A New History* (New York: Hill and Wang, 2000).

[9] For an example of a philosopher who rejects James's 'justification of faith' on the grounds that it is ultimately no better than 'an impressive recommendation of "wishful thinking"', see John Hick, *Faith and Knowledge*, ch. 2, 32–44.

types of non-evidential motivation for doxastic venture, open to varying moral evaluations. For example, making a faith-commitment to a religious doxastic framework merely on the basis of a private, self-concerned wish for a world as therein depicted *does* seem morally flawed. Commitment from such a motive seems unavoidably self-indulgent—though perhaps that verdict is fuelled by our response to cases where people allow themselves to take what they wish to be true when the issue *is* decidable on their evidence, and (J) applies, of course, only where the issue is essentially evidentially undecidable. In any case, however, there are types of non-evidential motivation that *do* seem morally acceptable. For example, the conviction that the highest forms of good are achievable only if the ventured faith-belief is true seems to be a morally weightier motivation for a faith-venture than any mere wish. Religious faith-commitments are often motivated by the inspiration resulting from one's experience of the relevant tradition, either through being formed in it from earliest youth or through being moved by encounter with it as an adult. *Prima facie*, there seems nothing morally base about being motivated in such ways to take religious faith-beliefs to be true. Moral distinctions may be drawn, then, amongst the possible types of motivation for supra-evidential ventures with respect to faith-propositions, and so (J) may be augmented by adding a third condition to the effect that such a venture will be morally permissible only if it is motivated by a morally acceptable type of motivation.

This addition to (J) is not enough to resolve our present difficulty, however. Perhaps many who committed themselves beyond their evidence to Nazi religion did so from morally questionable motivations—they may have been motivated, for example, by a desire to conform and by fear of the consequences of not doing so. But it is certainly conceivable that some made a Nazi faith-commitment through sincere conviction of the nobility of Nazi ideals—and venturing through motivation of that *type* is not *as such* morally flawed. It seems, that is to say, that it is possible to commit oneself to a morally objectionable faith-belief with a non-evidential motivation of a morally respectable kind. If this is correct, then a still further condition seems necessary if (J) is to be defended against the objection that it is too liberal.

It is easy enough to see what that further condition may be, given the context of commitment to integrationist values. For, integrationist values imply that morally permissible faith-commitments need to be integrated, not just with other evidentially justified factual beliefs, but also with justified *evaluative* beliefs or attitudes. This condition may be relied on to exclude Nazi religious faith-commitment, even if the motive for such commitment is of a morally acceptable kind. For, this condition further requires *that it be good* that Nazi gods should exist... and that is widely agreed not to be the case.

Two additional clauses seem to need to be added to (J), then, resulting in the following augmented thesis (J+):

(J+)   Where p is a faith-proposition of the kind exemplified by the propositions taken to be true in the context of theistic faith, it is morally permissible for people to take p to be true with full weight in their practical reasoning while correctly judging that it is not the case that p's truth is adequately supported by their total available evidence, if and only if:

  (i)  the question whether p presents itself to them as a genuine option; and

  (ii)  the question whether p is essentially evidentially undecidable; and

  (iii)  *their non-evidential motivation for taking p to be true is of a morally acceptable type;* and

  (iv)  *p's being true conforms with correct morality.*

To apply condition (iii) with the fullest confidence we would need a general theory of virtuous types of non-evidential motivation for faith-commitments. I shall simply assume that such a theory must be feasible, without making any attempt to develop it here.[10] For, we do clearly recognize that some non-evidential motivations are morally honourable, and others dishonourable, and it is thus clear that condition (iii) has real bite.

Condition (iv) requires more extended comment. A minor point first: a thoroughgoing integrationism might perhaps propose a broader version of condition (iv)—as requiring conformity with correct values *generally*, not just moral values. Though the idea that faith-commitments need to be integrated with (e.g.) properly held aesthetic values is of interest, I shall

[10] Robert J. O'Connell directs us back to James for what is needed here: see his discussion of 'Strata of the Passional' in *William James on the Courage to Believe*, ch. 7. Morally respectable passional motivations for faith-ventures will be identifiable with those that issue from a well-developed virtuous character, and will be distinguishable from those that are impulsive or merely temperamental.

here pursue the requirement of integration with value commitments with respect to moral values only.

I have stated condition (iv) as requiring the content of permissible supra-evidential ventures to conform to correct morality. Where such ventures involve commitment to factual claims (as they do in the case of religious theistic claims, under their commonsensical realist construal), conformity to correct morality is to be understood as requiring that it be morally good for those claims to be true. But what is meant by 'correct morality' here? Naïve forms of meta-ethical subjectivism aside, there is a gap between what a person *takes* correct morality to be and what correct morality *actually is*.[11] Condition (iv) as stated requires faith-commitments to conform to what correct morality *actually is*.

Given the gap between correct morality and what is taken to be so, the addition of condition (iv) does nothing to exclude the nightmare possibility that an individual reflective Nazi might find claims about the gods of Nazi religion to conform fully with *what he takes to be* correct morality. That will not render his faith-venture morally permissible, however. The morally consistent Nazi will simply be mistaken about what moral position is, in fact, correct. Actual claims about what moral positions are correct—as, indeed, actual claims about what factual beliefs are evidentially justified on all the available evidence—are fallible and can be made only from some situated perspective. The conditions stated in (J+) are objective conditions, and situated individuals can do no more than judge as best they can whether those conditions are satisfied for the particular faith-venture with which they are concerned. The possibility that such a best judgement may be mistaken can never altogether be excluded. People may thus reasonably suppose themselves morally entitled to make a given faith-venture when, in fact, they are not (and this may happen even when it is not their fault that their judgement is mistaken). Nevertheless, we may, I think, be reasonably confident of our ability to judge correctly whether the conditions imposed by (J+) do or do not obtain—and, in particular, whether condition (iv), the 'conformity with correct morality' condition, does or does not obtain.[12]

---

[11] The distinction between what one takes correct morality to be and what it actually is may be preserved under more sophisticated forms of meta-ethical non-realism and quasi-realism: it is not obviously the exclusive possession of moral realists.

[12] The nature of moral truth and the possibility of moral knowledge are, of course, contentious philosophical issues. The position I take here, however, is meant to assume no more than meta-ethical

# Implications for reflective faith-believers

What are the implications of thesis (J+) for reflective believers, concerned about the moral permissibility of their faith-ventures? Consider reflective theists, in particular. To satisfy themselves as best they can that their commitments are morally acceptable, they will need first to judge that the faith-propositions concerned present a genuine option—and, as we have seen, if those propositions are highest-order framing principles of a whole framework of faith-beliefs the option presented will certainly be forced, and may also in context count as living and momentous. Furthermore, the truth of such propositions will be persistently and essentially evidentially undecidable—which meets the second condition with which reflective theists need to be concerned. To be sure that a given faith-proposition meets this condition, however, reflective believers will need to be quite satisfied that its truth is not excluded by the truth of their other evidentially justified beliefs. Commitment to the truth of their foundational faith-propositions requires a venture beyond their evidence, but it must not require venturing contrary to it. Finally, reflective theists will need to satisfy themselves that the motivation for their venture is morally acceptable and that its content fits with their overall value-commitments, and, in particular, with what they take to be correct morality.

cognitivism (i.e. that moral claims are truth-apt) and the falsity of global moral scepticism. I shall, however, remark on one point of moral epistemology. Some philosophers might construe condition (iv) as the requirement that holding p to be true should conform to our *moral evidence*—and then go onto suggest that, once we recognize that evidence generally includes moral evidence, condition (iv) is redundant, since a faith-venture whose content conflicts with moral evidence will be ruled out by clause (ii), the 'evidential undecidability' condition. While the notion of moral evidence may seem sensible to some—rationalist moral foundationalists, for example—others will doubt whether any suitably intersubjective notion of moral evidence can be brought into play. Some basic moral judgements do indeed enjoy wide acceptance—but it is not clear that this involves shared awareness of the basic evidence of their truth, nor that such shared moral intuitions may properly be treated as evidence, assessable under a generally established moral evidential practice. In any case, the suggestion that condition (iv) may be redundant can be repudiated—even for those who *do* find it justifiable to think in terms of moral evidence. For, to put the point in terms of my Nazism example, condition (ii) requires the evidential undecidability of the claim *that Nazi gods exist*; whereas the force of condition (iv)—for those who wish to think in terms of moral evidence—will be to require that our moral evidence is consistent with the claim that *it is good that* Nazi gods should exist. If our moral evidence does indeed exclude the latter claim, it still leaves the truth of the former open. Given that condition (ii) is here met, the force of the moral evidence is to exclude *morally permissible faith-venture* in favour of the existence of Nazi gods: it is powerless to exclude the uncomfortable possibility that such gods might indeed exist.

As already noted, any situated reflective theist's confidence that his or her faith-commitment is morally permissible will rest on *fallible* judgements as to whether the conditions required for such permissibility are satisfied—namely, as I have now argued, the conditions of (J+). Faith-commitments should therefore not be made in a close-minded or dogmatic spirit, but in a manner open to the possibility of having to revise the judgements upon which one's assessment of them as morally acceptable depends. Yet—again, as already noted—it does not follow that such commitments can only be half-hearted or tentative. They involve taking foundational faith-propositions true with full weight in one's practical reasoning. But that wholehearted commitment should nevertheless be non-dogmatic, open in principle to revision. (It is a fallacy to infer that I must be committing myself less than wholeheartedly if I consciously recognize in principle that my commitment could be misplaced and may be withdrawn or revised. *Dwelling on* the likelihood of that eventuality may undermine full commitment, but I can consciously register the real possibility of revising my commitment without any such 'dwelling'.)

To regard their ventures as morally acceptable, then, faith-believers must (fallibly) judge them to satisfy the conditions of thesis (J+). That has the crucial implication that one could not judge one's faith-ventures to be morally acceptable unless one was able to integrate them into an overall coherent view of how things are and ought to be. According to (J+), people must conclude that they are doing wrong if they venture to take to be true faith-beliefs that do not, according to their own judgement, at least cohere with their overall evidence; furthermore, (J+) implies that they should also conclude that they are doing wrong if they commit to the truth of faith-beliefs that do not fit their own best theory of correct morality.

Thus, for example, even if (as the thesis of evidential ambiguity implies) the existence of the God of classical theism is consistent with all we know about what the world is like, it might still be wrong to take it to be true that such a God exists if, in fact, correct morality entails that an omnipotent Creator could not have a morally adequate reason for causing certain kinds of actual evils. For then, commitment beyond the evidence to the existence of an omnipotent and morally perfect Creator could not be integrated with commitment to correct morality. So, to make a faith-venture in favour of God's existence that they can regard as permissible, reflective theists must be able to endorse a moral theory under which all historical evils could be such that God has a morally adequate reason for permitting and/or causing them. Now, of course, many reflective theists think they *can* endorse such a moral position. My point is only that, if (J+)'s restrictions on permissible doxastic venture are correct, reflective theists who come to the conclusion that they *cannot* endorse such a position will no longer be able to regard themselves as morally justified in believing by faith in the classical theist's God. And they may then be prompted to consider the viability of theistic belief *according to some alternative theory of the nature of God*.[13] The force of the Argument from Evil, then, might best be understood as challenging the confidence of reflective theists in the possibility of integrating their classical theistic commitment with their overall value commitments.

Let me briefly elaborate further on this suggested refocusing of the Argument from Evil. In arguing for the plausibility of the evidential ambiguity of core classical theistic belief, I earlier claimed that one may consistently maintain, for any evils whatsoever, that there exists a morally adequate reason—generally unknown—why God permits them. I am not withdrawing that claim now. My present point depends on noticing that there is a distinction between (a) *allowing that it is not epistemically irrational* to hold that there is a morally adequate reason why God permits certain evils, and (b) *being able to endorse a moral position* according to which this is so. Anyone who accepts the ambiguity thesis with respect to the hypothesis of the existence of the classical theist's God will do the former; but they need not be able to manage the latter. For, one might well take the stance that, though there could indeed be a consistent moral theory—of a utilitarian kind, perhaps—that justified an omnipotent God in standing by while, to use Rowe's example mentioned earlier (Chapter 3), a fawn badly burnt in a forest fire dies a slow agonizing death, and although one is in no position to show that such a moral theory is not actually correct, nevertheless one could not oneself make a venture of commitment in favour of the basic principles of any such morality.

---

[13] See my 'Can There Be Alternative Concepts of God?' *Noûs*, 32 (1998), 174–88. It is of interest that the formulation James himself gives of the content of religious faith in 'The Will to Believe' is not explicitly theistic at all—even in a revisionary way. He says that 'religion says essentially two things. First, she says that the best things are the more eternal things, the overlapping things, the things in the universe that throw the last stone, so to speak, and say the final word. ... [Her] second affirmation is that we are better off even now if we believe her first affirmation to be true' (*The Will to Believe*, 25–6).

Finally—by way of an aside—let me remark on how condition (iv) may be understood when (J+) is applied to *moral* faith-ventures. My focus has been (and remains) on *religious* faith-ventures—but I have acknowledged that the question does, of course, arise as to what other varieties of faith-venture there may be. Basic moral commitments—and, indeed, evaluative commitments generally—seem a likely further case, at least on certain assumptions. We do, it seems, have some real choices about what basic values we adopt—and those options typically meet the criteria for 'genuineness'. Under any cognitivist meta-ethic, such choices are about what we take to be true in our practical reasoning. And, *pace* Kantian rationalism (and any attempted construals of foundational moral intuitions as properly basic within our evidential practice), basic value commitments seem in principle not to be rationally decidable on the evidence. There are, then, plausible (though not uncontentious) views according to which basic moral value commitments are commitments to the framing principles of a doxastic framework of moral beliefs, and must involve doxastic (or, maybe, sub-doxastic) venture. On those views, then, (J+) applies to our foundational moral beliefs—and its condition (iv) in such cases will then reduce to the requirement that those beliefs be mutually coherent.

## Coda: A reflection on Abraham as forebear in faith

I have argued, then, that to do the best they can to assure themselves of the moral probity of their faith-ventures, reflective theists will need to satisfy themselves that those ventures are morally well motivated and fit with their moral beliefs generally. This does not entail, however, that people somehow fix their moral beliefs first and then constrain their faith-ventures accordingly. The requirement that moral beliefs and faith-beliefs be properly integrated may be achieved by traffic in either direction: prospective faith-ventures may sometimes prompt revisions in moral and evaluative commitments, as well as, at other times, being curbed by such commitments. Ventures in commitment to foundational theistic beliefs thus need to develop in tandem with ventures in fundamental evaluative beliefs.

To illustrate this, I will continue the venerable tradition of reflecting on Abraham as forebear in faith. (It will be apparent, however, that what follows is not intended as commentary on Kierkegaard's famous reflections on Abraham.)[14]

Abraham's character may be seen as that of the spiritual genius determined to worship only what is truly worthy of it. Driven by that concern, Abraham rejects the religion in which he was brought up and 'invents' monotheism. An unconditioned Creator of all that is could (he believes) be a worthy object of worship in a way in which nothing humanly created, nor any finite thing in the natural world, could be. By faith he dares to commit himself to taking it to be true that there is such a Creator; that he, Abraham, stands in personal relationship with Him; and that the supreme good involves submitting himself wholly to the Creator's will.

In that faith, Abraham receives God's promise that he will be the father of many nations, and (contrary to natural expectation) his wife Sarah conceives and bears his son Isaac. Then he hears what he takes to be the voice of God commanding him to sacrifice Isaac. Now, at this point Abraham has to decide whether he will take the step of faith of acting on the belief that the voice he hears really is God's voice. Would such a step be morally permissible? Well, according to thesis (J+), Abraham must bring his moral judgements to bear—and what would those judgements be? For us, of course, the judgement that it would be utterly wrong to kill a child as a sacrifice to God (no matter what the circumstances) is exceedingly well entrenched. Any contemporary father who found himself seriously inclined to believe that God was calling on him to sacrifice his son ought to seek spiritual and psychiatric help. But with the character of Abraham we are immersed in ethico-theological cognitive archaeology. We are presented with one who has the faith that he should submit wholly to the will of the One Creator God, and ensure that his ultimate commitment rests there and only there. And we are presented with him as he has the understandable thought that perhaps Isaac—the child of the promise—has become more important to him than God Himself. And this concern manifests itself in the thought that he must show that he does indeed put God first, and that the only unambiguous way to do this is to sacrifice Isaac.

*In that context*, Abraham's preparedness to take it to be true that God was calling him to sacrifice Isaac may have been neither insanity nor a 'religious

---

[14] Søren Kierkegaard, *Fear and Trembling*, trans. Alastair Hannay (Harmondsworth, Middlesex: Penguin Books, 1985); first published 1843.

suspension of the ethical'. Abraham could reasonably suppose that his motivation for acting on the belief that God was calling him to sacrifice Isaac was morally sound and not excluded by *what he took to be* correct morality, *given* the stage of his character's development of faith-commitments and moral commitments. (What requires venture essentially beyond his evidence is Abraham's taking it to be true that the living God has his will revealed in an inner voice that commands the sacrifice of Isaac; for that venture to be morally permissible it must, according to (J+), have sound moral motivation and conform to correct morality. *So far as Abraham is best able to judge*, situated as he is at any early stage of our ethico-theological historical development, those conditions might reasonably be thought to be met, however clear it is that no one could now, in such circumstances, reasonably suppose so.)

But, as we know, though Abraham sets out on the journey to Mt Moriah with the definite intention of sacrificing Isaac, Isaac is not sacrificed, and lives to fulfil the promise. Something happens to reverse Abraham's initial conscientious belief that God was calling him to sacrifice Isaac; and the process which leads to this outcome provides, I think, an exemplary case of the way in which morally proper theistic faith-ventures develop in tandem with moral commitments constrained by the requirement that, at any given stage, they together form a properly integrated set of overall commitments.

Just as it was up to Abraham to decide whether to take it that the voice that he heard calling him to sacrifice Isaac was the voice of God, so too it was up to Abraham to decide whether the angel that called on him to stay his hand at the last moment was or was not an envoy of God's will. And Abraham could not have had evidence that would have enabled him to make this decision purely rationally. (Of course, the Biblical story is itself told straight: as if there were nothing in the least problematic about the idea that Abraham could hear God or God's angel calling from heaven. In fact, interpreting any experience as conveying divine messages requires going beyond what could non-question-beggingly be settled on the basis of evidence.) At that crucial moment when he is about to plunge the knife, Abraham *could* have thought to himself: 'Be resolute! I was bound to be tempted not to go through with this. But let me overcome that temptation, and resist the thought that if anything has to be sacrificed it could only be that ram caught over there in a thicket. Let me carry out my resolve to demonstrate once and for all that nothing matters more to me than God Himself.' But, in fact, Abraham takes the giant step of letting his original judgement that he could submit to God only if he sacrificed what was humanly most dear to him be overridden by a new perception that God does not require such demonstrations of submission. And that new perception, committed to through doxastic venture, is the foundation of the development of a theological ethic—an ethic of relationship with God in which sacrificing innocent human victims is altogether ruled out. It was at that moment of new perception, I suggest, that Abraham truly became forebear in faith to the theistic religious traditions.

I contend, then, that we can see here a paradigm case of the working out of the requirement that morally permissible faith-ventures should conform to correct morality. Steps of faith beyond one's evidence need to be constrained by moral judgements; but faith-ventures and ethical commitments undergo development in dynamic tension with each other, not only in the life of individuals, but also—and more significantly—in the life of faith-communities. The development of Abraham's faith and moral understanding is, of course, a paradigm from an early stage in the development of the theistic religious traditions. But the same principles may still apply to reflective theists within these traditions today—on a doxastic venture model of faith-commitments, anyway. Given the conditions for permissible supra-evidential venture stated in thesis (J+), reflective theists must ensure the conformity of their faith-ventures with basic moral values that they can endorse as correct—and they must thus respond to any conflict between their faith-beliefs and their moral beliefs by revising either the one or the other.

I have argued, then, that my James-inspired thesis (J) needs further conditions beyond those directly based on 'The Will to Believe' if it is to be considered as a plausible statement of the necessary and sufficient conditions on permissible faith-ventures of the kind involved in theistic faith. Those conditions require that permissible ventures should have moral clearance, and they imply that one may not regard oneself as morally justified in a faith-venture unless the proposition taken to be true and one's non-evidential motivation for taking it to be true fits with what one takes to be correct morality.

This brings my exposition and development of a potentially viable thesis on morally permissible doxastic (and sub-doxastic) venture in favour of faith-beliefs to a close. I turn now to consider, in the remaining two chapters, what arguments may be urged in favour of it.

# 8

# Arguments for supra-evidential fideism

Over the preceding three chapters, I have developed a James-inspired thesis that states sufficient and necessary conditions for morally permissible faith-ventures—that is, doxastic (or sub-doxastic) ventures with respect to faith-propositions of the type involved in theistic religion. This thesis expresses a modest *supra-evidential fideism* that respects a general presumption in favour of evidentialism but claims that it is inapplicable in the case of propositions that present options that are both existentially significant and unavoidable ('genuine'), and whose truth is *essentially* evidentially undecidable. I have argued that the *highest-order framing principles* of a doxastic framework may present such options. (If foundational theistic beliefs have that status, that explains their persistent evidential ambiguity.) A general functional definition of a faith-proposition has thus emerged: foundational faith-propositions are optional highest-order framing principles, practical commitment to which makes a morally significant difference to one's actions and way of life; and derivative faith-propositions are those that presuppose the truth of relevant foundational ones.

In the previous chapter, I made proposals designed to immunize this modest fideism from the objection that it is too liberal. I suggested that a defensible supra-evidential fideism should incorporate a commitment to integrationist doxastic values, thereby making it non-arbitrary to permit only supra- and not counter-evidential faith-ventures. I drew the conclusion that supra-evidential fideism needs therefore to accept that morally permissible faith-ventures must also carry epistemic entitlement (i.e. it needs to accept the moral-epistemic link principle). Its distinctive claim is thus that passionally, non-evidentially, motivated faith-commitments may, under certain conditions, be made *with epistemic entitlement*—that is, through the right use of epistemic rationality. (Supra-evidential fideism thus rejects epistemic evidentialism: it rejects the view that one can be epistemically entitled to take a faith-proposition to be true only if one is evidentially justified in holding it true.) I argued, finally, that a defensible supra-evidential fideism needs to be morally coherentist: faith-ventures must conform to correct morality, with the result that reflective faith-believers may not reasonably take their commitments to be morally permissible unless they judge both their motivational character and their content to fit their own best theory of correct morality.

All these features of a defensible moral coherentist supra-evidential fideism I have sought to express in my James-inspired thesis, which, in its final form, I refer to as 'thesis (J+)'. According to (J+), passionally motivated doxastic or sub-doxastic ventures in favour of the truth of persistently and essentially evidentially undecidable faith-propositions (faith-ventures, for short) are morally permissible and within the proper exercise of one's epistemic rationality when, and only when, the context is one of 'genuine' option, the non-evidential motivation is of a virtuous kind, and the faith-proposition's content conforms with correct morality.

This modest variety of fideism will be opposed by a moral evidentialism that rejects religious and similar faith-ventures, even though, as any sensible view must, it acknowledges exceptional cases where commitment beyond, or even against, the evidence is clearly morally justified. This kind of evidentialism is thus not absolutist—but it does take a hard line with respect to the permissibility of faith-ventures of the sort that, granted the thesis of evidential ambiguity, must be involved in theistic religious faith. That hard line typically results from a conviction that religious faith-ventures lead to more harm than good—that 'gods are mankind's most dangerous inventions'[1]—and that this net harm could be avoided if only people curbed their religious doxastic inclinations in line with the moral evidentialist principle.

If a James-inspired fideism of the kind expressed in thesis (J+) is to be vindicated, then, the rival hard-line evidentialist positions needs to be

---

[1] Slogan seen on a T-shirt. The sentiment is age-old, however: *tantum religio potuit suadere malorum*, Lucretius, *De Rerum Natura*, I, 101.

taken very seriously.[2] Supra-evidential fideists need to engage in debate with hard-line evidentialists. Each side of that debate accepts *broad* evidentialist commitments. What is at issue, in effect, is whether broad evidentialist commitments are wide enough to permit *certain sorts of* faith-venture, namely faith-ventures of the kind involved in religious commitment.

In this chapter, I shall consider various apparently promising arguments for preferring my modest version of supra-evidential fideism to its hard-line evidentialist rival. I shall conclude that none of them quite succeeds in making a decisive case. The debate thus threatens to end in impasse. In the next and final chapter I will consider what the implications are if the debate *does* end in impasse. Ought supra-evidential fideists to be satisfied, perhaps, with forcing the debate to a stalemate? And, if not, is there a way of breaking the impasse in favour of a morally and epistemically responsible fideism that will affirm the integrity of (some) religious faith-ventures?

## The importance of defending the epistemic permissibility of faith-ventures

I now take up, then, the question of how to argue for supra-evidential fideism as expressed in thesis (J+). What reasons may be given for concluding that faith-ventures are morally permissible if and only if they settle 'genuine' options, and their content and motivational character conforms to correct morality?

As already argued, to keep the door closed against their counter-evidential fideist cousins, supra-evidential fideists need to hold that morally permissible faith-ventures must also be *epistemically permissible*, in the sense that they carry epistemic entitlement. (For faith-ventures to carry epistemic

---

[2] Philosophers inclined towards fideism have not always given sufficient weight to the rival evidentialist position. For example, despite his rejection of what he takes to be James's actual position in 'The Will to Believe' (already referred to above, Chapter 7, *n.* 9), John Hick claims that, given the systematic religious ambiguity of the world, we may retain James's 'central insight' that 'it is wholly reasonable for the religious person to trust his or her own experience and the larger stream of religious experience of which it is a part' (*An Interpretation of Religion*, 227, 228). But Hick here fails to acknowledge the need to respond to the evidentialist contention that no such commitment should be made without adequate evidential support.

entitlement means only that they are made in accordance with the proper exercise of epistemic rational capacities. Recall, from Chapter 3, the importance of distinguishing epistemic entitlement as an agency-focused notion applicable to takings-to-be-true in practical reasoning from the propositional-attitude-focused notion of the positive epistemic status of a belief. This distinction opens up the precise conceptual space that supra-evidential fideism requires—the possibility that taking a proposition to be true in reasoning may carry epistemic entitlement even though the person concerned is in no position to certify the epistemic worth of his or her holding that proposition to be true.)

Supra-evidential fideists do not suppose, then, that the moral justifiability of those faith-ventures that are morally permissible derives from *any moral overriding* of the proper exercise of epistemic rationality. On this modest version of fideism, morally proper faith-ventures require no ethical suspension of the epistemic. Rather, those who make faith-ventures under the conditions stated in (J+) are held to be doing so with epistemic as well as with moral entitlement. And it is here—in claiming that faith-ventures can carry epistemic entitlement—that supra-evidential fideists disagree at root with hard-line moral evidentialists. Supra-evidential fideists and hard-line evidentialists agree that faith-ventures must carry epistemic entitlement in order to be morally permissible (they accept the moral-epistemic link principle). What they disagree about is whether faith-ventures can ever carry epistemic entitlement (they disagree over the thesis of epistemic evidentialism).

What is needed, then, for a vindication of supra-evidential fideism as expressed in thesis (J+), is a defence of the moral permissibility of faith-ventures meeting (J+)'s conditions *that also secures the epistemic permissibility of those ventures*, in the sense of their being made with epistemic entitlement, in accordance with the right use of our epistemic rational capacities. So, when I refer in what follows simply to the 'permissibility' of faith-ventures, it should be understood that the notion of epistemic as well as moral permissibility is generally in play.

Note also that, in what follows, I shall sometimes refer to the moral coherentist supra-evidential fideism expressed in (J+) just as 'fideism', and to the opposing view just as 'evidentialism'—but it must, of course, be understood that it is 'hard-line' moral evidentialism as applied to foundational faith-propositions that I have in mind.

## Strategies for supporting fideism

Supra-evidential fideists agree that, *in general*, one ought to commit oneself in one's practical reasoning to truths only when they enjoy sufficient evidential support as certified under the applicable evidential practice. Their claim that an exception should be made for certain foundational faith-propositions might at first seem to follow just from the *special status* of the options such propositions present—options that are forced and momentous and essentially unable to be settled purely by intellectual assessment of evidence. We may envisage the supra-evidential fideist arguing as follows:

If what has to be decided is whether or not to take it to be true (e.g.) that God is revealed in Jesus Christ, and if it really matters what decision is made (affecting the person's life significantly from the time of decision onwards), and if this decision could be not be resolved just by following a judgement as to evidential support, then how could it be wrong to let oneself decide through some morally respectable non-evidence-based motivation (one's 'heart is strangely warmed,' say, while hearing the Gospel preached)? The decision will inevitably be made one way or the other, and if the decision matters significantly, and cannot be made on the evidence alone, how could it be wrong to let it be settled on a decent passional basis? Where respecting rational assessment of the evidence alone in guiding one's practical commitment is in principle impossible, one may surely be quite within one's rights, both epistemically and morally, to rely on other sources of guidance?[3]

These rhetorical questions do not amount to a decisive argument, however. A forced decision whether or not to take proposition p to be true will, indeed, get made one way or the other (here, not to decide is to decide not to). And it is also true that if p's truth is essentially evidentially undecidable, a policy of deciding by simply mirroring one's judgement of evidential support cannot determine how that forced decision is to be settled. Yet, even if one has a decent non-evidential motivation for deciding to take p to be true, and the question is indeed 'momentous',

---

[3] Stephen T. Davis argues for the correctness of James's 'right to believe' doctrine along these lines—indeed, he does so more succinctly, and without rhetorical questions: ' ... if we have to decide (forcedness criterion) and if we cannot decide on the basis of the evidence (ambiguity criterion), it follows that we will have to decide on some basis other than evidence' (*Faith, Skepticism, and Evidence*, 151).

it still does not follow that it is permissible to venture to take p to be true. Evidentialism *could* apply here—as, indeed, the hard-line evidentialist maintains it does. The right decision *could* be to resist one's passional motivation to commit to p's truth, and resolve the forced option by *not taking p to be true* (even though one may perhaps continue at least for a while to have the non-evidentially caused *attitude* towards p that it is true). Even though a purely evidential basis for making such a forced decision is necessarily lacking, one may arguably still be required to 'respect rational assessment of the evidence in guiding one's practical commitment' by following the evidentialist principle that one may take p to be true only when its truth is well supported by the evidence. So the supra-evidential fideist's final assertion by rhetorical question in the passage above exhibits the complementary fault to the seductive error noted in Chapter 6, whereby a judgement of open evidence with respect to a proposition p was assumed by itself to entail deciding the forced option whether or not to take p to be true in the negative. The point is that *some normative policy* is needed for dealing with essentially evidentially undecidable forced options, with hard-line evidentialism and supra-evidential fideism offering rival hypotheses for what that policy should be.[4]

Supra-evidential fideists might perhaps maintain that the considerations expressed above, though they do not decisively favour fideism, nevertheless do reverse, for the special case of foundational faith-propositions, the usual presumption in favour of evidentialism. But whether that is so is difficult to determine—and, in any case, even if hard-line evidentialists do bear the onus of proof, perhaps they can meet it. So sensible supra-evidential fideists will prefer, if they can, to offer some substantive argument for favouring their hypothesis for the normative policy that applies to genuine options presented by foundational faith-propositions. I shall now consider three strategies for producing such an argument: an 'assimilation to personal relations cases' strategy, a 'consequentialist' strategy, and a *tu quoque* strategy.

---

[4] Davis's argument—see previous note—thus leaves it open that the way we should decide 'on some basis other than evidence' is *by following the evidentialist principle not to commit ourselves without evidential support*. It is thus not the succinct and obviously successful argument in favour of Jamesian fideism that he thinks it is. However, the fact that evidentialism is a normative policy which, when applied to an evidentially undecidable forced option, cannot fairly be represented as a policy of simply mirroring in one's practical reasoning the attitude that is rational on the evidence, points the way to the *tu quoque* strategy, to be considered shortly.

## An 'assimilation to personal relations cases' strategy: experimental ventures in interpersonal trust

The first fideist strategy I shall consider is to assimilate faith-ventures to cases of clearly permissible doxastic venture. As already remarked, the presumption in favour of evidentialism is defeasible. Clear examples where it is defeated arise in the sphere of interpersonal relations, where the preparedness to believe in advance beyond the evidence can sometimes be an important virtue, both epistemic and moral. Is it justifiable, then, to assimilate doxastic venture in favour of foundational faith-propositions to permissible doxastic ventures that occur in the context of personal relations?

Mundane interpersonal trust usually does not require venturing beyond our evidence—for example, the weight of our evidence *supports* our taking professionals to be reliable in performing their roles and our fellow citizens trustworthy in not gratuitously impeding our legitimate business. But there are situations—for example, in a developing intimate personal relationship—where we *could not* have sufficient evidence *at the outset* that a person who has proved trustworthy in minor matters will turn out to be trustworthy in some major respect. In such a case, though, it is generally morally admirable to take it to be true, necessarily beyond our evidence, that the person will prove trustworthy, and such behaviour tends to have good consequences. (Though it need not be conceded, of course, that what *makes* such behaviour morally right is solely the fact that it has good consequences.) Plainly, any sensible moral evidentialism needs to allow as exceptions doxastic ventures of this particular kind. Furthermore, taking another to be trustworthy beyond one's initial evidence seems compatible also with a sensible epistemic evidentialism, since relevant evidence can emerge only on the condition that such a venture is made. Such ventures are thus consistent with the proper exercise of epistemic rationality, and may carry epistemic as well as moral entitlement.

Commitment to foundational faith-propositions does not seem readily assimilable to this kind of interpersonal doxastic venture, however—for the following reason. When I take another to be trustworthy beyond my initial evidence, confirmatory or disconfirmatory evidence may subsequently emerge—my commitment is, in a sense, experimental.[5] With persistently and essentially evidentially undecidable foundational faith-propositions, however, there is no such possibility. In experimentally venturing to take another to be trustworthy, I open myself to acting on a valuable truth (if the person is indeed trustworthy) without risking an error that could not ever be corrected (if the person is not). Venture with respect to foundational faith-propositions, however, is no mere initial phase which may later be displaced by the emergence of confirmatory evidence for which it was a necessary precondition, and, if the commitment made is in fact in error, no evidence could ever emerge—within human history, anyway—to allow it to be corrected.

James does himself suggest that religious faith might properly be assimilated to experimental doxastic venture—at least for those for whom 'the more perfect and more eternal aspect of the universe is represented … as having personal form.' 'We feel', James says, 'as if the appeal of religion to us were made to our own active good-will, as if evidence might be forever withheld from us unless we met the hypothesis halfway'.[6] It is true that an initial venture in religious faith-commitment is often followed by experiences that may properly be interpreted *from within* a specifically religious evidential practice as confirming the truth of what has been accepted, but such confirmation, though psychologically reinforcing, does not count as *independent* evidence that could show the foundational framing principles that were the subject of the initial venture to have been evidentially justified. By contrast, in a case where one experimentally takes another to be trustworthy beyond one's evidence, just such independent evidence confirmatory of one's initial venture *can* emerge.

So, even if there may be something important to be learnt from the analogy between faith-ventures and ventures in interpersonal trust, one cannot satisfactorily establish supra-evidential fideism simply by arguing

---

[5] It would not generally be correct to describe people who take others to be trustworthy beyond their evidence as experimenting with or on those people; such a locution suggests that the action is performed *with the intention of* eliciting evidence relevant to the question of the other's trustworthiness, and, typically, no such intention is involved. Nevertheless, the commitment is experimental in the sense that making it is a necessary condition for the emergence of evidence which may (or may not) show it to be true that the person is indeed trustworthy.

[6] *The Will to Believe*, 27 and 28.

that faith-ventures are *just another instance* of a kind of doxastic venture which may unproblematically be made with both epistemic and moral entitlement—namely, taking another person to be trustworthy necessarily beyond one's initial evidence. With a foundational faith-proposition, a ventured commitment that was in fact in error could never be corrected in the light of future evidence. Taking another to be trustworthy beyond one's initial evidence does not have this feature, and this difference, hard-line evidentialists may maintain, is highly salient. An evidentialist normative policy towards optional foundational faith-propositions, they may urge, is to be preferred precisely because it guards against falling into such *irremediable* error. (I shall shortly return to the question whether this way of arguing for evidentialism actually succeeds. My present point is only a dialectical one: the fact that evidentialists may argue this way is enough to show that the attempted analogy cannot *alone* bear the burden of securing the fideist view.)

## The 'assimilation to personal relations cases' strategy: cases where 'faith in a fact can help create a fact'

Perhaps the present strategy can work by appeal to a different kind of case of clearly permissible doxastic venture in the context of interpersonal relations to which James draws attention.

> *Do you like me or not?* ... Whether you do or not depends, in countless instances, on whether I meet you half-way, am willing to assume that you must like me, and show you trust and expectation. The previous faith on my part in your liking's existence is in such cases what makes your liking come.[7]

Here, as James puts it, 'faith in a fact can help create a fact', and it would be 'an insane logic which should say that faith running ahead of scientific evidence is the "lowest kind of immorality" into which a thinking being can fall.'[8]

James's point seems decisive: a sensible evidentialism will have to make an exception for this kind of case. Doxastic venture is obviously morally permissible when taking proposition p to be true is a necessary constitutive

---

[7] *The Will to Believe*, 23–4.    [8] *Ibid.* 25.

condition for p's coming to be true, and p's coming to be true is itself morally desirable. Under such conditions, no misuse or setting aside of epistemic rationality is involved: indeed, as in the previous kind of case, such a venture is a necessary condition for the emergence of evidence relevant to the question of p's truth.[9] Could supra-evidential ventures with respect to foundational faith-propositions be properly assimilated to these cases of permissible doxastic venture where 'faith in a fact can help create a fact'?

One obstacle to this proposal is that the analogy does not fit classical theistic faith-propositions. The existence of the classical theistic God is patently not understood as a fact that comes about in part only through the doxastic ventures of those who take it to be a fact. A second obstacle is that the cases do not seem analogously evidentially undecidable. The existence of a general phenomenon such as the tendency for us to like those who anticipate our liking them is well supported by our total available evidence. To venture beyond my initial evidence that *you, in particular,* will like me seems thus to have a kind of higher-order evidential support not paralleled in the case of commitment to a foundational faith-proposition (and the same seems true of other types of case where 'faith in a fact can help create a fact'). Furthermore, if, with you and me in particular, what happens goes against the trend, evidence can and will emerge that you do not like me, and I will not remain in potentially damaging long-term commitment to a falsehood. We may thus envisage hard-line evidentialists making the same kind of response here as before: doxastic ventures essentially beyond one's *initial* evidence may be permissible when there is no risk of an error that could not later be corrected by further evidence. Foundational faith-propositions, however, are persistently and essentially evidentially undecidable, and so venture in their favour does carry just such a risk. If it is sensible to avoid the risk of such irremediable error, then an evidentialist policy with respect to such propositions is surely to be preferred. As I noted above, that contention needs further examination—but it is surely enough to block the attempt to settle in favour of fideism *just* by assimilating faith-ventures to permissible doxastic ventures in cases where 'faith in a fact can help create a fact'.[10]

That conclusion may need qualification, however. There is the intriguing possibility that a faith-proposition might be such that it is *both* essentially unable to be decided on the basis of evidence *and* such that a necessary condition for it to be true is that people should take it to be true. Certain kinds of *revisionary* theistic faith-beliefs may prove a case in point. Consider, for example, an understanding of God as evolving through the historical process—a God who is the alpha only through being the omega, the ultimate *telos* of the Universe's development. (Such a God would be 'Creator' only in the sense of being the Universe's Aristotelian final cause, while the notion of an efficient cause of the Universe as a whole would be rejected.) The proposition that a God of this revisionary kind exists may well be essentially evidentially undecidable, and the option to take it to be true that such a God exists might present a genuine option provided it could be shown *how it could matter* whether or not one committed oneself in practice to such a God's existence. One obvious way in which it could matter would be if there was reason to think that the existence of such a God amounted to, or was required for, the supreme good, and yet that supreme good could be realized (or even begin to be realized) only through the actions of those who venture beyond their evidence to take it to be true that the Universe has an ultimate divine *telos*. Then we would get just the unusual sort of case envisaged: commitment to the truth of a proposition necessarily and persistently unable to be confirmed by evidence would be required to help make that proposition true.[11] Yet, even if an

---

[10] Stephen T. Davis argues that James has *two* doctrines which he is inclined to confuse—a 'will to believe' doctrine 'that belief or faith is sometimes self-verifying, that is, the doctrine that a willingness to act as if p were true can at times either make p true or be a factor in making p true', and the 'right to believe' doctrine 'that in certain circumstances we are epistemologically justified in believing more than the evidence strictly warrants' (*Faith, Skepticism, and Evidence*, 92). These interpersonal cases support what Davis calls the 'will to believe' doctrine, but they also support a 'right to believe' in such cases, so that the real question is the one I have addressed, namely, whether there is sufficient analogy between the interpersonal and the religious cases to justify accepting the 'right to believe' doctrine for the latter.

[11] James himself has such a possibility in mind when he remarks, 'I confess I do not see why the very existence of the invisible world may not depend on the personal response which any one of us may make to the religious appeal. God himself, in short, may draw vital strength and increase of being from our very fidelity' ('Is Life Worth Living?' in *The Will to Believe*, 61). Compare also James's remark: 'The melioristic universe ... will succeed just in proportion as more people work for its success. If none work it will fail. If each does his best it will not fail' ('Faith and the Right to Believe', in *Some Problems of Philosophy: A Beginning of an Introduction to Philosophy* (New York: Longmans, Green, 1911), 229).

optional faith-commitment fits this condition, it remains true that such a venture will risk an error that could not in principle be corrected through further emerging evidence. Hard-line evidentialists, as already envisaged, may take that as sufficient reason to rule such ventures impermissible—but perhaps the special features of this kind of case defeat that view? Perhaps the value of the supreme good that could possibly come about only through supra-evidential commitment to a given faith-proposition is so great as to outweigh the risk of falling into evidentially irremediable error?

## A consequentialist strategy

This last suggestion suggests a cleaner strategy for the fideist to pursue—namely, the 'consequentialist' claim that, where committing oneself to foundational faith-propositions has the best consequences overall, such a venture must indeed be morally permissible.[12] For simplicity I shall consider only a maximizing Utilitarian version of this strategy. Applying Utilitarianism to our mental actions in taking propositions to be true in our practical reasoning, we get the result that, when forced to choose whether or not to take a faith-proposition to be true, our moral obligation is to choose whichever option yields the greater net increase in utility. Utilitarians therefore treat the evidentialist principle as a rule of thumb only. For Utilitarians, cases like that of the person who trusts beyond the initial evidence of the other's trustworthiness illustrate permissible doxastic venture because in these cases the basic moral imperative to maximize utility overrides the evidentialist rule of thumb. And Utilitarians will argue that, *whenever* the utilitarian calculation supports overriding the evidentialist principle, doxastic venture will be permissible—indeed obligatory. Potentially, then, consequentialism could provide a moral justification for doxastic venture with respect to faith-options that are essentially evidentially undecidable.[13]

---

[12] As already noted (Chapter 6, *n.* 17) Richard Gale has argued (*The Divided Self of William James*, Chapter 4) that James's own approach to the justification of faith is a consequentialist one, although deliberately masked in 'The Will to Believe'. For Gale, however, 'willing to believe' is a matter of intentionally self-inducing a desired belief. The consequentialist strategy I consider here, however, applies to doxastic venture as I have understood it—i.e. taking a proposition to be true beyond one's evidence in one's practical reasoning.

[13] Compare Joshua Golding, who argues that it may be rationally defensible (and therefore also morally permissible?) to live a religious life 'on the grounds that there is a certain great value or potential

Supra-evidential fideists will most probably need to reject this strategy, however, because it faces difficulty in meeting their requirement that doxastic venture with respect to foundational faith-propositions should be shown to be *epistemically* as well as morally permissible. Under this strategy, such ventures count as morally justified when they do because consequentialist considerations *simply override* epistemic ones. *Counter*-evidential commitment to faith-propositions might therefore, on occasion, be open to consequentialist justification. This unwelcome corollary could be avoided only if there were grounds for confidence that counter-evidential faith-commitment never in fact maximizes utility, even though supra-evidential faith-commitments sometimes do, and it seems doubtful that there could be such grounds.

In any case, this consequentialist strategy will, of course, be open to all the usual objections to consequentialist moral theories. A version of one of the standard objections—namely, that consequentialism fails to be action-guiding—is, I think, particularly problematic. Consider a paradigm foundational faith-proposition—say, that God is revealed in Jesus. Consequentialism will enjoin taking this proposition to be true beyond (or, as I have just noted, against) our evidence if and only if so doing yields greater increase in net utility than not so doing. But how may we determine whether this condition obtains? Arguably, this cannot be done without begging the question. Arguably, we will hold that better consequences flow from Christian commitment only to the extent that we are already inclined towards such commitment and are viewing the world from a Christian perspective. Those who think that Christian commitment is wrong because it ventures beyond the evidence will, from their perspective, be able to tell a plausible enough story about how *resisting* Christian commitment has the better consequences—a story Christians may properly dispute, but only from within their Christian perspective. What is true of Christian commitment is, I suspect, true generally: people will, in general, think that the best overall outcome results from doxastic venture in favour of a particular optional foundational faith-proposition only if they are already inclined to view the world from the perspective of commitment to its truth.

value to be gained by being religious' even if 'it is not rationally defensible to have a full-blown or confident belief in God' (*Rationality and Religious Theism*, 3, 4). Golding's position thus seems to be a version of supra-evidential fideism, supported by appeal to the good consequences of (sub-doxastic) practical commitment to religious claims.

Decisive consequentialist justifications for doxastic ventures with respect to *particular* faith-propositions seem unlikely to be available, then. But perhaps there could be a decisive higher-order consequentialist justification for supra-evidential fideism as such? Such a justification would, however, have to defeat the likely evidentialist claim that it is precisely our willingness to commit ourselves in practice beyond our evidential support that leads to all the trouble caused by religion, and that a greater increase in net utility would result if we ceased such venturing. Defeating that claim would inevitably require dealing with many particular historical cases—and then the problem of circularity mentioned in the previous paragraph will block any possibility of progress in what would anyway be an impractically exhaustive survey of the track record of foundational faith-ventures. In any given case, there will be no non-question-begging basis for confidence that beneficial effects of doxastic venture will outweigh detrimental ones.[14]

## A note on Pascal's Wager

It might be supposed, however, that Pascal's Wager provides a means of overcoming this problem, and it is therefore worth pausing briefly to explain why it does not.

Consider a—in one respect, non-standard—version of Pascal's Wager which attaches infinite reward to *practical commitment* to the truth of God's existence, should God actually exist, even if that commitment should be sub-doxastic. (The standard version, of course, attaches the reward to the *state* of actually believing that God exists.) Any non-negligible probability that such practical commitment will yield infinite reward then dominates. This reasoning may seem at first to make no question-begging theistic assumptions—but appearances here are, I think, illusory.

Attaching infinite reward to the option of taking God's existence to be true can mean only that such an action is (at least a necessary)

---

[14] As already noted in Chapter 7, it is possible to contrive cases where some powerful agency attaches such high extrinsic reward to some (as it happens, psychologically feasible) doxastic venture with respect to some foundational faith-proposition that any detrimental effects of the risk of holding a falsehood are massively overridden. Those cases will clearly be exceptional, however; in general it will be quite opaque just how to assess the expected utility of doxastic venture with respect to any given faith-proposition.

condition for achieving one's true fulfilment, a personal supreme good for the sake of which all else should reasonably be sacrificed. In that case, however, the claim that practical commitment to God's existence carries the chance of infinite reward *does* beg the question against a reasonable naturalist, non-theistic, point of view, according to which the only true fulfilment limited human beings can achieve requires that one does *not* take any form of supernaturalist classical theism to be true. Whereas the traditional theist holds that the real possibility of true fulfilment belongs to an eternal order of existence distinct from the natural order, a suitably non-nihilistic naturalist will hold that it is a real possibility achievable only within the natural order. So, the classical theist holds that one can have a chance of true fulfilment only by living in the light of a commitment to one's destiny in a supernatural realm under a supernatural God; but the naturalist holds that that chance is available only to those who live by commitment to the recognition that whatever fulfilment we can attain is achievable only within the natural historical order. Either side can thus offer a 'Pascal's Wager'; and that entails, of course, that each of these Wager-arguments fails as a vindication of the supra-evidential venture it recommends.[15] So even if—to return to a scenario envisaged earlier—it may possibly be that the supreme good can be achieved only if people make supra-evidential ventures with respect to certain particular faith-propositions, the seriousness of the risk of error should those faith-propositions actually be false cannot rightly be regarded as outweighed, since it *could* be the case that, to the contrary, the supreme good can emerge only if people *resist* just those doxastic ventures.

---

[15] Alan Hájek provides an excellent account of Pascal's Wager plus a survey of objections ('Pascal's Wager', in Edward N. Zalta (ed.), *The Stanford Encyclopedia of Philosophy* (Spring 2004 Edition), <http://plato.stanford.edu/archives/spr2004/entries/pascal-wager/>). The objection to the Wager I have sketched here is a version of the 'many gods' objection—expanded to include an optimistic naturalism as a live hypothesis. Hájek's own objection suffices to show that Pascal's main argument (which Hájek calls 'The Argument from Generalized Expectations') is invalid, and could be repaired only if the utility of salvation were somehow unsurpassably enormous yet still finite. Hájek points out that even the strategy of doing the best one can to *avoid* believing in God may reasonably be assigned some small probability of causing belief in God: so that strategy has infinite expected utility, given that the reward of believing in God if God does indeed exist is literally infinite. The account I give here might be seen as suggesting a reply to this objection—namely, that the defender of Pascal characterize the reward in terms of 'ultimate fulfilment' (which could be understood to be a finite utility, but one that could not be bettered). As I have noted, however, that line of reply simply lands us right back with the 'many gods' objection.

## The *tu quoque* strategy

A further fideist strategy is the *tu quoque* strategy. Its key idea is that everyone inescapably makes faith-ventures of the kind the fideist holds to be morally and epistemically permissible—including would-be hard-line evidentialists themselves, whose rejection of religious faith-ventures may thus be met with a terse 'you too'. No one can fail to be committed supra-evidentially to the truth of *some* highest-order framing principles, and such commitment must therefore carry epistemic and moral entitlement.

Now, human beings are indeed universally committed to the truth of certain highest-order framing principles (e.g. the existence of an external world, the existence of other minds, basic logical and arithmetical truths) even though establishing the truth of these commitments on the basis of external evidence without circularity is impossible. But, as already remarked, these deeply habituated commitments do not present anyone, this side of insanity, with any sort of *option*. It is as if we are hardwired to take these foundational propositions to be true—so no real question of whether we are either epistemically or morally entitled to make such commitments can arise. Hard-line evidentialists may thus respond to the fideist's *tu quoque* by making it clear that their policy is intended to apply only when foundational faith-propositions present a real option. Hard-line evidentialism might thus be expressed as the view that whenever we are not naturally compelled to be committed to the truth of propositions that function as highest-order framing principles, but have an uncompelled choice about whether or not to make such a commitment, we should refrain from doing so. So called 'parity' arguments that seek to place commitment to foundational religious faith-propositions on a par with commitment to such principles as the existence of other minds and the external world thus fail, since they miss the important distinction between compelled and uncompelled commitments.[16]

---

[16] Note that if there are theists for whom taking their foundational theistic beliefs to be true is as compelled as (e.g.) taking their perceptual experience to be of a mind-independent world of objects in space and time, then a 'parity' argument *will* succeed. If there are any such theists, they are quite untypical, however. As already noted in Chapter 4 (*n.* 36), even those theists who do have experiences in which they are aware of God's presence would generally not assimilate that experience to ordinary perceptual experience, because (on reflection) they recognize that they are choosing to interpret their experiences in a religious way when that interpretation is not unavoidable for them. (Ordinary

## Is hard-line evidentialism self-undermining?

The *tu quoque* strategy might not, perhaps, be so easily dismissed. James himself maintains that for the evidentialist 'to say … "Do not decide, but leave the question open," is *itself* a passional decision'.[17] If that is so, then evidentialists will have to admit that *their own commitment* rests on *uncompelled* doxastic venture. But, then, surely their commitment undermines itself? Surely, in making their commitment, hard-line evidentialists are doing precisely what hard-line evidentialism holds should not be done? In which case, do we not have here a decisive vindication of fideism *via* a proof that evidentialism is self-referentially incoherent?

Matters are not quite so straightforward.

Evidentialists may reply that they have *rational arguments* for their hard-line view that supra-evidential ventures with respect to foundational faith-propositions are epistemically (and, hence, morally) impermissible. Indeed, we have already seen what one such argument might be: evidentialists may claim that commitment to the truth of a foundational faith-proposition risks error beyond all possibility of correction in the light of future evidence, and that is a risk one ought not to take (to do so would be a serious loss of rational, epistemic, integrity). Maybe, however, any such argument will rest on one or more premises that are neither able to be established on the evidence by rational argument, nor self-evident, nor admissible as basically evident under the applicable evidential practice. In that case, the ultimate motivation for commitment to hard-line evidentialism *will* need to be passional (non-evidential), and a case for the claim that hard-line evidentialism is incoherent because it is self-undermining might at least get off the ground.

The following passage suggests that James may have had just such a point in mind:

perceptual experience may, of course, require active interpretation of raw data by the mind—but the mind's activity is here both subconscious and involuntary, whereas in the religious case people may become conscious that they are choosing to place a religious construal on their experience.)

[17] The degree of importance James himself attached to this observation may be indicated by the fact that he incorporates it *into the very statement* of the fideist thesis he defends in 'The Will to Believe': 'Our passional nature not only lawfully may, but must, decide an option between propositions, whenever it is a genuine option that cannot by its nature be decided on intellectual grounds; for to say, under such circumstances, "Do not decide, but leave the question open", is *itself a passional decision* …' (*The Will to Believe*, 11, my emphasis).

Believe truth! Shun error!—these, we see, are two materially different laws; and by choosing between them we may end by colouring differently our whole intellectual life. We may regard the chase for truth as paramount, and the avoidance of error as secondary; or we may, on the other hand, treat the avoidance of error as more imperative, and let truth take its chance.[18]

The suggestion may be, then, that only our passional, non-evidential, inclinations can settle whether we take it that we should guard against falling into radical evidentially irremediable error at the cost of potential loss of commitment to vital evidentially inaccessible truth (the preference that underlies hard-line evidentialism) or, conversely, be prepared to risk such irremediable error for the sake of a chance of gaining such truths (the preference that underlies fideism). The hard-line evidentialist sees 'giving in' to passional motivation as a serious loss of rational epistemic integrity; while the fideist sees a ban on passional resolution of religious and similar options as a serious loss of our *overall* integrity as beings who are more than purely rational animals. But, if this is how things stand, evidentialists must make an exception of their own passionally motivated commitment—and that appears, on the face of it, to be a serious weakness in their position.

It is important to realize, however, that the accusation that hard-line evidentialism is self-undermining *because it is incoherent* cannot be sustained. For it is at least *consistent* to hold that passionally motivated supra-evidential commitment is permissible *only* to whatever is required to secure commitment to hard-line evidentialism itself, and that, once that passional step is taken, any further passional resolution of essentially evidentially undecidable options is thereby excluded. (For example, if an ultimately passional preference to avoid risk of evidentially irremediable error is indeed the rational basis for commitment to hard-line evidentialism, then hard-line evidentialists may consistently allow that risk to be taken in

---

[18] *The Will to Believe*, 18. James makes the point more generally than required for our context here, where attention is restricted to essentially evidentially undecidable options presented by highest-order framing principles.

It is of interest that James's general point that different agents may 'value truth and disvalue falsehood very differently from one another' is 'happily accommodated' by the 'Cognitive Decision Theory' (CDT) outlined by Philip Percival in 'The Pursuit of the Epistemic Good', in Michael Brady and Duncan Pritchard (eds), *Moral and Epistemic Virtues* (Oxford: Blackwell, 2003), 29–46. CDT 'approaches the question "What, given his evidence, should A believe?" in the manner in which classical decision theory approaches the question "What, given his limited knowledge of the relevant contingencies, should A do?". Like its practical counterpart, it sees the problem as one of pursuing some valued quantity [namely, truth] under uncertainty' (43–4).

this case, while maintaining that such a risk need be, and may be, taken *only here* so that epistemic risk of this very kind may be minimized.)[19]

So, if commitment to hard-line evidentialism does ultimately rest on passional resolution of some essentially evidentially undecidable genuine options, it does not follow that it falls into incoherence. Hard-line evidentialism might, nevertheless, be judged unreasonable. For, it might seem unreasonable to suppose that the proper exercise of an obviously general capacity for passional resolution of essentially evidentially undecidable options should be as singularly restricted as the hard-line evidentialist maintains. (Compare the unreasonableness of puritan restrictions on the proper exercise of sexual capacities.)

In reply, however, hard-line evidentialists may protest that they are not 'singularly restricting' the proper exercise of our capacity for passionally motivated supra-evidential venture. They are not absolutists, after all, and they admit that doxastic venture is quite proper in (e.g.) interpersonal cases of the kind discussed earlier in this chapter. Their rejecting supra-evidential venture with respect to options posed by all foundational *religious* (and similar) faith-propositions may be indeed something of a hard line: but it is not unreasonably arbitrary. Their view is that our human capacity for passionally motivated venture beyond the evidence does have a proper sphere of operation—but when it is exercised in favour of religious (and similar) faith-propositions it is trespassing beyond that proper sphere.

For this response to escape the charge of arbitrariness, however, there will need to be some *principled* difference between religious and other cognitive ventures. (To return to the analogy: sexual puritans will be able to reply to the allegation that their restrictions are arbitrary by urging that they accord with the 'natural' reproductive purpose of sexuality.) One way in which hard-line evidentialists might maintain there is nothing *ad hoc* about their allowing passional foundations for commitment to their view that religious (and similar) cognitive ventures are impermissible, would be to argue that those passional foundations are *basic evaluative commitments*,

---

[19] Compare James:

'I have said ... that there are some options between opinions in which [the] influence [of our passional nature] must be regarded both as an inevitable and as a lawful determinant of our choice.

'I fear here that some of you my hearers will begin to scent danger, and lend an inhospitable ear. Two first steps of passion you have indeed had to admit as necessary,—we must think so as to avoid dupery, and we must think so as to gain truth; but the surest path to these ideal consummations, you will probably consider, is from now onwards to take no further passional step (*The Will to Believe*, 19).'

and that it is generally true that such commitments can be entered into only passionally. (This reply appeals to a view—already noted as plausible in the previous chapter—that basic evaluative propositions may present essentially evidentially undecidable genuine options. For this view to be correct, of course, it will have to be right to reject both the Kantian dream of deriving morality from consistency in the exercise of practical reason alone, and also the view that *all* truly basic moral commitments are naturally compelled.) Hard-line evidentialists may thus maintain that their rejection of supra-evidential commitments applies only to foundational faith-propositions with *factual* content (such as the proposition that God exists and is revealed in Jesus). When our capacity for passionally motivated cognitive venture is exercised in commitment to foundational claims about *how things are*, it trespasses beyond its proper sphere: the cognitive ventures evidentialists need to make, however, are a matter of practical commitment only to *how things ought to be*. Or so evidentialists themselves may maintain.

This suggestion returns us to the view that supra-evidential fideism and hard-line evidentialism are opposed evaluative theses, resting ultimately on opposing passionally motivated evaluative preferences, neither of which can be shown to be rationally superior to the other. On this view, hard-line evidentialists may escape the charge that their position is self-undermining; but they also fail to make a rationally compelling case against fideism.

Hard-line evidentialists might hope to contest this verdict on the debate by arguing that their position is the rationally compelling one because it follows from a maxim that will be accepted by anyone who is serious about achieving the epistemic goal of gaining truth and avoiding error—namely, the maxim that we ought not to commit ourselves to the truth of factual propositions when doing so risks error that is *evidentially irremediable*, that is, in principle unable ever to be corrected in the light of emerging evidence. That plausible maxim does not, however, give any reason to prefer evidentialist over fideist policy *with respect to foundational faith-propositions that present a forced option*, as such propositions do when they function as highest-order framing principles for a whole doxastic framework. To see why, consider the Evangelical Christian example once again (on the assumption, of course, that it does present a persistently evidentially undecidable genuine option). To rely on passional promptings to commit oneself to the truth that Jesus is the saviour does indeed risk irremediable error; but to follow the evidentialist imperative equally risks irremediable loss of commitment to the truth, should it actually be true that Jesus is saviour. It is indeed true that suspending judgement will avoid risking *having an attitude* that is irremediably in error—but as, *ex hypothesi*, the option here is forced, the practical implication of suspending judgement is that one *does not* commit oneself to this foundational faith-proposition's truth, and that stance carries a risk of failing to be committed to the truth—a risk that could not in principle be corrected in the light of future evidence. *Once the emphasis is placed on practical commitment in the context of a forced option*, there is no real difference between risking an erroneous commitment and risking failure to be committed to the truth, and where the option is persistently evidentially undecidable, *either of these eventualities* will be evidentially irremediable.[20] Thus, the injunction to avoid any risk of evidentially irremediable misalignment of one's practical commitments with the truth simply cannot be followed when an option is both forced and persistently evidentially undecidable. Evaluative commitments that yield that injunction cannot, then, tell in favour of hard-line evidentialism over supra-evidential fideism with respect to foundational faith-propositions.

## Attitudes to passional doxastic inclinations

Must we return, then, to the view that supra-evidential fideism and hard-line evidentialism rest on opposed passional evaluative preferences, with no means of showing that one set of preferences is more rational than the other? To answer this question, it is important to form a view about what precisely the opposed preferences are that divide the two sides. As I have been at pains to point out, fideists of the supra-evidential kind are at one with evidentialists in their concern for epistemic integrity—for the right use of the relevant human capacities in the pursuit of the epistemic goal of grasping truth and avoiding error. Their disagreement with hard-line evidentialists has to do with *what the relevant human capacities are*. For, supra-evidential fideists and hard-line evidentialists have opposed attitudes to our capacity for *passional inclinations towards taking foundational faith-propositions to be true*.

---

[20] Compare George Mavrodes's observation that 'where the possibility of remaining uncommitted disappears, as it does in the forced option, the distinction [between giving priority to avoiding error over believing truth and the converse] vanishes too' ('James and Clifford on "The Will to Believe"', *The Personalist*, 44 (1963), 194).

Evidentialists think such inclinations cannot responsibly be trusted in pursuit of the epistemic goal; fideists think they may responsibly be trusted—at least sometimes, under the conditions expressed in thesis (J+).

Hard-line evidentialists might now hope to show that their position is, after all, the rationally compelling one. They might claim that their distrust of religious (and similar) passional doxastic inclinations is the rationally appropriate attitude. And they might argue for this on the *factual* grounds that passional doxastic inclinations cannot ever function, non-accidentally, as guides to truth.

Is this argument successful? It is clearly generally true that passional doxastic inclinations cannot function as guides to truth. After all, they get counted as passional only because they are *not* evidential—not generally apt as indicators of the truth.[21] Supra-evidential fideists will have no quarrel with the *general* claim that those with serious epistemic goals should ignore such inclinations. Fideists contend, however, that in the very special case of a foundational faith-proposition, it can be consistent with the proper pursuit of serious epistemic goals to let ourselves follow passional promptings. Believing by faith may thus be seen as resting on a preparedness to trust in our passional nature as a guide to truth in the limiting case where truth is otherwise inaccessible, and an important forced decision must be made at the level of practical commitment. Hard-line evidentialists, by contrast, insist that the failure of passional doxastic inclinations to be generally apt indicators of truth applies as much as anywhere to the case of essentially evidentially undecidable faith-propositions such as (we are continuing to assume) are exemplified in theistic faith.

Fideists and evidentialists agree, then, that commitment to foundational faith-propositions must carry epistemic entitlement if it is to be morally justified. They also agree that making such a commitment through passional doxastic inclination can be epistemically responsible only if there is a real possibility that such inclinations may lead us non-accidentally to otherwise unobtainable vital truths. They disagree as to whether this condition is met. Perhaps the debate can be resolved, then, by settling this disputed factual question? We have plenty of evidence that passional doxastic inclinations

---

[21] Recall (from Chapter 5) that the notion of a passional cause for belief, or a passional motivation for practical commitment to the truth of a proposition, is to be interpreted broadly enough to include *all* types of causes and motivations that do not consist in providing the believer with grounds *in accordance with the applicable evidential practice* for holding or taking the proposition believed to be true.

are not generally apt indicators of truth—indeed, as noted, that is why we class them as passional. We also have good empirical grounds for identifying the exceptional cases (such as the interpersonal cases of permissible doxastic venture, and the cases where 'faith in a fact can help create a fact', discussed earlier). Can the question whether passional doxastic inclinations may properly be treated as guides to truth *in the special case of foundational faith-propositions* be settled on the basis of evidence and argument? Or must this question itself ultimately be settled on a passional basis—and, if so, what view should then be taken of the debate between fideist and evidentialist?

## Epistemological externalism again: a presumption in favour of fideism?

Consider first how supra-evidential fideists might try to argue for the epistemic propriety of reliance on passional promptings as to foundational religious truths. They cannot, of course, appeal to the past epistemic success of such faith-ventures in aligning commitment with the truth: short of putative post-mortem existence, there could be no knowledge of any such successes, since the truth of the faith-propositions concerned is in principle beyond evidential determination. (True, many people who have made ventures in faith have lived good and flourishing lives, and it might thus be claimed that the experiment of trusting to their passional doxastic inclinations has paid off. But their successful lives could count as adequate evidential support for the truth of their foundational faith-propositions only from within the doxastic framework that has those propositions as its framing principles.)

Fideists might try, however, to exploit the epistemological externalist insight of Reformed epistemology. They might observe that a purely passional conviction of, for example, the truth of the Christian Gospel could result from the proper functioning of the very mechanisms God intended for (chosen) human beings to come to commit themselves to it.[22] In

---

[22] See my earlier discussion of Reformed epistemology in Chapter 4. As I noted there, Reformed epistemologists themselves effectively see their position as conforming to a suitably broad evidentialism: they brook no talk of following passional doxastic inclinations, holding rather that certain religious beliefs grounded directly in experience can be properly basic. As previously argued, however, the evidential practice that allows certain theistic beliefs to count as basically evident in experience is internal to the relevant theistic doxastic framework, and so cannot externally certify commitment to it as a whole.

which case, the evidentialist stopper on passional doxastic inclinations might, potentially for *any* foundational faith-proposition, block our only means to knowledge. Would it then follow that hard-line evidentialism is epistemically irresponsible?

I noted earlier (Chapter 4) that Reformed epistemology's externalism cannot show that evidentially ambiguous Christian belief *actually does* have epistemic worth—only that it would *if* Christian beliefs are true. I therefore concluded that Reformed epistemologists are, in effect, fideists in denial, and stand in need of just the kind of general defence of epistemic entitlement to doxastic venture in favour of foundational faith-propositions that I am now attempting.

The question now, though, is whether epistemological externalism might prove useful *in arguing that supra-evidentialism should rationally be preferred to hard-line evidentialism*. Unfortunately, the same basic problem emerges as beset Reformed epistemology. The most that can be established is a conditional claim, when a categorical one is required. *If* it is true that, in the case of genuine options posed by foundational faith-propositions, passional doxastic inclinations are mechanisms whose proper function (e.g. through divine intention) is to inculcate true beliefs not accessible through evidential mechanisms, then hard-line evidentialism will indeed be epistemically misguided. But that does not establish, of course, that hard-line evidentialism *is* epistemically misguided.

Fideists might suggest, however, that appealing to epistemological externalism at least creates a presumption in their favour. If there is a real possibility that passionally motivated venture may bring our commitments into alignment with evidentially inaccessible truths, it is then a *prima facie* consideration against evidentialism that following its maxim will ensure that we fail to grasp any such truths.

## Scepticism about passional doxastic inclinations as guides to truth: how passions may be schooled

Hard-line evidentialists may, however, seek to turn the tables by maintaining that *there is no real possibility* that passional doxastic inclinations should function as guides to evidentially inaccessible truth. It is irrational, they will say, for supra-evidential fideists to accept the guidance of what they themselves agree not to be a generally apt indicator of truth just because there can be no other source of guidance. A bad guide does not become a good guide through being the only one available. There is thus a strong presumption *against* supra-evidential fideism. Or so hard-line evidentialists may maintain.

To reply to this presumptive defeater of their position, fideists will need to give positive grounds for the claim that treating passional doxastic inclinations as guides to truth in the restricted case of foundational faith-propositions is *not* epistemically irresponsible. How might such grounds be provided?

There is, I think, a tendency for fideists to be tempted at this point into overreaching themselves dialectically. Since their key point is that passional doxastic inclinations may, under the right conditions, properly be followed without abandoning the epistemic goal, it is easy for them to think that what they *really* want to say is that such inclinations need to be included *as a kind of evidence in their own right.*[23] Now, no doubt there is a case for granting that certain kinds of emotional states do indeed constitute evidence for the truth of certain claims. No doubt, for example, an immediate feeling of

---

[23] Fideists who give in to this temptation may then, of course, find themselves transformed into evidentialists who share something like the following view from Paul Helm:

'I am questioning the sole applicability of what I have called naturalist evidentialism to matters to do with the reasonableness of theistic belief and arguing that our moral nature may sometimes be needed to properly evaluate the total evidence that is available to us, including the evidence for and of certain moral facts. We might miss or resist such evidence. That is, the argument is not that we can, by invoking our moral nature, justifiably ignore certain kinds of evidence, or justifiably leap the gaps in our evidence, but that our moral nature is needed to assess the total evidence, and so to assess the force of that evidence. Such a procedure is not inconsistent with attempting to be as objective as one's overall outlook permits. But it does involve allowing one's judgement to be affected by one's wants and interests, as well as requiring that one's wants and interests are kept under review'. (*Faith with Reason*, 98)

Note also the interpretation Wainwright places on James:

'The views James advocates (meliorism, indeterminism, the religious hypothesis, and even pluralism) are not adequately grounded in epistemic reason *if* epistemic reasons are restricted to what philosophers have typically regarded as such. James, however, thinks that the only *generic* concept of a good epistemic reason is the concept of the kind of consideration that, when taken into account, tends to eliminate cognitive disturbance in the long run. Standard epistemic considerations are likely to do so. But so are the sorts of subjective grounds James appeals to. *Hence they are good epistemic reasons.*' (*Reason and the Heart*, 99; the last emphasis is mine)

The Jamesian fideism I defend emphatically does not treat non-evidential causes for faith-beliefs as providing good epistemic reasons (even in some suitably broader or 'generic' sense) for practical commitment to their truth: rather they provide the motivation for such a commitment beyond evidential support—a commitment which, under the right conditions (stated in (J+)), is made with both moral *and* epistemic entitlement, where commitment with epistemic entitlement is a matter of commitment consistent with the right exercise of one's epistemic capacities.

being under threat in another person's presence is often good evidence that the person is hostile and not to be trusted—and, even though unconscious inference from perceptions of the person's demeanour and behaviour will be involved in such a case, it may be reasonable to treat beliefs based on such feelings as properly basic. Feelings that involve intuitions of the truth of propositions will count as *evidence*, however, *only when they can be brought within an applicable normative evidential practice.* That will require, at a minimum, that the veridicality and defeasibility conditions of such intuitions be open to wide intersubjective agreement within the relevant community. Where subsumption under an evidential practice is not possible, however, 'feelings' as to truths, however subjectively compelling, will not count as evidence, and will rightly be classified as passional doxastic inclinations.

When it comes to the kind of passional doxastic inclinations involved in religious faith (and in any relevantly similar contexts), it is clear that such inclinations cannot properly be treated as intuitions of basically evident truths within some *generally applicable* evidential practice. As already noted, they may have that status *from within* the perspective of commitment to a particular religious doxastic framework under a *religiously specific* evidential practice. But, external to any such commitment, they will properly count as passional, as non-evidential. For, patently, people have intimations of the truth of a wide variety of different, and mutually incompatible, foundational religious truths, and only the most absurdly optimistic of ecumenists could hope to bring all such doxastic inclinations within the ambit of a single intersubjectively agreed evidential practice. But, in that case, how may fideists show that it is not irrational to treat strictly passional doxastic inclinations as guides to truth in the special case of foundational faith-propositions? There seems to be this dilemma: either treat religious doxastic inclinations as basic evidence, or else accept that they are indeed passional and thus never properly treated as guides to truth.

There is, I suggest, a way through the middle of this apparent dilemma. Though it may at first seem paradoxical, there can be epistemically rational aspects to passionally motivated faith-ventures. When people venture to commit themselves through passional motivation they do so in a dynamic and evolving context—in this respect, the analogy with ventures in interpersonal trust is quite apt. Passionally motivated faith-ventures are thus open to modification—and not merely on random whim, but through processes that have an epistemically rational aspect to them. One such rational aspect results from the need for faith-ventures at least to be consistent with—even though they necessarily cannot be confirmed by—independent external evidence. Imagine, for example, someone who ventures commitment to the existence of the God of the Biblical literalists, and who later realizes that this is inconsistent with independent evidence about (e.g.) the age of the Earth. Under the supra-evidential fideism expressed in (J+), she is then morally obliged to withdraw or modify her initial faith-venture—and it will have emerged that, even though she may have sincerely judged the option for or against the existence of the Biblical literalists' God to be evidentially undecidable, that judgement was in fact mistaken. (As already noted in Chapter 6, judgements as to whether any particular venture meets the conditions required for permissible faith-ventures—and in particular, the evidential undecidability condition—are always fallible.)

Moreover, a commitment that settles *what really is* a persistently essentially evidentially undecidable option—and which thus will never run against contrary evidence—can also come to be modified *in response to changing passional inclinations*. To explain how this may be so, let me reflect briefly on the notion of passional causes of holding, and passional motivations for taking, propositions to be true.

It is mistaken to hold that there can be no epistemically rational ways of dealing with beliefs—and, more broadly, motivations to take propositions to be true in reasoning—that have passional rather than evidential causes. Consider the case of basic evaluative beliefs, on the assumption that such beliefs are indeed passionally rather than evidentially caused. On this assumption, even if we are automatically furnished with *some* basic evaluative commitments, other basic evaluative matters do present real options which may be settled only on the basis of intuitions that count as passional because they cannot be subsumed under any established evidential practice. Such passional evaluative intuitions may nevertheless be dealt with rationally. First, they are subject to the constraint of mutual logical coherence. Secondly, they need to fit appropriately with evidentially-based factual beliefs. (Exactly what that notion of appropriate fit amounts to is a nice question which I will here simply mention: it does seem clear, however, that beliefs about what the facts are can, in some sense, reasonably constrain evaluative beliefs.)[24] Third, when we commit ourselves to basic evaluative beliefs through passional intuitions, we do so *in community*, and are subject to critical pressures from others as we proceed to live out those commitments. It is thus a living community (and it is another nice question of how its membership is to be defined) that provides the context in which the coherence requirements on basic evaluative commitments work themselves out, and passional motivations for such commitments are suitably schooled.

That rough sketch is, of course, but one view of the rationality of evolving evaluative commitments—it will be opposed by those who hold that evaluative beliefs *are* subject to a general evidential practice, either because they think that foundational evaluative claims can be shown *a priori* to be true or because they think that such claims can be properly basic, grounded in our direct intuitive experience of their truth.[25] My purpose is only to show that, *if* one holds the—at least plausible—view that basic evaluative claims require passionally motivated commitment, one does not thereby lose all grip on the idea of dealing broadly rationally with the making and revising of those foundational commitments.

It will be clear where this train of thought is leading: similar considerations may apply to passionally motivated foundational faith-commitments with factual content. We may envisage how a process of making, and living with, such passionally motivated faith-ventures may be fit to count as a mechanism to lead us to truth. (Not, of course, that these considerations establish that any passionally driven process *is* truth-conducive; the claim

---

[24] It does seem somehow incoherent, for example, to recognize that a certain way of living causes serious suffering to sentient beings and yet fail to place any negative evaluation on that way of living—though the incoherence is clearly not strictly logical. To make sense of the notion of fact/value coherence while retaining a fact/value distinction will require, I think, appeal to some overriding, *itself evaluative*, principle about how one's evaluations should relate to one's factual commitments—and that might be supplied by an ethic of right relationship. So, for example, judging that an action causes serious suffering and yet placing no—even *prima facie*—negative evaluation on that action will be incoherent because someone with that combination of judgements and evaluations would not be in a right relationship with how the world is.

[25] As already indicated, the question whether basic evaluative intuitions should be classified as passionally caused beliefs or as intuitions of the basic evidence of the relevant truths in experience depends on whether those intuitions can be brought under a generally applicable evidential practice, and that in turn will require wide intersubjective agreement about when such intuitions are true in the relevant community. In the case of basic moral intuitions, it is clear enough that the relevant community encompasses a significant lack of intersubjective agreement with respect to at least some such basic intuitions; in which case, those intuitions will count as passional.

is only that such a process has features which exclude *a priori* insistence that it *cannot* be truth-conducive.) I have, in effect, already illustrated this possibility in my reflections on Abraham at the end of the previous chapter. However, let me reinforce the point with a couple of further examples.

Imagine a person who, through passionally motivated supra-evidential venture, comes to be practically committed to the truth of the claim that there exists a God who, amongst other properties, requires retributive punishment for human sin and exacts it through the death of Christ ('the God of Penal Substitution'). As she continues to live with that commitment, she may, provided she does not circumscribe her community too tightly, encounter considerations which question the justice of Penal Substitution. Her (as we are here assuming, ultimately passional) responses to that encounter may lead her to moral commitments inconsistent with belief in such a God. This may prompt a change in the kind of God she is passionally motivated to believe in—as, indeed, is necessary if she is to regard her faith-venture as justified under (J+)'s condition (iv). The process she goes through seems clearly to be *a possible* vehicle of non-accidental progress towards the truth, even though, on our current assumptions, her shift in belief will not be describable as a response to new evidence.[26]

Or, for a somewhat different kind of case, imagine someone committed to Evangelical Christianity who undergoes, after much anguish and struggle in the attempt to avoid it, the break-up of his marriage. He is surprised to find that his fellow Evangelicals regard him as a failed Christian (their attitude is basically, 'shape up or shift out'), whereas some of his more liberal Christian friends are forgiving and supportive. This causes a change in his passional motivations, so that he now finds intuitively attractive foundational Christian claims of a significantly different character from those that used to seem intuitively compelling to him, and he may then choose to make a correspondingly altered faith-venture.

These cases illustrate how passionally motivated faith-ventures are always experimental in a certain sense. The experiment is not, and could not be, directed at enabling rational modification of initial commitments in the

---

[26] Contrast this case with that of a person who amends his initial faith-commitment to the existence of the God of Penal Substitution because he comes to the conclusion that Scripture does not sustain the penal substitutionary theory of the Atonement. Here the shift is in response to his assessment of the evidence, albeit, of course, within a specific theistic evidential practice that takes certain sources as authoritative.

light of evidence as to their truth in accordance with the norms of an evidential practice; rather, it is directed at discovering whether and how one's initial passional motivations may shift in the light of the experience of living out commitment in accordance with them. People of faith may view their potentially changing passional promptings as a test of initial faith-ventures and a potential path to their modification. In the context of faith in God, one's initial passional inclination to believe will be seen as a gift of God's grace, and any shifts in those inclinations (towards, for example, new understandings of the God in whom one believes) will potentially count as further gifts of grace. There is *some* analogy here with the scientist who trusts (suitably regimented) sense-experience as a source of basic evidence against which initial theoretical commitments are tested. But, as noted above, the parallel is not so close as to equate passional doxastic inclinations with intuitions of what is basically evident in experience. Some account will, of course, be needed *of which passional changes should be responded to with shifts in commitment and which should not.* That account will include—as (J+) requires—that a changed passional inclination should be of a morally respectable type and incline towards a truth-claim that conforms with correct morality. It may also be necessary to respect the norms of discernment prevailing in the community that shares the relevant tradition of faith—though there is, of course, a wide diversity of such communities even within the same broad religious tradition, and changes in passional religious inclinations might often prompt a shift in one's identification with a particular community of faith. Judgments about when to shift commitment in line with passional changes will thus always be risky—but they need not be completely arbitrary. Our Evangelical who suffers a marriage break-up will thus have *some* basis on which to judge whether he is right to modify the content of his basic Christian commitment in the light of changing passional inclinations caused by his experience of how he is treated by various purported followers of Christ.

I conclude, then, that the moral coherentist and supra-evidential features of modest fideism—plus the fact that passional promptings of the truth of particular faith-claims can change with experience and be responded to non-arbitrarily with modifications in commitment—seem enough to overturn any *a priori* allegation that passional experience *could not* be a fit guide to evidentially inaccessible truths, even though it must be granted that passional doxastic inclinations are not themselves a form of *evidence* for such truths. It will, however, be a necessary condition for passional inclinations to conduce to truth that they not be followed dogmatically, but with an open mind (though this does not entail, as I have already remarked in Chapter 6, that passionally motivated faith-ventures may only be, merely, tentative).

## The significance of scientific theories of passional motivations for faith-commitment

Considerations such as the above indicate what may be behind Pascal's remark (quoted by James) that 'Le coeur a ses raisons que la raison ne connaît pas'.[27] Nevertheless, the parallels between shifts in commitment to factual claims based on changing evidence and shifts based on changing passional motivations may be regarded as superficial, in the light of what is held to be adequate a posteriori evidence that only the former kind of process actually conduces to truth. I shall assume that this evidence is indeed generally adequate (even though science, too, has its passional aspects): the question here, however, is whether it is adequate with respect to the special case of foundational faith-propositions that are permanently and essentially evidentially undecidable. Do we have sufficient evidence to show that it is not a real possibility that passionally motivated commitment to the truth of such faith-propositions should conduce to truth, and that the epistemic goal is therefore better served by the hard-line evidentialist policy of resisting faith-ventures?

   Evidentialists may argue that, so long as we have some reasonably well confirmed explanation of the origin of our passional promptings towards religious (and similar) faith-beliefs that applies on the assumption that all such beliefs are false, we may exclude the hypothesis that there is a real possibility that they are mechanisms whose proper function is to align our commitments with the truth. Freudian and Marxian explanations provide examples of such theories. Recent evolutionary anthropology and psychology provide further examples which perhaps have a greater claim to be scientifically well confirmed. I have already mentioned (in Chapter 4) the theory that religious beliefs—when they concern supernatural agents, anyway—arise as a side-effect of our evolved capacities for forming

---

[27] The Will to Believe, 21.

beliefs about agents. Thus, our best scientific explanation of our having supernaturalist religious doxastic inclinations (including the inclination to take classical theism to be true) holds even if those doxastic inclinations do in fact systematically incline us towards falsehood.

As grounds for favouring moral evidentialism over supra-evidential fideism as applied to religious doxastic inclinations, this argument begs the question, however. Evidence from evolutionary psychology may indeed indicate that our tendency to form beliefs about supernatural agents is a side-effect of the evolutionarily selected proper functioning of certain human cognitive capacities. But it is fallacious to infer that such a tendency is therefore merely a gratuitous and peripheral aspect of human nature, since the assumption that core human nature is exhausted by a purely biological, evolutionary characterization of it may obviously be contested. From a theistic religious perspective—indeed, from all non-naturalist religious perspectives—'properly functioning' human nature may extend well beyond what evolutionary biology can recognize as such. From *within* a particular non-naturalist religious perspective it may be quite reasonable to interpret any well-confirmed scientific theory as to how religious belief would arise even though it were false as displaying a mechanism whose proper function is the production of true belief. It is open to classical theists, for example, to maintain that what counts *for science* as a side-effect of our evolved cognitive agency module, is exactly the mechanism God intended to bring about (limited) awareness of his supernatural presence. So, if hardline evidentialists are to maintain their view that our evidence indicates that religious doxastic inclinations cannot be trustworthy guides to truth, they will have to exclude any such theistic interpretation. It follows that a naturalist/atheist stance has to be presupposed if this argument in favour of hard-line evidentialism as the only epistemically responsible position is to go through. And so the question is begged against all supra-evidential fideists who reject a purely naturalist view of the world.[28]

---

[28] Some framing principles to which people may be passionally inclined (including some that may count as religious) do *not* involve postulating supernatural agents. So it might be suggested that our best scientific explanations of how people acquire *these kinds* of passional doxastic inclinations do not support the conclusion that *those* inclinations are epistemically untrustworthy. Science will count doxastic inclinations as passional, however, if and only if the intuitions involved do not fit into any scientifically respectable evidential practice. Their failure to fit into a scientific evidential practice is then *tantamount* (for science) to their being epistemically untrustworthy. And, of course, anyone committed to naturalism is thereby committed to the view that the correct scientific explanation of

## An impasse?

So, what should we conclude, then, on the question which, I have suggested, is at the root of the debate between hard-line evidentialists and supra-evidential fideists—namely, the question whether there is a real possibility that passional doxastic inclinations could be apt indicators of the truth in the special case of essentially evidentially undecidable foundational faith-propositions?

I have argued for the failure of both *a priori* and *a posteriori* evidentialist attempts to exclude the real possibility that passional religious doxastic inclinations should conduce to evidentially inaccessible vital truths. The supra-evidential fideist view that this *is* a real possibility seems then to be *undefeated*—but it is not *established*. To be sure, on certain non-naturalist religious views of the world, the epistemic goal would indeed be met by following such inclinations. But the fideist cannot non-question-beggingly assume such religious perspectives, any more than the evidentialist can non-question-beggingly assume a naturalist/atheist perspective in regarding the debate as settled by natural scientific explanations of non-naturalist religious belief. Disagreement about whether it is epistemically responsible to trust passional inclinations to take foundational faith-propositions to be true is thus readily resolvable: the trouble is that it is resolvable both ways! The essential evidential ambiguity of the choice between theism (or any similarly non-naturalist view of the world) and naturalism/atheism seems thus to block, in principle, any non-circular rational resolution of the basic question at issue between supra-evidential fideists and hard-line evidentialists.[29]

---

the occurrence of any foundational *non-naturalist* doxastic inclination will presuppose such inclinations to be systematically mistaken. Naturalists will, however, have to admit (and allow that science admits) just one exception: namely, the passional inclination to take a naturalist view of the world. The fideist *tu quoque* is thus sustained. I shall return to this point again later.

[29] In his recent stimulating 'revisiting' of the work of William James, Charles Taylor makes essentially the same point: 'James clarifies why it ['the epistemological-moral issue of the ethics of belief] always seems to end in a standoff.' 'The agnostic view propounds some picture ... of the universe and human nature. This has going for it that it can claim to result from "science", with all the prestige that this carries with it. It can even look from the inside as though this was all you need to say. But from the outside it isn't at all clear that what everyone would agree are the undoubted findings of modern natural science quite add up to a proof of, say, materialism, or whatever the religion-excluding view is' (*Varieties of Religion Today: William James Revisited* (Cambridge, MA: Harvard University Press, 2002), 53–4).

If this interpretation is correct, then the debate ends in impasse: neither side is able to show that its opponents are taking an epistemically irresponsible position. But if rational argument cannot in principle settle the choice between supra-evidential fideism and hard-line evidentialism, then commitment on this question must ultimately be passionally motivated. The fideist's *tu quoque* is thus sustained: but there is a problem in using it to show any epistemic fault in the opposing evidentialist position. The problem is that the passional venture or ventures required to undergird commitment to hard-line evidentialism *are likely to meet the fideist's own criteria for epistemically responsible doxastic venture* as expressed in conditions (i) and (ii) in (J+). *So long as hard-line evidentialists acknowledge the need for an exception to their principle when it comes to the doxastic ventures implicated in their own evidentialist commitment*, fideists can have no epistemic complaint against them. And if the key foundational passional venture that hard-line evidentialists need to make is to a naturalist world-view, then it will be clear enough that (J+)'s conditions (i) and (ii) are met, since naturalism does present a genuine, and in principle evidentially undecidable, option. Indeed, its doing so is merely the flip-side of the genuine, essentially evidentially undecidable option presented by theism.

So, the debate between hard-line evidentialist and supra-evidential fideists appears to end in impasse—at least on the interpretation for which I have argued, and on the assumption that its resolution would require that one side show that commitment to the other is epistemically irresponsible. If that conclusion is correct, what are the implications? Might it be enough to justify faith as doxastic venture that the fideist is able to force the debate to an impasse in which neither side can be defeated by rational, evidence-based argument? But *is* it, anyway, really correct to conclude that the debate does end altogether in such an impasse? Might we accept that neither side can show the other to be *epistemically* irresponsible while nevertheless maintaining that further *non-epistemically evaluative* considerations might favour supra-evidential fideism? These are the issues I shall pursue in my final chapter.

# 9

# A moral preference for modest fideism?

What conclusion may we draw as to the merits of the version of fideism developed in the foregoing chapters?

A modest James-inspired fideism that holds believing by faith to be permissible if, and only if, the conditions of thesis (J+) are satisfied meets many standard objections to fideism.

In the first place, it does not construe believing by faith as involving either directly or indirectly self-induced evidentially unsupported doxastic attitudes; rather, it understands the cognitive venture of faith as practical commitment to the truth of a proposition motivated by an *existing* passional, non-evidential, inclination to hold it true. What is proposed is a model of faith as involving doxastic (or, conceivably in some cases, sub-doxastic) venture—choosing to let oneself take to be true in one's practical reasoning a proposition whose truth, as one recognizes, lacks sufficient support from one's total evidence.

In the second place, this version of fideism places tight constraints on allowable faith-ventures. (J+)'s 'genuineness' requirement ensures that practical commitment to faith-propositions that lack sufficient evidential support will not be admissible when such commitment is in the context of an avoidable or unimportant choice. (J+)'s 'evidential undecidability' condition rules out counter-evidential commitments—commitments contrary to the weight of one's evidence. Furthermore, given that *essential* evidential undecidability is required, (J+) narrows the proper objects for permissible faith-venture down considerably. (Arguably, it is only the highest-order framing principles of whole frameworks of faith-beliefs that can be the proper objects of faith-venture. Within such a framework, beliefs may be held with evidential justification, but practical commitment to their truth will remain ultimately dependent on faith-venture with respect to the relevant framing principles.) Finally, the requirements for faith-ventures to have non-evidential motivations of a morally respectable kind, and for their content to conform to correct morality, block morally objectionable ventures that otherwise meet the first two conditions.

This modest version of fideism, then, concedes much to moral evidentialism—indeed, it insists that a morally proper faith-venture must remain within the ambit of serious epistemic concern, even though (necessarily) it lacks external evidential certification. This type of fideism is, however, in principle powerful enough to vindicate (certain) religious (and similar) commitments beyond evidential support. (Fideism of this character will thus, of course, be otiose with respect to religious commitments, if such there be, whose truth *can* be established under the canons of an externally applicable evidential practice. Since Chapter 3, however, my discussion has been with the scope of the assumption that this condition does not apply to theistic religious commitments.) If thesis (J+) is correct, then, the fideism it expresses potentially provides a 'justification of faith', under a doxastic venture model of faith.

I say that the fideism expressed in (J+) *potentially* justifies ventures in religious faith beyond the evidence advisedly. For many *actual* religious faith-ventures will be excluded as impermissible under (J+)'s constraints. (J+) thus provides criteria which may be used to overcome the 'irregularly conjugated verb' problem with which I began: under (J+) there can be no suspicion that all that makes a faith-venture virtuous is that it is *my* commitment or the commitment of *my group*. This is a robust fideism that places genuinely objective conditions on morally permissible faith-ventures.

## Implications of accepting (J+) for orthodox and revisionary theistic faith-ventures

What verdict on the moral permissibility of faith-ventures in favour of some variety of classical theism would result from accepting (J+) is an interesting question.

As noted in Chapter 7, (J+)'s 'conformity with correct morality' condition (iv) imposes considerable constraint on the kind of content that a virtuous supra-evidential religious faith-commitment can have. Some may even maintain that this constraint excludes classical theism altogether, leaving open only revisionary versions of theistic faith. This will be judged to be the case, in particular, by all those who find that they cannot commit themselves to any moral theory that could provide a morally adequate reason for an all-powerful agent to permit the occurrence of certain actual, (e.g. horrendous), evils.

I noted in Chapter 6 the pluralistic implications of the fideism expressed in (J+). Under (J+) different and mutually incompatible faith-ventures are likely to be equally morally permissible. Thus, those who rely on their judgement that their own faith-venture meets (J+)'s conditions will need to recognize that it is highly likely that others may be *equally* morally justified in making faith-ventures *incompatible* with their own. Faith-ventures should thus be made in a non-dogmatic, non-doctrinaire spirit—though that does not imply that they may be entered into only tentatively. Moral tolerance amongst those with different religious (or similar) commitments will thus be required by those who accept (J+). And this tolerance will need to extend to those who refrain from any religious commitments. Since it is a permissibility thesis, (J+) leaves it open that people might quite properly *not* commit themselves on the basis of *their own actual* passional religious intimations—through a stronger passional inclination towards a naturalist world-view, for example.

It does seem clear, however, that (J+)'s moral pluralistic implications will constrain the content of morally permissible faith-ventures *via* (J+)'s condition (iv). Again, the effect on the possibility of regarding any orthodox theistic religious faith-commitment as morally permissible will be significant, given the prevalence of exclusivist elements in such commitments. How, for example, will it be possible to meet (J+)'s moral coherence condition in venturing to take it to be true that God saves only those who accept Jesus as Saviour, if one is also committed to the moral permissibility of doxastic venture with respect to (e.g.) foundational Muslim theistic beliefs? Christian exclusivism will be defensible, I suspect, only on the assumption that correct morality is *internal* to specifically Christian commitment, so that no one with religious commitments incompatible with Christianity could satisfy (J+)'s condition (iv). Such an assumption seems quite unjustified: I shall not, however, pursue the large issue hereby raised. I do wish to emphasize, however, that any account of correct morality as purely internal to a specific set of religious commitments will have the effect of negating the independent force of (J+)'s fourth constraint. For that reason, proponents of the version of fideism expressed in (J+) will be committed to rejecting all such 'religiously internal' theories of morality.[1]

There is, then, an important connection between the present project of defending a modest moral coherentist supra-evidential fideism and various projects in progressive and revisionary theology. If theistic faith-commitment can be morally acceptable only if it is non-doctrinaire and tolerant, what implications does that have for its content? In what sense, if at all, can an authentic theism be pluralistic?[2] What are the prospects for revisionary theism—that is, for believing in God according to some alternative to the classical conception of the divine? Can there be *religiously adequate* alternative theories of the nature of God as revealed in the theistic religious traditions? Might commitment to God's existence under some alternative conception turn out to be morally preferable to commitment to any form of classical theism? To attempt to answer these important questions would be a major undertaking, well beyond my present scope. I suggest, however, that the present inquiry may supply a vital platform from which to launch attempts to deal with these further projects in progressive theology. For, all such projects will *inter alia* presuppose a general theory of the moral permissibility of religious faith-commitments, and that is exactly what the fideism expressed in (J+) provides.

## The apparent fideist/evidentialist impasse and its implications

As a sensible version of fideism, then, (J+) has much to commend it. It remains disputable, however, whether even so modest a version of fideism ought to be accepted. In the previous chapter I investigated arguments aimed at showing that a moral coherentist supra-evidential fideism should

---

[1] I am indebted to Imran Aijaz for drawing my attention to the importance of this point.
[2] Here a natural place to start would be with a critical investigation of the pluralistic hypothesis proposed by John Hick in Part 4 of his *An Interpretation of Religion*.

be preferred to its hard–line evidentialist rival. That investigation suggested that the debate ends in impasse. The most promising fideist strategy is a *tu quoque*, obliging evidentialists to concede that their own evidentialist commitment must ultimately rest on passionally motivated foundations. That strategy meets with some success—but it is not the clincher it may at first seem.

As I have argued, fideists cannot establish that commitment to hard–line evidentialism is epistemically irresponsible. On the account I have given, it is indeed true that hard–line evidentialism rests on passionally motivated ventures—in particular, a venture in favour of the naturalist perspective necessary to support the claim that, this very case excepted, there is no real possibility that passional motivations should conduce to evidentially inaccessible factual truths. But this passional venture *meets the fideist's own conditions for epistemically justifiable doxastic venture*. So the exceptions hard–line evidentialists thus have to make to their own moral evidentialist principle, though they might seem self-undermining, do not introduce any *epistemic* fault. On the other hand, neither can evidentialists non-question-beggingly establish that supra-evidential fideism is an epistemically irresponsible position. Supra-evidential fideism is not excluded under the plausible policy of seeking to avoid risk of irremediable misalignment between one's practical commitments and the truth, since *no one* can avoid such a risk when facing options that are both in principle evidentially undecidable and *forced*. Furthermore, it could in fact serve epistemic goals to trust to (some) religious and quasi-religious passional doxastic inclinations in making foundational faith-commitments, should a non–naturalist (e.g. theistic) view of the world turn out to be correct. And a process of evolving passionally motivated faith-commitments, while not a matter of revision in the light of evidence, nevertheless can have rational features that fit with the real possibility that such a process might (on a theistic view of the world, say) lead a person to the truth. Accordingly, given that both sides accept the moral-epistemic link principle under which faith-commitments are morally permissible only if they carry epistemic entitlement, it may well seem that the whole debate must end in impasse.

Suppose that assessment is correct: what are the implications? If neither supra-evidential fideists nor hard–line evidentialists can provide epistemically rational grounds for preferring their side of the debate, what should we conclude about the morality of believing by faith? What will become, in particular, of the desire of reflective theists who accept the evidential ambiguity of their faith-commitments to be assured of their moral probity in continuing to take those faith-beliefs to be true through non-evidential motivation?

If the debate does end in impasse, then it amounts to a case of irresolvable fundamental moral disagreement. The proper response to the impasse will thus fall under whatever general policy applies to dealing with such disagreements. Such a policy will be essentially political, since it concerns the question how people who take opposed moral stances should relate to one another in a single community or polity. An attractive policy is to affirm people's right to take either side of a fundamental moral disagreement, under conditions of mutual respect and tolerance (though there are, of course, important questions about the proper limits of such tolerance). (Note that such a policy does *not* entail any subjectivist or relativist dissolution of disagreement by making the opposed positions each morally correct relative to its own context. Indeed, such a relativist move *undermines* the attempt to secure the virtue of tolerance across fundamental moral disagreements, since relativism is powerless to exclude the moral permissibility of intolerance relative to any context that accepts it.)

If this response is made to the impasse, those who make religious and similar faith-ventures that meet the criteria set by (J+) may then be able to defend their right to believe *just in a broadly political sense.* For, this response will affirm a *modus vivendi* that respectfully tolerates the existence of irresolvable difference on the question whether any religious or quasi-religious faith-ventures may be morally permissible. Such an outcome will bring relief from politically extreme evidentialists, if such there be, who try to refuse practising fideists the right to be wrong (by hard-line evidentialist lights, that is).[3] Such an outcome will make possible what James describes as 'the intellectual republic' in which none of us 'issue[s] vetoes to the other' nor 'band[ies] words of abuse'.[4]

Nevertheless, the question whether one may be morally and epistemically entitled to make faith-ventures will remain essentially unresolved. Those who make theistic faith-ventures may be assured of no more than

---

[3] Historically the boot has frequently been on the other foot. Under this political response to the impasse, committed people of religious faith need equally to respect the hard-line evidentialist view that all religious faith-ventures are morally wrong.

[4] *The Will to Believe*, 30.

the impossibility of their evidentialist opponents *establishing* that religious faith-venturing is epistemically, and thus also morally, unreasonable. This assurance that their position is undefeated may, as I have just suggested, provide theist faith-venturers with sufficient *political* vindication—and that might seem victory enough.[5] Yet a positive moral vindication of religious and similar faith-ventures that conform to (J+)'s conditions will still be lacking. A moral evidentialist *veto* on religious faith-ventures may be unwarranted, but the evidentialist *opinion* on their moral status stands unrefuted.

So if the debate really does end in impasse, we have no answer to the following—it seems existentially vital—question: Does the highest morality liberate us from enthralment to all forms of religion or quasi-religion that require cognitive commitments in principle beyond evidential support, as the hard-line evidentialist maintains? Or is the fideist correct in holding that the highest morality permits us—or perhaps even requires us—to trust certain of our passional doxastic inclinations in making such faith-commitments? If the debate ends in impasse, the upshot is just that we must live with radical disagreement over the worth of human religious and quasi-religious impulses to make morally significant commitments to essentially evidentially undecidable foundational claims about the sort of world we inhabit. One need have no dispute with that, however, to maintain a vital interest in trying to push the debate further. Reflective theists, in particular, may feel the need for a positive moral vindication of their specific religious ventures while in no way disputing the need for political tolerance of those with differing religious or, indeed, anti-religious commitments. I may be satisfied that people with my sort of religious commitments ought to be politically entitled to maintain them, without thereby being satisfied that my continuing those commitments is, in fact, morally right. It would be good to be finally free of any nagging suspicion that the evidentialist might be right in rejecting religious faith-ventures as morally misguided.

---

[5] A political philosophical defence of religious freedom will evidently be required for such vindication to be complete—and, of course, such a defence may justify religious tolerance beyond the boundaries here envisaged to include, for instance, even some counter-evidential faith-ventures. For a recent discussion of the Christian case for supporting a version of liberalism, see Philip L. Quinn, 'Can Good Christians Be Good Liberals?' in Andrew Dole and Andrew Chignell (eds) *God and the Ethics of Belief: New Essays in Philosophy of Religion* (Cambridge: Cambridge University Press, 2005), 248–76.

# Beyond impasse? Direct moral evaluation of the fideist/evidentialist debate

Supra-evidential fideism and hard-line evidentialism are, of course, contradictory *moral* theses. So the question is whether it should be the one or the other that features in our best theory of correct morality. Reflective theists (who accept the evidential ambiguity of theism) would like to be able to assure themselves that it is supra-evidential fideism as expressed in thesis (J+) that properly belongs in our best overall moral theory.

We have seen that one strategy for gaining this reassurance leads to impasse. That strategy was this: show that commitment to the hard-line evidentialism that rejects thesis (J+) is *epistemically* irresponsible, and so infer (given that morally responsible commitments must be epistemically responsible) that hard-line *moral* evidentialism is false. If that strategy leads to impasse, perhaps an alternative strategy will move the debate beyond it. And it is clear what that alternative might be: address the moral issue between fideism and evidentialism *directly*—that is, rather than *via* the moral-epistemic link principle and an attempt to show that hard-line evidentialism lacks epistemic entitlement. It may be, that is, that although fideists have to concede that hard-line evidentialism cannot be shown to be *epistemically* misguided, they can provide grounds for holding that it is *morally* misguided.[6]

I will thus conclude my inquiry with a brief discussion of the prospects for providing the moral reassurance that reflective theists require by taking the debate between fideism and evidentialism directly into moral territory. One obvious route to direct moral resolution of the debate will be to apply one's favoured moral theory. In the previous chapter, I considered—and set aside—one example of this approach, namely the attempt to vindicate fideism by appeal to consequentialism. (I argued that the consequences for net utility of religious doxastic venturing are unlikely to be agreed between fideists and evidentialists. I also pointed out that any consequentialist vindication of fideism threatened to do too much by licensing the ethical suspension of the epistemic, something emphatically opposed

---

[6] Note that this assumes (I think, obviously correctly) that the converse of the moral-epistemic link principle is generally false: i.e. it is not the case that the fact that practical commitment to a certain position carries epistemic entitlement entails that it also carries moral entitlement.

by supra-evidential fideists. The type of fideism consequentialism might vindicate is thus not the fideism expressed in thesis (J+).)

It seems most unlikely, however, that a decisive vindication of supra-evidential fideism might derive from some general moral theory agreed on either side of the debate. Nevertheless, it may be possible to collect a set of moral considerations favouring acceptance of (J+)—even if defenders of hard-line moral evidentialism can parry these considerations, and the debate remains without an outright winner. With such considerations at least identified, reflective theists' concern for the morality of their stance in the face of evidential ambiguity will be significantly relieved. For, supporters of the modest fideism expressed in (J+) will then be able to explain what it is about this position that leads them to a moral preference for it over hard-line evidentialism.

In the remainder of this chapter, then, I will briefly discuss three types of moral consideration that seem to favour supra-evidential fideism over hard-line evidentialism—namely, (1) the suggestion that fideism expresses a more balanced and authentic self-acceptance than evidentialism; (2) the claim that hard-line evidentialism arises from an unwarrantedly dogmatic attachment to a naturalist view of the world—and may even count as a failure in love; and (3) the claim that those who accept that basic moral values rest on passional commitment will end up with a doubtfully coherent overall position if they also (as hard-line evidentialists) reject religious faith-ventures in favour of the claim that the world is a moral as well as a natural order.

## Self-acceptance and authenticity

The first moral consideration in favor of fideism is the suggestion that hard-line evidentialists lack the virtue of self-acceptance: they lack authenticity because they fail to be 'true to who they really are'. Hard-line evidentialists reject commitment on the basis of passional, non-evidential, religious doxastic inclinations. But religious doxastic inclinations are (typically) not deliberately self-induced: they are part of how people find their own developed characters—their own nature—to be. (In this respect they seem on a par with basic moral intuitions.) To ban practical commitment to their truth may thus seem a policy of self-repression. As I put it in the previous chapter, it may seem that, in the name of rational integrity, hard-line evidentialists compromise our *overall* integrity as beings who are more than purely rational animals.

Evidentialists will reply, however, that it is unfair to portray them as 'inauthentically' repressing natural passional doxastic inclinations. Their commitment to certain basic values is as passional as anyone else's basic value commitments. Indeed, their commitment to rational integrity itself may well be ultimately passionally motivated. Furthermore, like anyone else they need to make the forced in principle evidentially undecidable choice (as we are assuming it to be) between a naturalist and a theistic view of the world. Their venture in favour of naturalism must thus be passionally, non-evidentially, motivated (although, as we have seen, from the naturalist perspective they are then able to make a rational, evidence-based case for the unreliability of non-naturalist religious doxastic inclinations as guides to the truth). Evidentialists might thus claim that they are as self-accepting as the next person: it is just that they find themselves with a different set of basic passional doxastic inclinations from those religious people possess.

So far as they go, these points are well taken. It is important to notice, however, that people could be committed to the value of rational integrity and to a naturalist world-view *without being hard-line evidentialists*—without holding, that is, that it is morally impermissible to make religious faith-ventures. One may consistently be *a naturalist and a supra-evidential fideist* who accepts thesis (J+). One's stance would then be expressible thus: I commit myself in accordance with my own passional prompting towards a naturalist world-view, and from that perspective I see non-naturalist religious passional inclinations as systematically misleading, and it would thus be epistemically irresponsible *for me* to 'give in' to any such inclinations I may have; however, since I recognize that a judgement of the epistemic worth of non-naturalist religious inclinations depends on the *prior* choice between naturalist and non-naturalist (e.g. theistic) views of the world, I accept that others who have inclinations towards non-naturalism are epistemically and morally entitled to commit themselves in accordance with them, provided that all the conditions of thesis (J+) are met. This stance parallels, of course, the religious fideist's moral tolerance of others' commitment to a naturalist view of the world—provided, that is, that the religious fideist concedes (as some may not) that it would not be *morally* bad for the world actually to be as the naturalist supposes.

What we are interested in, however, is the attempt to draw a moral contrast between supra-evidential fideism and *hard-line* evidentialism—the application of moral evidentialism to religious faith-propositions. Naturalists who irenically compare themselves to theists, making the point that those in each camp are simply being true to the basic passional promptings they find they have, are not *so far* hard-line evidentialists. That requires the further step of denying that it can be morally permissible to make *religious* faith-ventures, even though (as hard-line evidentialists must concede) a faith-venture in favour of a naturalist world-view is permissible.

Hard-line evidentialists may thus seem guilty of unfairly discriminating amongst naturally occurring passional doxastic inclinations. They may reply, however, that there is nothing *unfair* about their attachment to the value of rational integrity in making foundational factual commitments in accordance with the evidence, and therefore nothing unfair about seeking to minimize reliance on passional, non-evidential, promptings when making such commitments. Given the essential evidential ambiguity of the choice between naturalist and theistic world-views, the only way to minimize such reliance is to yield to the passional inclination to hold a naturalist world-view, recognizing that *once within that perspective* it will indeed count as epistemically irrational, and morally deficient, to surrender to any further (in particular, religious) passional doxastic inclinations. The fact that hard-line evidentialists make an exception for their own naturalist faith-venture results, then, not from any unfair self-favouring, but from the fact that allowing this exception is the only way to carry out a policy of keeping to the absolute minimum reliance on non-evidential motivations for commitment to the facts.

Perhaps we will get a better grip on the idea that the hard-line evidentialist position is insufficiently self-accepting by considering the case of those who combine religious doxastic inclinations they recognize to be non-evidential with a strong attraction to the value of making practical commitments to the truth of factual claims only to the extent of their evidential support. People in this situation have passional promptings that seem in tension. Such people, it seems, cannot literally be *wholly* self-accepting. But, then, *virtuous* self-acceptance is not to be equated with accepting oneself however one finds oneself to be. Self-acceptance may sometimes exemplify the vice of complacency or smugness, for example. Virtuous self-acceptance is accepting aspects of the self *that ought to be accepted*—aspects that might thus be identified as belonging to the authentic self. Virtuous self-acceptance thus requires that one gives one's passional inclinations their due. But what is their due? When one is inclined both to value the evidentialist principle and also to a religious view of the world, do both inclinations equally express one's authentic self, and, if not, which takes priority if one is to be virtuously self-accepting?

As we saw in formulating (J+)'s moral conditions (in Chapter 7), passional inclinations may be of more or less morally admirable types. So, in a particular case, a self-reflective person might realize (for example) that his inclinations towards hard-line evidentialism stem from a desire to conform to peer expectations, while his religious doxastic impulses arise from long-term and stable experience of their content as expressing a noble and challenging view of the world. Such a person would then be able to answer the question which of these passional inclinations was more true to his authentic self, *for his own particular case*. For a *generally* persuasive case for the claim that hard-line evidentialism is morally defective because it blocks virtuous self-acceptance, there would need to be good reason to think that the passional motivations undergirding hard-line evidentialism are *always* of a morally inferior kind. And that does not seem plausible. Indeed, if we consider in turn the prompting towards valuing 'evidential integrity', the prompting towards a naturalist world-view, and any number of (though not just *any*) religious and quasi-religious doxastic impulses, it seems clear that *each* is capable of belonging to morally admirable types of non-evidential motivation for commitment.

Nevertheless, it might yet be claimed that if people with religious doxastic inclinations also endorse hard-line evidentialism, they are allowing one passional motivation to become too dominant. In yielding to their desire for evidential integrity they are extinguishing the power of other passional motivations that ought to be given a fairer chance of influencing practical commitments. The prompting towards evidential integrity in our practical commitments is obviously noble and good. But when it gives rise to hard-line evidentialism, it may seem, that prompting overreaches itself. It is a mistake to suppose that broadly evidentialist and non-evidential religious promptings are somehow *as such* in conflict: they come into conflict only when the desire for epistemic integrity goes so far as to insist that, even in the case of an existentially significant forced and essentially evidentially undecidable option, the evidentialist imperative must be applied even to a morally impeccable religious doxastic inclination. *That* is the hard-line evidentialist position—and that position seems unbalanced. The supra-evidential fideist, by contrast, seems to have the balance right, admitting a strong prompting towards respect for evidence while recognizing its limits when it comes to essentially evidentially undecidable genuine options, and making a case for the virtue of passionately motivated faith-venture that (as I was at pains to emphasize in Chapter 7) remains within the scope of serious epistemic concern.

These considerations do, of course, fall short of a decisive moral argument in favour of supra-evidential fideism over hard line evidentialism. The less 'balanced' position might yet be the correct one. Nevertheless, there is material here for serious advocacy in favour of supra-evidential fideism. This version of fideism may be recommended as enabling acceptance, in a judicious balance, of two widespread kinds of inclination found in developed human character—the inclination towards respect for evidence in making practical commitments about the facts, and inclinations towards overall views of the world whose truth could not in principle be established rationally on the basis of evidence.

## Hard-line evidentialism as grounded in doctrinaire naturalism

Hard-line evidentialists may, however, retort that they, too, allow acceptance of the two aforementioned kinds of inclinations: it is just that *their* 'judicious balance' allows passionately motivated practical commitment to only one world-view, the naturalist one. In response, fideists may perhaps suggest that hard-line evidentialism rests on a *doctrinaire* or *dogmatic* commitment to the naturalist world-view, and that dogmatic commitment to any optional view of the world is a moral fault. Commitment to naturalism as such need not be doctrinaire, of course—but non-doctrinaire naturalists will be naturalist supra-evidential fideists, not naturalist hard-line evidentialists.

This fideist perspective on the rival position is easily explained. As we have seen, *once* one is committed to the naturalist view of the world, there is *then* good reason to favour the view that passional religious doxastic inclinations are not apt guides to otherwise inaccessible vital truths. *Prior* to settling the choice between naturalist and theistic world-views, however, the question whether passional religious doxastic inclinations may guide us to vital truths *remains open*. But in holding that it is epistemically—and, hence, morally—impermissible to make religious faith-ventures, hard-line evidentialists ignore how things stand prior to determining the issue between naturalism and theism. Effectively, they take it that this prior position may properly be ignored, given that they have themselves settled in favour of naturalism. But, fideists will claim, to ignore the prior position in this way is to make a mistake—the mistake of being dogmatic. The hard-line evidentialist commitment to naturalism thus contrasts with that of non-dogmatic naturalists who retain the recognition that their own world-view commitment is a faith-venture that resolves a genuine option that could, equally permissibly, be resolved in favour of a theistic world-view.

Commitment to a naturalist view of the world is inevitably a doxastic (or sub-doxastic) venture in which one takes to be true what could not in principle be supported by evidence independent of such commitment. Hard-line evidentialists have no choice but to concede this, and must, of course, suppose that their own commitment to naturalism carries moral entitlement. Now, fideists will, of course, hold that a venture in favour of naturalism is permissible only if the conditions of (J+) are met. And, as I have already argued, accepting (J+) has pluralist consequences: those who take themselves to be entitled under (J+) to make a particular faith-venture will need to recognize that others could be equally entitled to make different, and incompatible, faith-ventures. So, naturalists will need to recognize that those who make incompatible ventures in favour of theistic world-views may meet the conditions of (J+). Of course, naturalists need not—and should not—concede that *every* theistic faith-venturer ventures with moral entitlement. Sometimes (J+)'s condition (iii) will fail—the type of passional motivation driving the theistic venture will be morally flawed. And sometimes it will be condition (iv) that is violated: correct morality will rule out the particular content of some theistic faith-ventures (indeed, I have already hinted at the possibility that, given their moral commitment, all *classical* theistic faith-ventures will, for some people, be ruled out under this condition). The point is, however, that it is highly implausible that committed naturalists could reasonably suppose that *no* theistic faith-venture could meet (J+)'s conditions. Dogmatic adherence to naturalism is thus unwarranted.

Furthermore, those who make faith-ventures that they judge to meet the conditions of thesis (J+) should do so in a spirit of openness to the possibility of revising their faith-commitments—*inter alia*, in the light of changing passional promptings. In Chapter 8, I argued that such openness—which, importantly, must not be equated with tentativeness of commitment—is required if faith-ventures are to be made with serious epistemic concern, as supra-evidentialists are committed to holding they should be. From the fideist point of view, any approach which lets passional promptings settle vital essentially evidentially undecidable options dogmatically, once and for all, is not consistent with taking those promptings seriously as guides to evidentially inaccessible truth.

Hard-line evidentialists, however, *do* dogmatically close off the possibility of revising their foundational naturalist faith-commitment. They take their passionally driven step, and then foreswear in the name of epistemic rational integrity all further passionally driven ventures. Their stance is to 'forget' that they ever had to make any passional commitment. This stance, their fideist opponents may suggest, may be motivated by a morally dubious desire to avoid the vulnerability and responsibility entailed by the risk of making faith-ventures. Much is at stake when we are faced with a Jamesian genuine option. We will naturally seek clear and reliable guidance in making so significant a decision—and the (necessary) failure of our epistemic rationality to provide evidence-based guidance will cause anxiety. Fideists may accuse hard-line evidentialists of dealing with that anxiety in a morally questionable way—namely, by urging that we may still do the rational thing by resisting all our purely passional inclinations as to the fundamental facts of our existence. This strategy, the fideist may claim, is morally dubious because it requires self-deception (studiedly 'forgetting' that commitment to a naturalist view of the world is itself passionally motivated); and also because it involves a kind of bad faith in which, out of fear, we suppress our recognition of our freedom to embrace the sheer contingency of our historically situated and potentially shifting passional religious (and similar) doxastic inclinations. There is a disturbing messiness about making serious commitments to religious and quasi-religious faith-propositions through passionally motivated doxastic venture: non-evidential causes sustain a wide variety of mutually incompatible beliefs, and we will be tempted to avoid the mess by taking the evidentialist stance that no such causes can possibly be guides to truth. But—the fideist may claim—the evidentialist urge to avoid the messiness is a temptation towards an inauthentic way of existence. Authentic human existence requires the courage to risk epistemically uncertifiable optional commitments. The morality of authenticity thus favours fideism—or so the fideist might maintain.

In reply, hard-line evidentialists might claim that they need fall into no self-deception or bad faith. They may concede that they themselves rest ultimately on passionally motivated doxastic venture in favour of a naturalist world-view. They may acknowledge the reality of our freedom to make commitments either in accordance with, or in resistance to, our passional doxastic inclinations generally. They may even agree that authentic human existence requires the courage to risk epistemically uncertifiable optional commitments. But they *themselves* exercise that courage, they will maintain, in passional commitment to a naturalistic view of the world that justifies keeping the messiness of passional commitment to the absolute minimum. That venture involves a risky renunciation of tempting religious and ideological impulses—and, it seems to them, exhibits heroic human integrity.

This reply, however, does not address the charge of dogmatism. For, just such a position as sketched in this reply is held by the non-doctrinaire committed naturalist who is also a supra-evidential fideist and thus morally tolerates (at least some) religious faith-ventures. From the perspective of the supra-evidential fideist, as I have argued, *dogmatic* faith-ventures show a failure of epistemic concern. But for hard-line evidentialists themselves, of course, dogmatic attachment to a naturalist view of the world is precisely what serious epistemic concern requires—for (they will maintain) we will be able to curb the epistemic distraction that the passional represents only when that foundational commitment is held utterly secure. The consideration that hard-line evidentialism rests on a dogmatic faith-venture in favour of naturalism is thus clearly not decisive. But it is a recommendation in fideism's favour that articulates what it is that fideists themselves find attractive about their view.

This outcome is hardly surprising, if there is indeed (as I argued in Chapter 8) an impasse over the question whether hard-line evidentialism is an epistemically responsible position. The hard-line evidentialists' dogmatic commitment to naturalism, of which fideists complain, is, for hard-line evidentialists, an epistemic merit. Fideists might perhaps enhance advocacy of their position, however, by suggesting that a dogmatic faith-venture in favour of naturalism is not only an epistemic failure, but also a failure in love.

Charles Taylor has recently suggested that James's defence of fideism may be understood as 'building on the Augustinian insight that in certain domains love and self-opening enable us to understand what we would never grasp otherwise'.[7] Augustine's principle *Non intratur in veritatem, nisi per caritatem*[8] may help identify just what it is that is morally flawed about dogmatic faith-ventures. A morality of love—of right relationship—may thus favour supra-evidential fideism over hard-line evidentialism. The suggestion (canvassed in the previous section) that fideism offers a more balanced self-acceptance than hard-line evidentialism might naturally be couched in terms of what the right kind of self-love requires. What is now immediately pertinent is the suggestion that, in the dogmatic adherence to naturalism which justifies their moral intolerance of religious faith-ventures, hard-line evidentialists are failing in the love of others. For, as I noted in Chapter 8, the 'schooling' of passional doxastic inclinations is something that takes place within a community where people are open to the influence of others in reviewing their commitments. Those who are doctrinaire and who make faith-ventures dogmatically, however, remove themselves from the kinds of mutual engagement that persons of faith ideally ought to have with one another—forms of mutual engagement and respectful conversation that may well be crucial for human moral and religious development. In thus cutting themselves off from others, they fail in love.

If considerations such as these do indeed show hard-line evidential-ism (based as it seems to be on a dogmatic commitment to a naturalist world-view) to be morally flawed, then it is worth noting that they may take us far enough to conclude that people *ought* to commit themselves in accordance with their own passional doxastic inclinations under the conditions expressed in thesis (J+), rather than merely be morally permit-ted so to do—which is all that thesis (J+) claims. Direct moral advocacy

---

[7] *Varieties of Religion Today*, 47.

[8] 'One does not enter into the truth except through love.' Quoted by Taylor from Augustine *Contra Faustum*, lib. 32, cap. 18.

of thesis (J+) against hard-line evidentialism might, that is, result in a strengthened, less irenic version of (J+).[9] Committing oneself (in a properly non-doctrinaire spirit) to one's morally authentic passional religious and quasi-religious promptings under (J+)'s conditions might turn out to be morally obligatory—if, for example, it emerged that resisting such promptings was indeed a failure in love. That would not, of course, render any *particular* faith-venture obligatory: the obligation would be to commit oneself in accordance with one's authentic non-evidential doxastic inclinations, *whatever they happen to be* (always assuming, of course, that (J+)'s conditions are fully met). Those passionally inclined to atheist/naturalist views of the world would meet their obligations by committing themselves accordingly: but they would not be justified in holding non-naturalist religious faith-ventures to be either epistemically or morally impermissible.

## Coherence amongst moral and religious passional commitments

A third moral consideration in favour of supra-evidential fideism is the suggestion that there is something not fully coherent about accepting that foundational moral commitments have a non-evidential, passional, basis while taking a hard-line evidentialist position about foundational factual commitments of a religious and similar kind.

My main focus in this inquiry has been on our entitlement to commit ourselves to religious, particularly theistic, claims. I have stressed, however, that this is but a paradigm case of faith-commitment generally: the fideism expressed in (J+) applies in principle to passionally motivated commitment to *any* essentially evidentially undecidable claim that presents a genuine option. Non-religious examples of such faith-ventures are to some degree controversial. Arguably, certain metaphysical commitments qualify (e.g. to libertarian free will, to moral realism), although some might consider that

---

[9] Note O'Connell's claim that James's justification of faith 'falls into a shambles' if we fail to notice its dependence on James's 'robust streak of deontologism': 'Central to any rightly formed character ... James contends, is the freely developed capacity for making ... ultimate choices [such as involved in faith-commitments] ... in the "strenuous" moral mood—a mood which ... makes us actually "want" a world that makes austere, sometimes even shattering demands on the slumbering hero dwelling in each one of us' (*William James on the Courage to Believe*, 125).

these questions are purely theoretical and cannot give rise to the kinds of morally significant genuine options with which (J+) is concerned. Less controversially, basic moral options require passional resolution—that will be the case, at any rate, if meta-ethical cognitivism is assumed, and rationalist forms of moral foundationalism are rejected. Many will thus take it for granted that it is morally permissible to settle options for basic *moral* commitments through inclinations that count as passional, rather than evidential.

But if one accepts passionally motivated doxastic venture in favour of basic moral claims, might it not then be discordant to maintain the hard-line evidentialist stance towards religious claims? It is true that foundational moral commitment is commitment to how things ought to be, while foundational religious commitment is (under realist assumptions, anyway) commitment to how things are. It is thus not simply arbitrary to admit doxastic venture with respect to the former while rejecting it with respect to the latter. Nevertheless, there seems something perverse about such a stance *when it comes to the specific case of those foundational religious claims that function to ground the hope that seeking to live in accordance with morality is not a pointless goal.* But that *does* seem to be a key role for religious belief—perhaps within all religious traditions, but certainly within the theistic ones.[10] Theistic religious belief does not, *pace* certain non-realists, simply reduce to moral belief: but it does make a claim about the world being, in a certain sense, a moral as well as a natural order. It affirms that the world is such that living morally well is not a mere ideal, but amounts to living in harmony with how things are, at the most ultimate and profound level. Such a claim is indeed evidentially ambiguous, and able to be embraced only through a faith-venture that is likely to meet all (J+)'s conditions.[11] And

---

[10] Compare Tim Chappell's view that the virtue of faith consists in its 'instantiat[ing] responsiveness to two basic goods; truth, and ... "practical hope"', where 'the condition of practical hope is the condition of believing that I am not, either continually or typically, confronted with situations in which my endeavours, both practical and intellectual, are either doomed to disaster from the start or else can make no possible difference' ('Why Is Faith a Virtue?' 548).

[11] There is little doubt that there can be morally respectable passional motivations for taking it to be true that moral commitment is not ultimately pointless, nor that such commitment will cohere with correct morality. One is inclined to intone with Sarastro: *Wen solche Lehren nicht erfreun verdienet nicht ein Mensch zu sein* (Mozart, *Die Zauberflöte*) [whoever does not delight in this teaching is not worthy of being human].

Compare Robert Adams ('Moral Faith', *Journal of Philosophy*, 92 (1995), 75–95) who notes the moral importance of commitment to beliefs such as that 'the good of different persons is not so irreconcilably competitive as to make it incoherent to have the good of all persons as an end' (81); and that 'actual

now my point is that to take the hard-line evidentialist stance by rejecting commitment to such a claim, while allowing passional commitment to basic moral claims, does not seem to belong to a *fully* coherent overall moral position. The notion of 'full coherence' appealed to here is, however, clearly more than strictly logical coherence, and hard-line evidentialists will no doubt protest that, whatever it is, they do not share it. From their perspective, there is nothing discordant about accepting passionally motivated commitment to basic moral claims themselves, but not to claims about the world that would secure the worth of moral commitment. They are willing—even eager—to accept that people should lead the moral life without commitment to any foundational truths about the world that justify the hope that so doing has real point. So this third consideration, like the first two, fails to be decisive. Yet, again like the first two, it does provide material for advocating fideism, by drawing attention to a feature of the fideist position aptly understood as commending it as a moral stance superior to the rival hard-line evidentialist view.

## Conclusion

Contrary views of human nature and the world undergird the clash between supra-evidential fideist acceptance and hard-line evidentialist rejection of religious (and similar) faith-ventures. Fideists take it that passional doxastic inclinations in favour of religious (and similar) claims do have the potential to lead us to commitment to vital evidentially inaccessible truths. Evidentialists take it that the world is not like that: passional promptings have no truth-conducive potential, not even in the context of essentially evidentially undecidable genuine options.

I have argued that, when these contrary factual commitments are evaluated epistemically, neither emerges as decisively preferable on grounds that

---

causal circumstances are not so adverse, all things considered, as to preclude realization of the moral ends' (83). Adams does not, however, suggest that such claims require *religious* faith-commitment. Yet defending just that view may be what Adams needs to meet the criticism made by Jonathan Adler—namely that we do not need to venture beyond our evidence in order to commit ourselves to views about the world which secure the point of morality. Adler put his point thus: 'reflections on the Prisoner's Dilemma, and far from that alone, show that a great deal of morality can be based on the solid, but minimal, foundations of reasonable self-interest, appreciation of the benefits and vulnerabilities of co-operation, and a normal range of intelligence and sentiments' (*Belief's Own Ethics*, 226).

could be agreed between the opposing sides of the debate. Evidentialists cannot establish that it is epistemically irresponsible to take the fideist view that passional doxastic inclinations may lead us to evidentially inaccessible vital truths. But then neither can fideists establish that commitment to the contrary evidentialist view lacks epistemic entitlement—provided, that is, that evidentialists acknowledge that their claim that passional doxastic inclinations cannot conduce to evidentially inaccessible truths ultimately depends on a faith-venture in favour of a naturalist view of the world and (therefore) requires a qualification that admits that undergirding venture as the sole exception.

In this final chapter, I have argued that arriving at such an impasse may be enough to secure a requirement for a mutual, broadly political tolerance between supra-evidential fideism and hard-line moral evidentialism. And that may indeed be sufficient to achieve a worthwhile rehabilitation of fideism of the James-inspired supra-evidential, moral coherentist variety I have articulated in thesis (J+). I have suggested, however, that direct *moral* considerations may be produced which at least recommend the supra-evidential fideist over the hard-line evidentialist position, such as the consideration that fideism involves a more balanced self-acceptance of developed human nature. Furthermore, hard-line evidentialism seems to rest on *dogmatic* commitment to naturalism: but, from a fideist perspective, it is arguable that making any faith-venture dogmatically is an epistemic failure, and even, perhaps, a failure in love towards others. Finally, I have suggested that hard-line evidentialism as applied to certain kinds of religious claim may not be fully coherent if combined with the view that commitment to the truth of basic moral claims requires doxastic venture. Fideists will think it perverse to hold that, although we commit ourselves to basic claims about the good and the right by faith, we would do wrong to take it be true, essentially beyond any possible evidence, that the world is a moral order having real features that ground the hope that commitment to the good and the right is not ultimately pointless.

None of these considerations, however, decisively defeats the hard-line moral evidentialism that rejects religious faith-ventures as epistemically and morally impermissible. These considerations do, however, make it intelligible that people fully committed to the epistemic goal may have a serious moral preference for supra-evidential fideism over the hard-line moral evidentialism that rejects religious faith-ventures, allowing only supra-evidential venture in favour of a naturalist view of the world. Reflective theists will thus be able to assure themselves that the claim that their faith-ventures are morally justifiable—provided they meet (J+)'s conditions—is not simply undefeated by evidentialist argument, but deserving of positive endorsement.

# Bibliography

Adams, Robert, 'Moral Faith', *Journal of Philosophy*, 92 (1995): 75–95.

Adler, Jonathan, *Belief's Own Ethics* (Cambridge, MA: MIT Press, 2002).

Alston, William P., 'A "Doxastic Practice" Approach to Epistemology', in M. Clay and K. Lehrer (eds), *Knowledge and Skepticism* (Boulder, CO: Westview Press, 1989), 1–30.

——, *Perceiving God: The Epistemology of Religious Experience* (Ithaca, NY: Cornell University Press, 1991).

—— 'Belief, Acceptance and Religious Faith', in Jeff Jordan and Daniel Howard-Snyder (eds), *Faith, Freedom and Rationality: Philosophy of Religion Today* (Lanham, MD: Rowman & Littlefield, 1996), 3–28.

Amesbury, Richard, 'Fideism', in Edward N. Zalta (ed.), *The Stanford Encyclopedia of Philosophy* (*Summer 2005 Edition*), <http://plato.stanford.edu/archives/sum2005/entries/fideism/>.

Atran, Scott, *In Gods We Trust: The Evolutionary Landscape of Religion*, Evolution and Cognition (New York: Oxford University Press, 2002).

Bishop, John, *Natural Agency: An Essay on the Causal Theory of Action* (Cambridge: Cambridge University Press, 1989).

—— 'Naturalising Mental Action', in Ghita Holmström-Hintikka and Raimo Tuomela (eds), *Contemporary Action Theory, Volume 1*, Synthèse Library (Dordrecht: Kluwer Academic Publishers, 1997), 251–66.

—— 'Can There Be Alternative Concepts of God?' *Noûs*, 32 (1998): 174–88.

—— 'Faith as Doxastic Venture', *Religious Studies*, 38 (2002): 471–87.

—— 'Believing by Faith and the Concept of God', in Ree Boddé and Hugh Kempster (eds), *Thinking Outside the Square: Church in Middle Earth* (Auckland: St Columba's Press and Journeyings, 2003), 1–11.

—— 'On the Possibility of Doxastic Venture: a Reply to Buckareff', *Religious Studies*, 41 (2005): 447–51.

—— 'The Philosophy of Religion: A Programmatic Overview', *Philosophy Compass*, 1 (2006), 506–34 <http://www.blackwell-synergy.com/doi/full/10.1111/j.1747-9991.2006.00039.x>.

—— and Aijaz, Imran, 'How to Answer the *De Jure* Question about Christian Belief', *International Journal for Philosophy of Religion*, 56 (2004), 109–29.

BonJour, Laurence, *Epistemology: Classic Problems and Contemporary Responses* (Lanham, MD: Rowman and Littlefield, 2002).

—— 'Internalism and Externalism', in Paul K. Moser (ed.), *The Oxford Handbook of Epistemology* (New York: Oxford University Press, 2002).

Boyer, Pascal, *Religion Explained: The Evolutionary Origins of Religious Thought* (New York: Basic Books, 2001).

Braine, David, *The Reality of Time and the Existence of God: The Project of Proving God's Existence* (Oxford: Oxford University Press, 1988).

Braithwaite, R. B., 'An Empiricist's View of the Nature of Religious Belief', in Basil Mitchell (ed.), *The Philosophy of Religion* (Oxford: Oxford University Press, 1971), 72–91.

Buckareff, Andrei, 'Can Faith Be a Doxastic Venture?' *Religious Studies*, 41 (2005): 435–45.

Burleigh, Michael, *The Third Reich: A New History* (New York: Hill and Wang, 2000).

Chappell, Tim, 'Why is Faith a Virtue?' in Charles Taliaferro and Paul J. Griffiths (eds), *Philosophy of Religion: An Anthology* (Malden, MA: Blackwell, 2003), 546–52. (Originally published in *Religious Studies*, 32 (1996): 27–36.)

Chignell, Andrew, 'Epistemology for Saints', <http:/www.christianitytoday.com/bc/2002/002/10.20.html>, accessed 2005.

Clifford, William Kingdon, 'The Ethics of Belief', in Leslie Stephen and Frederick Pollock (eds), *Lectures and Essays of the Late William Kingdon Clifford*, Volume 2 (London: Macmillan, 1879), 177–211.

Code, Lorraine, *Epistemic Responsibility* (Hanover, NH: University Press of New England, 1987).

Cohen, L. Jonathan, *An Essay on Belief and Acceptance* (Oxford: Clarendon Press, 1992).

Conee, Earl, 'The Basic Nature of Epistemic Justification', in Earl Conee and Richard Feldman (eds), *Evidentialism: Essays in Epistemology* (Oxford: Clarendon Press, 2004), 37–52.

—— and Richard Feldman, 'Internalism Defended', in Earl Conee and Richard Feldman (eds), *Evidentialism: Essays in Epistemology* (Oxford: Clarendon Press, 2004), 53–82.

Conee, Earl, and Feldman, Richard (eds), *Evidentialism: Essays in Epistemology* (Oxford: Clarendon Press, 2004).

Craig, William Lane, *The Kalām Cosmological Argument* (New York: Barnes and Noble, 1979).

Crumley, Jack S. (ed.), *Readings in Epistemology* (Mountain View, CA: Mayfield, 1999).

Cupitt, Don, *Taking Leave of God* (London: SCM Press, 1980).

Davis, Stephen T., *Faith, Skepticism, and Evidence: An Essay in Religious Epistemology* (Lewisburg: Bucknell University Press, 1978).

—— *God, Reason, and Theistic Proofs* (Grand Rapids, MI: W. B. Eerdmans Publishers, 1997).

Dole, Andrew, and Chignell, Andrew, 'The Ethics of Religious Belief: A Recent History', in Andrew Dole and Andrew Chignell (eds), *God and the Ethics of Religious Belief: New Essays in Philosophy of Religion* (Cambridge: Cambridge University Press, 2005), 1–27.

Draper, Paul, 'The Skeptical Theist', in Daniel Howard-Snyder (ed.), *The Evidential Argument from Evil* (Bloomington, IN: Indiana University Press, 1996), 175–92.

Earman, John, *Hume's Abject Failure: The Argument against Miracles* (New York: Oxford University Press, 2000).

Evans, C. Stephen, *Faith Beyond Reason: A Kierkegaardian Account* (Grand Rapids, MI: W. B. Eerdmans Publishers, 1998).

Feldman, Richard, 'The Ethics of Belief', in Earl Conee and Richard Feldman (eds), *Evidentialism: Essays in Epistemology* (Oxford: Clarendon Press, 2004), 166–95.

——— 'Clifford's Principle and James's Options', *Social Epistemology*, 20 (2006): 19–33.

Flew, Antony, 'The Presumption of Atheism', in id., *The Presumption of Atheism, and Other Philosophical Essays on God, Freedom and Immortality* (London: Elek for Pemberton, 1976), 13–30.

Fodor, Jerry A., *The Mind Doesn't Work That Way: The Scope and Limits of Computational Psychology* (Cambridge, MA: MIT Press, 2000).

Gale, Richard M., *The Divided Self of William James* (Cambridge: Cambridge University Press, 1999).

Golding, Joshua L., 'Toward a Pragmatic Conception of Religious Faith', *Faith and Philosophy*, 7 (1990): 486–503.

——— *Rationality and Religious Theism* (Aldershot, Hants and Burlington VT: Ashgate, 2003).

Goldman, Alvin, 'What Is Justified Belief?' in George Sotiros Pappas (ed.), *Justification and Knowledge: New Studies in Epistemology* (Dordrecht, Holland: D. Reidel, 1979), 1–23.

Greco, John, 'Virtue Epistemology', in Edward N. Zalta (ed.), *The Stanford Encyclopedia of Philosophy* (*Winter 2004 Edition*), <http://plato.stanford.edu/archives/win2004/entries/epistemology-virtue/>.

Griffiths, Paul J., 'Religious Identity: Introduction', in Charles Taliaferro and Paul J. Griffiths (eds), *Philosophy of Religion: An Anthology* (Malden, MA: Blackwell, 2003).

Gutting, Gary, *Religious Belief and Religious Skepticism* (Notre Dame, IN: University of Notre Dame Press, 1982).

Hájek, Alan, 'Pascal's, Wager', in Edward N. Zalta (ed.), *The Stanford Encyclopedia of Philosophy* (Spring 2004 Edition) <http://plato.stanford.edu/archives/spr2004/entries/pascal-wager/>

Helm, Paul, *Faith with Reason* (Oxford: Oxford University Press, 2000).

Hick, John, *Faith and Knowledge*, 2nd edition (Ithaca, NY: Cornell University Press, 1966).

_____ 'Eschatological Verification Reconsidered', *Religious Studies*, 13 (1977): 189–202.

_____ *An Interpretation of Religion: Human Responses to the Transcendent* (London: Macmillan, 1989).

Houston, J., *Reported Miracles: A Critique of Hume* (Cambridge: Cambridge University Press, 1994).

Howard-Snyder, Daniel (ed.), *The Evidential Argument from Evil* (Bloomington, IN: Indiana University Press, 1996).

_____ and Paul K. Moser (eds), *Divine Hiddenness: New Essays* (Cambridge: Cambridge University Press, 2002).

Hume, David, *Enquiry Concerning Human Understanding* (ed.) P. H. Nidditch, 3rd edition (Clarendon Press, Oxford, 1975).

Insole, Christopher, 'Kierkegaard: A Reasonable Fideist?' *Heythrop Journal*, 39 (1998): 363–78.

James, William, 'Faith and the Right to Believe', in id., *Some Problems of Philosophy: A Beginning of an Introduction to Philosophy* (New York: Longmans, Green, 1911), 221–31.

_____ 'Is Life Worth Living?' in id., *The Will to Believe and Other Essays in Popular Philosophy, and Human Immortality* (New York: Dover, 1956), 32–62.

_____ 'The Sentiment of Rationality', in id., *The Will to Believe and Other Essays in Popular Philosophy, and Human Immortality* (New York: Dover, 1956), 63–110.

_____ 'The Will to Believe', in id., *The Will to Believe and Other Essays in Popular Philosophy, and Human Immortality* (New York: Dover, 1956), 1–31.

_____ *Pragmatism* (Cambridge, MA: Harvard University Press, 1975).

_____ *Essays in Philosophy* (Cambridge, MA: Harvard University Press, 1978).

Johnson, David, *Hume, Holism and Miracles* (Ithaca, NY: Cornell University Press, 1999).

Jordan, Jeff, 'Pragmatic Arguments and Belief', *American Philosophical Quarterly*, 33 (1996): 409–20.

Kaplan, Mark, *Decision Theory as Philosophy* (Cambridge: Cambridge University Press, 1996).

Kenny, Anthony, *What Is Faith? Essays in the Philosophy of Religion* (New York: Oxford University Press, 1992).

Kierkegaard, Søren, *Concluding Unscientific Postscript*, trans. David F. Swenson and Walter Lowrie (Princeton: Princeton University Press, 1968).

_____ *Fear and Trembling*, trans. Alastair Hannay (Harmondsworth, Middlesex: Penguin Books, 1985); first published 1843.

Kretzmann, Norman, 'Evidence against Anti-Evidentialism', in Kelly James Clark (ed.), *Our Knowledge of God: Essays on Natural and Philosophical Theology* (Dordrecht: Kluwer Academic Publishers, 1992), 17–38.

Kvanvig, Jonathan L., *Warrant in Contemporary Epistemology: Essays in Honor of Plantinga's Theory of Knowledge* (Lanham, MD: Rowman & Littlefield Publishers, 1996).

Mackie, J. L., *Problems from Locke* (Oxford: Clarendon Press, 1976).

—— *The Miracle of Theism: Arguments For and Against the Existence of God* (Oxford: Oxford University Press, 1982).

Madden, Peter, 'Introduction', William James, *The Will to Believe and Other Essays in Popular Philosophy* (Cambridge, MA: Harvard University Press, 1979).

Malcolm, Norman, 'The Groundlessness of Belief', in R. Douglas Geivett and Brendan Sweetman (eds), *Contemporary Perspectives on Religious Epistemology* (New York: Oxford University Press, 1992), 92–103. (Originally published in Stuart C. Brown (ed.), *Reason and Religion* (Ithaca, NY: Cornell University Press, 1977), 143–57.)

—— *Thought and Knowledge: Essays* (Ithaca, NY: Cornell University Press, 1977).

Mavrodes, George I., 'James and Clifford on "the Will to Believe"', *The Personalist*, 44 (1963): 191–8.

McKim, Robert, *Religious Ambiguity and Religious Diversity* (Oxford: Oxford University Press, 2001).

Miller, Barry, *From Existence to God: A Contemporary Philosophical Argument* (London: Routledge, 1992).

Morris, Thomas V., 'Agnosticism', *Analysis*, 45 (1985): 219–24.

Nielsen, Kai, 'Wittgensteinian Fideism', *Philosophy*, 42 (1967): 191–209.

—— *God, Scepticism, and Modernity* (Ottawa: University of Ottawa Press, 1989).

O'Connell, Robert J., *William James on the Courage to Believe*, 2nd edition (New York: Fordham University Press, 1997).

Penelhum, Terence, 'Reflections on the Ambiguity of the World', in Arvind Sharma (ed.), *God, Truth, and Reality: Essays in Honour of John Hick* (New York: St Martin's Press, 1993), 165–75.

—— *Reason and Religious Faith* (Boulder, CO: Westview Press, 1995).

Percival, Philip, 'The Pursuit of the Epistemic Good', in Michael Brady and Duncan Pritchard (eds), *Moral and Epistemic Virtues* (Oxford: Blackwell, 2003), 29–46.

Peterson, Michael L. and VanArragon, Raymond J. (eds), *Contemporary Debates in Philosophy of Religion* (Malden, MA: Blackwell, 2004).

Phillips, D. Z., *The Concept of Prayer* (London: Routledge & Kegan Paul, 1965).

—— *Faith and Philosophical Enquiry* (London: Routledge & Kegan Paul, 1970).

Plantinga, Alvin, 'Reason and Belief in God', in Alvin Plantinga and Nicholas Wolterstorff (eds), *Faith and Rationality: Reason and Belief in God* (Notre Dame: University of Notre Dame Press, 1983), 16–93.

\_\_\_\_ 'Is Belief in God Properly Basic?' in R. Douglas Geivett and Brendan Sweetman (eds), *Contemporary Perspectives on Religious Epistemology* (New York: Oxford University Press, 1992), 133–41. Originally published in *Noûs*, 25 (1981), 41–51.

\_\_\_\_ *Warrant: The Current Debate* (New York: Oxford University Press, 1993).

\_\_\_\_ *Warranted Christian Belief* (Oxford: Oxford University Press, 2000).

Plantinga, Alvin, and Nicholas Wolterstorff (eds), *Faith and Rationality: Reason and Belief in God* (Notre Dame: University of Notre Dame Press, 1983).

Pojman, Louis, 'Faith without Belief?' *Faith and Philosophy*, 3 (1986): 157–76.

\_\_\_\_ 'Faith, Doubt and Belief, or Does Faith Entail Belief?' in Richard M. Gale and Alexander R. Pruss (eds), *The Existence of God* (Aldershot, Hants, Burlington, VT: Ashgate/Dartmouth, 2003), 1–15.

Putnam, Hilary, *Mind, Language, and Reality* (Cambridge: Cambridge University Press, 1975).

Quinn, Philip L., 'Can Good Christians Be Good Liberals?' in Andrew Dole and Andrew Chignell (eds), *God and the Ethics of Belief: New Essays in Philosophy of Religion* (Cambridge: Cambridge University Press, 2005), 248–76.

Rowe, William L., 'The Problem of Evil and Some Varieties of Atheism', *American Philosophical Quarterly*, 16 (1979): 335–41.

Ruben, David-Hillel, *Action and its Explanation* (Oxford: Clarendon Press, 2003).

Russell, Bertrand, *History of Western Philosophy: and its Connections with Political and Social Circumstances from the Earliest Times to the Present Day* (London: Allen & Unwin, 1946).

Schellenberg, J. L., *Divine Hiddenness and Human Reason* (Ithaca, NY: Cornell University Press, 1993).

Scriven, Michael, *Primary Philosophy* (New York: McGraw-Hill, 1966).

Smart, J. J. C., and Haldane, John, *Atheism and Theism* (Oxford: Blackwell, 1996; 2nd edition 2002).

Sosa, Ernest, *Knowledge in Perspective: Selected Essays in Epistemology* (Cambridge: Cambridge University Press, 1991).

\_\_\_\_ 'Knowledge and Intellectual Virtue', in id., *Knowledge in Perspective* (Cambridge: Cambridge University Press, 1991), 225–4.

Swinburne, Richard, *The Coherence of Theism* (Oxford: Clarendon Press, 1977, revised 1993).

\_\_\_\_ *The Existence of God* (Oxford: Clarendon Press, 1977, 2nd edition 2004).

\_\_\_\_ *Faith and Reason* (Oxford: Clarendon Press, 1981, 2nd edition 2005).

\_\_\_\_ *Miracles* (London: Collier Macmillan, 1989).

Swinburne, Richard *Responsibility and Atonement* (Oxford: Clarendon Press, 1989).

——*Revelation: From Metaphor to Analogy* (Oxford: Clarendon Press, 1992).

——*The Christian God* (Oxford: Clarendon Press, 1994).

——*Providence and the Problem of Evil* (Oxford: Clarendon Press, 1998).

——'Plantinga on Warrant', *Religious Studies*, 37 (2001): 203–14.

Talbott, Thomas, *The Inescapable Love of God* (USA: Universal Publishers/ uPUBLISH.com, 1999).

Talbott, William, 'Bayesian Epistemology', in Edward N. Zalta (ed.), *The Stanford Encyclopedia of Philosophy (Fall 2001 Edition)*, <http://plato.stanford. edu/archives/fall2001/entries/epistemology-bayesian/>.

Taliaferro, Charles, *Contemporary Philosophy of Religion* (Malden, MA: Blackwell, 1998).

Taylor, Charles, *Varieties of Religion Today: William James Revisited* (Cambridge, MA: Harvard University Press, 2002).

Tertullian, *De Carne Christi*, trans. Ernest Evans (London: S.P.C.K., 1956).

Tilghman, Benjamin R., *An Introduction to the Philosophy of Religion* (Oxford: Blackwell, 1994).

Tillich, Paul, *Dynamics of Faith* (New York: HarperCollins, 1957; 2001 edition).

Vanden Burgt, Robert J., *The Religious Philosophy of William James* (Chicago: Nelson-Hall, 1981).

Wainwright, William J., *Reason and the Heart: A Prolegomenon to a Critique of Passional Reason* (Ithaca, NY: Cornell University Press, 1995).

Williams, Bernard, 'Deciding to Believe', in id., *Problems of the Self: Philosophical Papers 1956–1972* (Cambridge: Cambridge University Press, 1973), 136–51.

——'The Makropulos Case: Reflections on the Tedium of Immortality', in id., *Problems of the Self: Philosophical Papers 1956–1972* (Cambridge: Cambridge University Press, 1973), 82–100.

Wittgenstein, Ludwig, *On Certainty* (ed.) G. E. M. Anscombe and G. H. von Wright, trans. Denis Paul and G. E. M. Anscombe (Oxford: Blackwell, 1969).

Wolterstorff, Nicholas, *John Locke and the Ethics of Belief* (Cambridge: Cambridge University Press, 1996).

Wykstra, Stephen J., 'Rowe's Noseeum Arguments from Evil', in Daniel Howard-Snyder (ed.), *The Evidential Argument from Evil* (Bloomington, IN: Indiana University Press, 1996), 126–50.

——'On Behalf of the Evidentialist: A Reply to Wolterstorff', in D. Z. Phillips and Timothy Tessin (eds), *Philosophy of Religion in the 21st Century* (New York: Palgrave, 2001), 64–84.

Wynn, Mark, *Emotional Experience and Religious Understanding: Integrating Perception Conception and Feeling* (Cambridge: Cambridge University Press, 2005).

# Index

Abraham, forebear in faith 170–3
acceptance
  believing acceptance 110 n.17
  contrasted with belief 34 n.12
  and inner assent 41 n.
acting on an assumption 34 n.12, 39–40,
  42–3, 110, 113
Adams, Robert 226 n.11
Adler, Jonathan 63 n.10, 115 n.25, 132 n.,
  226 n.11
aesthetic values 165
affective states, influencing judgements of
  evidential support 74 n.29, 96 n.,
  198–9
agency-focused notions, see epistemic
  evaluation
agent-causation 36
agnosticism 77–8
Aijaz, Imran 85 n.12, 94 n.29, 211 n.1
alpinist 136, 153
Alston, William 2 n., 34 n.12; 81 n.88 n.17,
  89
ambiguity thesis, see evidential ambiguity,
  of theism
Aquinas 41 n., 93 n.27, 105 n.7; see also
  faith, Thomist model
argument from divine hiddenness 73 n.29
argument from evil 70 n.21, 72
  and argument from divine
    hiddenness 73 n.29
  and the gift of faith 116 n.
  and moral constraints on theistic
    faith-ventures 168–9, 210
argument from religious experience 72
atheism, presumption in favour of 77
atheology, see natural atheology
Atran, Scott 91 n.23
Augustine 44 n., 224
authenticity 217, 219, 223

bad faith 222–3
Bayesianism 36 n.13, 128
basically evident beliefs, see belief(s),
  basically versus inferentially evident

belief(s)
  avowal of 39, 41 n.18
  basically versus inferentially evident 19,
    23, 86; see also belief(s), properly
    basic
  causal, see causal beliefs
  conceptually related to evidential
    support 115 n.25
  contrasted with acceptance 34 n.12
  control over, see doxastic control
  culpable and inculpable, see doxastic
    responsibilities
  degrees of 12, 128–9, 131, 134, 138,
    142 n.
  detection of 153
  ethics of, see ethics of belief
  evaluative 114, 164, 170, 192–3, 200–1,
    226
    constrained by factual beliefs 200–1
  held on authority 62
  moral, see belief(s), evaluative
  ordinary and philosophical senses of 6 n.,
    29–30
  partial, see partial beliefs
  passional causes of, see passional causes of
    belief
  perceptual 84, 87, 88–92, 130 n., 189
  properly basic 86, 93, 95
    specified by norms of evidential
      practice 66, 88
  rational causes of 113
  responsibility for, see doxastic
    responsibilities
  self-induced 32, 118–9, 153, 185 n.12
  suspension of 71 n., 78 n., 130, 132, 139,
    194
  tentative 148, 168
  theistic see theistic beliefs
  thick versus thin 48 n.23
  well-founded 58 n.5
belief policies 31 n.
believing at will, impossibility of 30
believing by faith
  defined 3–4, 7

believing by faith   *(cont.)*
  not a matter of voluntarily inducing
    belief 11–12, 117
  *see also* doxastic venture; sub-doxastic
    venture
Biblical literalists 136 *n.*14, 152, 157, 200
blameworthiness, in relation to beliefs, *see*
  doxastic responsibilities
BonJour, Laurence 61 *n.*
Boris, with correct beliefs about Second
  Coming 61 *n.*
Boyer, Pascal 91 *n.*23
Braine, David 70 *n.*19
Braithwaite, Richard 83 *n.*10
Buckareff, Andrei 111 *n.*18
Burleigh, Michael 163 *n.*8

Calvin, John 93 *n.*27, 104
Cartesian doubt 89, 90
causal beliefs 107 *n.*
causal theory of action, applied to
  takings-to-be true 38 *n.*
cause, final 184
Chappell, Tim 106 *n.*9, 226 *n.*10
Chignell, Andrew 1 *n.*, 98 *n.*
circularity, epistemic, *see* epistemic
  circularity
Clifford, William Kingdon 45 *n.*, 64 *n.*,
  123, 145
Code, Lorraine 31 *n.*
Cognitive Decision Theory 191 *n.*
cognitive evidentialism 64 *n.*; *see also*
  evidentialism
cognitivism 83, 144–5, 167 *n.*, 170
Cohen, Jonathan 34 *n.* 12, 39 *n.*, 41 *n.*
coherence
  abandoned under counter-evidential
    fideism 156
  of evaluative beliefs 200–1
coherentism, *see* foundationalism,
  epistemic, contrasted with
  coherentism, holism
commitment, practical (to truth-claims)
  compelled and uncompelled 90–2,
    116–18, 189
  *see also* experimental commitments;
    faith-commitment; taking to be
    true
Connee, Earl 27 *n.*3, 28 *n.*5, 58 *n.*5,
  63 *n.*10
consequentialism

as justifying faith-ventures 15, 118,
  137 *n.*17, 152–3, 185–7, 215–6
objected to as failing to guide action 186
cosmological argument 72
counter-evidential fideism, *see* fideism,
  counter-evidential
Craig, William Lane 70 *n.*19
creationism 136 *n.*14, 152
credences, *see* partial beliefs
Cupitt, Don 55 *n.*

dark night of the soul 120
daunting tasks 154
Davis, Stephen T. 72 *n.*27, 118 *n.*28,
  127 *n.*7, 148 *n.*, 178 *n.*, 179 *n.*, 184 *n.*
deciding for oneself as deciding for all 50
deciding to believe, *see* believing at will
decision theory 128, 131, 191 *n.*
*de facto* and *de jure* objections to Christian
  belief 49 *n.*25
degrees of belief, challenge to forced
  options in practical reasoning 128–9,
  131
*de jure* question, in relation to
  faith-beliefs 49, 52
Descartes, René 41 *n.*, 90
devils, as possessing faith 105, 111 *n.*19
disambiguation, of the world, as between
  theism and naturalism 71, 102 *n.*,
  141
Divine Command Theory
  (meta-ethical) 85 *n.*12, 210–11
dogmatism
  to be avoided in faith-ventures 148–9,
    168, 204, 210, 222
  in evidentialist commitment to
    naturalism? 220–2
  not implied by full
    faith-commitment 120
Dole, Andrew 1 *n.*
doubt, *see* Cartesian doubt; faith, involving
  doubt and risk
doxascope (belief detector) 153
doxastic control 8, 28–41, 51
  direct, impossibility of 30, 117
  in formulation of evidentialism 63–4
  indirect (at 'first locus') 31–2, 118
  and inner assent 41 *n.*
  in practical reasoning (at 'second
    locus') 35–41, 111; *see also* doxastic
    venture

doxastic frameworks
  defined 19, 79–80
  moral 170
  theistic 80–1, 138–9
    in isolationist epistemology 81–2
    in Reformed epistemology 96
    under integrationist values 158
  see also framing principles
doxastic practice
  defined 20, 81
  sensory perceptual, as compared with
    theistic 88–92
  theistic
    psychologically avoidable 91, 96,
      97–8
    requiring genuine venture 92
doxastic responsibilities
  as arising from control over practical
    reasoning 35, 38, 42
  as epistemic (a standard view) 31–2, 42,
    48, 51–2
  exercised culpably or inculpably 59 n. 6,
    65 n., 93 n.28
  as moral responsibilities in relation to
    faith-beliefs 44–51, 75
  as practical responsibilities 44, 46
doxastic venture
  conceptual possibility of 111, 135
  conscious and unconscious 107–8
  counter-evidential 135–6, 137 n.17,
    146
    dangers of 155–6
    not absolutely prohibited 152–5, 158
    open to consequentialist
      justification 186
  defined 9, 11–12, 19, 78–9, 106–7
  distinct from 'leap', self-induced
    belief 112, 116–9, 208
  as embracing evidential deficiency 109
  as entailing recognized lack of evidential
    support 108
  epistemic entitlement to 162
  in favour of faith-propositions 145
  freely chosen 116
  in moral commitment 170
  moral permissibility of 122
    extrapolated from cases of
      interpersonal trust 145–6, 180–1
    general account eschewed 146
    implications of epistemological
      externalism for 64–5

linked to permissibility of
    counter-evidential venture 151
  subject to evidentalist
    presumption 123, 125
  see also Jamesian fideism
  in personal relations 14–15, 145–6,
    180–5, 199
  presupposing belief already held 117,
    119, 208
  psychic resources needed for 115–6
  psychological possibility of 102, 111–9
  relative to norms of implicitly accepted
    evidential practice 107, 156
  required for theistic faith-
    commitment 92, 96–100, 101
  supra-evidential 137; see also Jamesian
    fideism
  see also faith, doxastic venture model
doxastic voluntarism 51 n.; see also doxastic
  control
Draper, Paul 72 n.26
duck-rabbit 71

Edwards, Jonathan 74 n.29
egotism 106
emotions
  as causes of belief 114
  their significance for religious
    belief 115 n.24
epistemic capacities, right exercise
  of 161–2, 177, 194, 198 n.
epistemic circularity
  in natural theology and atheology 71–3
  in Plantinga's answer to de jure question
    about Christian belief 94–6
epistemic concern (to gain truth and avoid
  error) 152, 156, 160–2, 193–5, 198,
  204, 212; see also ethical suspension of
  the epistemic
epistemic entitlement
  defined 20, 56–61
  not uniformly sufficient for morally
    permissible practical
    commitment 69 n.18
  required for morally permissible
    supra-evidential venture 161, 177,
    186
  see also moral-epistemic link principle
epistemic evaluation, agency- versus
  propositional-attitude-focused 19,
  56–7, 60–2

epistemic evaluation, agency- *versus*
    propositional-attitude-focused  (*cont.*)
  applied to scepticism about perceptual
    beliefs  90
  in critique of Plantinga's theory of
    warranted Christian belief  96
  as opening conceptual space for
    supra-evidential fideism  177
epistemic evidentialism
  argument for  58–60
  component in moral evidentialism  64
  defined  20, 161
  denied by Jamesian fideism  161–2
  as expressing integrationist ideal  161
  externalist critique of  60–2
  in relation to isolationist
    epistemology  84–5
  met in cases of interpersonal trust  180
  met when taking p to be true is necessary
    for p's coming to be true  182–3
epistemic insulation  157–8; *see also*
    isolationist epistemology
epistemic justifiability  26–8, 58 *n*.3; *see also*
    epistemic entitlement; epistemic
    evidentialism; evidential justification;
    faith-beliefs, justifiability of, as
    epistemic issue
epistemic worth, of a belief  60–1; *see also*
    externalism, epistemological
epistemological imperialism  89
epistemology, isolationist, *see* isolationist
    epistemology
epistemology, Reformed, *see* Reformed
    epistemology
error
  risk of  181–3, 185, 190, 191–2, 193
    compared with risk of loss of truth  194
ethical evidentialism  64 *n*.; *see also* moral
    evidentialism
ethical suspension of the epistemic  27 *n*.2,
    53–4, 69 *n*.18, 152–5, 158, 161–2,
    177, 186
ethics of belief  44–7; *see also*
    faith-commitment, ethics of
evaluative beliefs, *see* beliefs, evaluative
Evans, C. Stephen  97 *n*.34, 135 *n*.
evidence
  broad and narrow notions of  66, 157
  counterbalanced  132 *n*.
  does not decide, *see* evidential
    undecidability

going beyond but not against  132, 156
moral  167 *n*.
*see also* epistemic justifiability; evidential
    practice; evidential support
evidential ambiguity
  defined  20
  of theism
    affecting debate between fideists and
      evidentialists  206
    consistent with epistemic worth of
      theistic belief  95
    defended as plausible  70–4, 102, 226
    implications of, for reflective
      theists  74–5, 77, 92, 169, 176 *n*.
    as necessary  140–3
    responses to
      fideist  2, 78, 99–100, 101–2
      in terms of specifically theistic
        evidential practice  78–99
evidential justification
  defined  21, 58–9, 62
  governed by objective norms  65–6
  not entailed by epistemic
    inculpability  59 *n*.6, 65 *n*., 93 *n*.28
  as related to doxastic venture  106–7
evidential practice
  defined  21, 57–8
  entitlement to  88–9
  moral  167 *n*.
  objective norms implicit in  65–6
  and passional beliefs  114 *n*.23, 199, 201
  presupposed by doxastic venture  107
  presupposed by evidentialist
    requirements  65
  rational empiricist  10, 24, 66–8
    applied to theistic beliefs  68–70, 79
    extended in Reformed
      epistemology  86–7
  theistic  79–99, 147, 199
evidential proportion *versus* evidential
    deficiency models of faith, *see* faith,
    evidential proportion models; faith,
    evidential deficiency models
evidential support
  commitment beyond  107, 132; *see also*
    doxastic venture; sub-doxastic venture
  as determining rational attitudes  130
  inferential and non-inferential (basic)  19,
    23, 66
  judgement of, influenced by affective
    states  74 *n*.29

lack of, as undermining belief 115
mirrored in practical
    commitment 132–3, 178–9
evidential undecidability
    defined 21, 130
    entailed by forced options 131–3
    essential ('in principle') 115 n.25, 134,
        139
        of commitment to theistic framing
            principles 140–5
        of choice between realism and
            non-realism 160
        role in defence of Jamesian
            fideism 178–9
    inapplicable, given partial beliefs 131
    in Jamesian formulation of
        fideism 123–4, 134
evidentialism
    broad and narrow versions 66 n., 87 n.
    and coherence requirements on
        belief 156–7
    defined 21
    distinctive features of present
        account 63–4
    implications of, when evidence is
        open 133, 179
    and integrationist doxastic values 161
    presumption in its favour 123, 179
    see also epistemic evidentialism; moral
        evidentialism
evil, argument from, see argument from
        evil
    absorbed 72
evolutionary psychology, as explaining
        religious beliefs 91, 204–5
exclusivism, religious 149, 210–11
experimental
    commitments 181, 202–3
    practical reasoning 39–40, 42, 110, 145,
        146
explanation, of religious beliefs 204–5
external world, belief in 189
externalism, epistemological 9, 11, 16, 28,
        60–1
    in Calvin's model of faith 104
    in defending fideism 64–5, 97,
        196–7
    in Reformed epistemology 92–9

fact/value distinction 201 n.24
faith

Abraham, exemplar of 170–3
active component of 105–6
authentic 120
Calvin's model 104–5, 106 n.8, 108
Christian 103–6, 135
cognitive component of 104, 138
counter-evidential 135, 155
doxastic venture model 101, 103,
    106–11, 120, 136, 209; see also fideism
evaluative-affectional component of 105
evidential deficiency models 109, 119
evidential proportion models (purely
    fiducial venture models) 108, 109–10
in a fact, helping to create that
    fact 182–5
as free 111 n.19, 116–7
as gift and act 103–4, 111 n.19, 116, 203
Hick's account of 109 n.15
as hope 110 n.18
involving doubt and risk 106, 109, 222
Kierkegaard's definition of 109
as knowledge 104–5, 109 n.14
meritorious 105
Plantinga's A/C model 97, 108
possessed by devils 105
requiring full commitment to truths 110,
    120
resulting from religious inquiry 111 n.19
sub-doxastic venture model 110–11, 119
Swinburne's pragmatist model 110 n.18
theistic 103; see also theistic beliefs
Thomist model 104 n., 105, 108,
    111 n.19
Tillich's account 109
as a virtue 106 n.9, 226 n.10
faith-beliefs
    causes of 114–5
    defined 7, 21, 48, 138
    theistic beliefs as paradigm of 6–7, 48,
        225
    integrated with moral beliefs 164–5, 170
    justifiability of
        as epistemic issue 26–8, 33, 41–2,
            51–2, 53, 148 n.; see also evidential
            ambiguity, of theism; evidential
            justification; evidential practice
        as metaquestion 4–6, 8, 26
        as moral issue 4, 8, 33, 35, 46–52
        see also moral-epistemic link principle;
            moral evidentialism
    see also theistic beliefs

faith-believers, reflective *see* reflective
    believers
faith-commitment
    ethics of 8, 22, 50, 52, 53, 64
    to basic factual claims 15–16, 193
    to basic moral claims 16, 193
    *see also* faith-ventures
faith-propositions
    as cognitive component of faith 104
    defined 7, 22, 174
    foundational, as highest-order framing
        principles 141–4, 146, 147, 167,
        193
    as presenting evidentially undecidable
        genuine options 138
faith-ventures
    assimilated to ventures in interpersonal
        trust 180–2, 199
    assimilated to/compared with
        experimental ventures 183–5, 203
    consequentialist justifications for, *see*
        consequentialism
    counter-evidential, *see* fideism,
        counter-evidential
    defined 13, 22, 137 *n.*16, 147
    epistemic entitlement to 162, 177, 186
    evaluated ('irregularly conjugated verb'
        problem) 3, 209
    moral, evaluative 170, 192–3, 200–1,
        225–6
    moral permissibility of 147
        inclusive of counter-evidential
            venture? 151–5
        judged only fallibly 148, 166, 168
        rejected by hard line
            evidentialists 174–5
        *see also* Jamesian fideism
    non-dogmatic 148–9, 168, 204, 210,
        222
    non-religious examples 225–6
    open to modification, change 15,
        199–200, 203, 222
    passionally motivated 16, 74 *n.*29,
        115–6, 133, 137, 199
    religious variety distinguished in
        principle 192–3
    supra-evidential, *see* Jamesian fideism
fallibilism
    in judging moral permissibility of
        faith-ventures 148, 200
    moral 166

in rational empiricist evidential
    practice 68
falsifiability, of theistic beliefs *see* theistic
    beliefs, falsifiability of
fawn, caught in forest fire 72, 169
Feldman, Richard 27 *n.*3, 29 *n.*, 32 *n.*,
    51 *n.*, 58 *n.*5, 63 *n.*10, 132 *n.*
fideism
    counter-evidential 19, 135–7, 214 *n.*
        as abandoning coherence
            requirements 156
        excluded (non-arbitrarily) by Jamesian
            fideism 136, 152, 156, 160–2
        implications of accepting 155–7
        inconsistent with integrationist
            doxastic values 158–9
        not absolutely morally
            excluded 152–5
        open to consequentialist
            justification 186
        popular with Christian
            evangelicals 162 *n.*
        rejection in need of defence 76, 152
    definitions of 3, 7, 22
    isolationist 85–6, 159–60
    Jamesian (supra-evidential, moral
        coherentist) *see* Jamesian fideism
    moral coherentist 23, 175; *see also*
        Jamesian fideism
    objected to 102, 208–9
        as accepting bad guides to
            truth 197–8; *see also* moral
            evidentialism
        as condoning wishful thinking 2, 163
        as too liberal 2–3, 13–14, 151, 163–4
    supra-evidential 25, 156; *see also* Jamesian
        fideism
    Wittgensteinian 80 *n.*3
Flew, Antony 77 *n.*
Fodor, Jerry 158 *n.*
forced option, *see* option, Jamesian
form of life 82 *n.*7
foundationalism, epistemic, contrasted with
    coherentism, holism 28 *n.*4, 67–8
framing principles
    defined 22, 80
    highest-order 13, 23, 189
        appealed to in response to 'degrees of
            belief' challenge 142
        functioning differently from ordinary
            factual claims 144

presenting essentially evidentially
    undecidable options 141
relevance for Jamesian fideism 147
universality of commitment
    to 189–90
moral 170
presenting forced options 129, 138–40
sub-doxastic commitment to 140, 143

Gale, Richard 112, 118 n.28, 136 n.15,
    137 n.17, 153 n., 185 n.12
genuine options 123, 125–9, 167, 178, 222
Golding, Joshua 48 n.24, 111 n.18,
    185 n.13
Goldman, Alvin 28 n.5
grace, divine 116 n., 118 n.30, 203
Great Pumpkin objection 88, 89, 92, 93
Griffiths, Paul J. 160
Gutting, Gary 80 n.3

Hájek, Alan 188 n.
Haldane, John 70 n.21
hard line moral evidentialism, see moral
    evidentialism, hard line
Heil, John 154 n.
Helm, Paul 31 n., 48 n.23, 108–9, 198 n.
heretics, treatment of 44–5
Hick, John
    his account of faith 109 n.15
    his religious pluralism 211 n.2
    his thesis of religious ambiguity 71 n.
    on James's will-to-believe thesis as
        defending wishful thinking 163 n.9
    as neglecting force of
        evidentialism 176 n.
    on post-mortem eschatological
        verification 140 n.
    on theistic doxastic framework as 'total
        interpretation' 142 n.
hiddenness, divine 71 n., 73 n.29, 94 n.29,
    99
historical claims, implicated in expanded
    theism 69, 146 n.
holding true, see taking to be true,
    contrasted with holding true
holism, see foundationalism, epistemic, as
    contrasted with coherentism, holism
Holy Spirit, operation of, in Calvin's and
    Plantinga's models of faith 93 n.28,
    104–5
holy water 119 n.30

hope, grounded by theistic belief 226–7
human nature 205
Hume, David 64 n., 73 n.28, 107 n., 128
hyperbolical doubt see Cartesian doubt

idolatry 162 n., 171
imagination 154
impasse, in debate between fideists and
    evidentialists 206–7, 212–14, 223–4,
    228
imperialism, epistemological 89
inner assent 41 n.
Inquisitor case 44–5, 46, 47
Insole, Christopher 135 n.
integrationism 23
integrationist values 157
    integration of faith-beliefs with scientific
        beliefs 152, 200
    integrationist doxastic values 14,
        157–60, 168
    moral integration of faith-beliefs 164–6,
        168, 170, 171–3
integrity, epistemic and general 190–1,
    217, 223
internalism, epistemological 27, 60
isolationist epistemology 10, 79–82
    committed to theistic framing principles
        as highest-order 142
    compared with Reformed
        epistemology 87, 96
    defined 23
    entailed by non-realism 82–4, 159
    implicitly fideistic 85–6
    not committed to isolationist
        semanticism 80 n.3
    not entailed by framework structure of
        theistic beliefs 82, 139
    unable to meet moral evidentialist
        requirements 84–5

(J₁), thesis 124
(J), thesis 147
(J+), thesis 165, 175
James, William
    on belief in a personal God 181
    as defending the right to believe 117 n.,
        184 n.
    on distinguishing seeking truth from
        avoiding error 191
    on evidentialism as passionally
        motivated 190, 192 n.

James, William  (*cont.*)
  on faith in a fact helping to create that
    fact 182
  on genuine options 123, 125–9
  on God as dependent on human
    faith-ventures 184 *n*.11
  on the impasse between fideism and
    evidentialism 206 *n*.29
  on the intellectual republic 213
  his notion of religion in 'The Will to
    Believe' 169 *n*.
  on passional nature as causing belief 45,
    114, 115 *n*.24, 198 *n*.
  as providing a justification of faith 112
  quoting Pascal on 'reasons of the
    heart' 204
  his 'robust streak of deontologism' 225 *n*.
  on self-induced belief 119 *n*.30
  use of 'overbelief' 137
  his will-to-believe thesis
    Gale's consequentialist
      interpretation 118, 153 *n*.,
      185 *n*.12
    as ignoring notion of
      probability 129 *n*.
    as including counter-evidential
      venture 137 *n*.17
    as involving tentative
      commitment 148 *n*.
    as justifying wishful thinking 163 *n*.9
    as requiring supplementation 173
    as restricted to highest-order framing
      principles 144 *n*.
    weak and strong versions of 149 *n*.28
    'will to believe' *versus* 'right to believe'
      versions 184 *n*.
Jamesian fideism 123–8, 174–5
  [formulated as thesis (J₁) 124; (J), 147;
    (J+), 165]
  accepting evidentialist
    presumption 123, 125, 178–9,
    200, 209
  affirming supra-evidential
    venture 137, 152
  allegedly condoning objectionable
    faith-ventures 155, 163–5
  allegedly lacking actual
    application 128–9, 134, 138–44
  applied to Abraham, forebear in
    faith 170–3

claiming epistemic entitlement 157,
  161–3, 177, 186, 198 *n*.
compatible with non-doctrinaire
  naturalism 217, 223
defended [*NB in order of presentation*]
  in virtue of restriction to
    undecidable genuine
    options 178–9
  by appeal to personal relations
    cases 180–5
  by *tu quoque* strategy 179 *n*.,
    189–90, 206 *n*.28, 207, 212
  on consequentialist grounds 185–7
  by alleged self-referential
    incoherence of
    evidentialism 190–2
  by appeal to epistemological
    externalism 197
  as morally preferable to
    evidentialism 18, 207, 215–16,
    228–9
  as balanced response to passional
    doxastic motivations 220
  as conforming to morality of
    authenticity 223
  as required by love 224
  as fitting with taking basic moral
    commitments as
    passional 225–7
excluding counter-evidential
  venture 136, 151–2
implications for reflective
  believers 167–70
implicit in Reformed
  epistemology 96–100
itself resting on passional
  commitment 207
meeting 'degrees of belief'
  challenge 142–4
merits summarised 208–9
as modest variety of fideism 175,
  177
not implying ethical suspension of the
  epistemic 177, 186
opposed by hard line moral
  evidentialism 175, 193–4, 206–7
as permissibility or deontological
  thesis 149, 224–5
presupposing realism and integrationist
  doxastic values 162

qualified by moral admirability of
    passional motivation 163–4, 165,
    203
qualified by moral correctness of
    content 165, 167 *n.*, 202–3
rejecting epistemic evidentialism 161
resting on trust in our passional nature
    as a guide to truth 195, 197–8
restricted to faith-propositions 146–7
supporting moral pluralism 149, 210,
    221
Jesus as personal Saviour, presenting forced
    option 127, 129, 132, 143–4, 193–4
Jordan, Jeff 64 *n.*, 137 *n.*17
juror, ignoring inadmissible evidence 37
justifiability *see* faith-beliefs, justifiability of

Kantian ethics 170, 193
Kaplan, Mark 36 *n.*13, 110 *n.*16
Kenny, Anthony 77 *n.*, 94 *n.*31
Kierkegaard, Søren 109, 135 *n.*, 171
knowledge
    'animal' *versus* 'reflective' 105 *n.*5
    not needing definition 27 *n.*2
    understood under externalism 60 *n.*, 61,
        94 *n.*29, 95, 104
Kretzmann, Norman 87 *n.*

language game 82 *n.*7, 85 *n.*12, 139, 144
leap of faith 3, 4, 97, 99, 102, 116
liberalism, political 214 *n.*
libertarianism (metaphysical) 225
liking and being liked 182–3
living option, *see* option, Jamesian
Locke, John 34 *n.*11, 63 *n.*9, 64 *n.*
locus of doxastic control, *see* doxastic
    control
logic, insane 182
logical positivism 144
love, as favouring fideism 224
loyalty (in face of apparent evidence of
    betrayal) 27 *n.*2, 53–4, 69 *n.*18, 154
Lucretius 175 *n.*

Mackie, J. L. 70, 72, 105 *n.*5
McKim, Robert 70 *n.*22, 71 *n.*, 148 *n.*
Madden, Peter 149 *n.*28
Malcolm, Norman 80 *n.*3, *n.*5, 82 *n.*7, *n.*8
Martians 152
Mavrodes, George 194 *n.*

melioristic universe 184 *n.*11
Miller, Barry 70 *n.*19
miracles, argument from 73
modularity of mind 158 *n.*
momentous option, *see* option, Jamesian
monotheism 171
moral disagreement 18, 213
moral entitlement to faith-beliefs 49,
    52
moral-epistemic link principle 8, 24, 55–8
    argued for on realist grounds 54–5,
        85 *n.*13
    combined with epistemic
        evidentialism 62
    component in moral evidentialism 64,
        212
    retained by Jamesian fideism 161,
        176–7, 212
moral evidentialism 62–5
    absolutist, seen to be incorrect 19, 123,
        145, 152
    defined 24, 52
    factored into two components 62–4, 79,
        161
    hard-line 11, 15, 22, 175, 179, 192,
        219–20
        as avoiding irremediable error 182–3,
            185, 190, 191–2
        as exhibiting heroic integrity 223
        as itself resting on a faith-
            venture 15–17, 189–92
            of a dogmatic kind 220–2, 223
            in favour of an evaluative rather
                than factual claim 193, 194
            in favour of naturalism 207, 218,
                220, 228
            meeting fideist requirements 207,
                212
        facing impasse with Jamesian
            fideism? 206–7, 212–14, 223–4,
            228
        failing in love? 224
        failing in self-acceptance,
            authenticity? 216–20, 222–3
        misguided if theistic beliefs have
            external epistemic worth 197
        non-absolutist 192
        not concordant with taking basic
            moral commitment as
            passional 226–7

moral evidentialism   (*cont.*)
  rejecting passional inclinations as
      guides to truth 16, 194–5, 218,
      227–8
  as risking loss of truth 16, 193–4
  as self-undermining 190–4
  supported by scientific explanation of
      religious belief? 205
  unbalanced (allowing dominance by
      one passional
      motivation)? 219–20
  and isolationist epistemology 85
  partly affirmed by Jamesian
      fideism 136–7
  and Reformed epistemology 87–99,
      196–7
  subject to exceptions 180, 182
moral integration, of faith beliefs 164–5,
      171–3
moral realism 166, 225
morality
  highest ideals of, as related to
      religion 214, 215
  internal to religious
      commitments 210–11
  as rationally based 170, 193, 227 *n.*
Morris, Thomas V. 77 *n.*
Moser, Paul 73 *n.*29
motivation, for faith-ventures, *see* passional
      causes of belief
Mozart 226 *n.*11
myth of the given 68

natural atheology, epistemic circularity
      of 71–3
natural theology, epistemic circularity
      of 71–3
naturalism, naturalist world-view 17, 24
  evidentially ambiguous, in relation to
      theism 73
  held dogmatically by hard line
      evidentialist? 220–2, 224
  non-doctrinaire, consistent with
      fideism 217–8, 223
  as passionally motivated 205 *n.*, 207, 217
  presupposed by argument against
      passional inclinations as guide to
      truth 205
Nazi faith-commitment 163–5, 166,
      167 *n.*
Newman, John Henry 74 *n.*29

Nielsen, Kai 80 *n.*3, 82 *n.*8
noetic structure 80
Norman, clairvoyant as to President's
      whereabouts 61 *n.*
non-cognitivism, *see* cognitivism
non-realism, in relation to religious beliefs,
      *see* realism
non-evidential causes of belief, *see* passional
      causes of belief
non-inferentially evident beliefs, *see*
      basically evident beliefs
'noseeum' assumption 72

O'Connell, Robert J. 144 *n.*, 165 *n.*, 225 *n.*
option, Jamesian
  defined 125
  evidentially undecidable, *see* evidential
      undecidability
  forced 125–7, 193–4, 212
      'degrees of belief' challenge to 128–9
      as generating evidential
          undecidability 131–3, 134
      as generated by framing
          principles 139–40
  genuine *see* genuine options
  living 125–6
  momentous 125–7
other minds, belief in 189
'ought' implies 'can' 51 *n.*
overbelief 137

Pascal, Blaise 118, 204
Pascal's Wager 118, 187–8, 119 *n.*30
'parity' argument (comparing religious to.
      e.g., perceptual beliefs) 11, 88–92,
      189
partial beliefs 12, 36
  accommodated in thesis of
      evidentialism 62–3
  as challenge to evidential
      undecidability 131, 134
  as challenge to forced options 128–9,
      134
  degree of, determined by evidence
      130
  excluded in forced options 132, 142–3
  excluded when evidence necessarily
      absent 143
  inconsistent with authentic faith 110,
      120
  problematic 110 *n.*16, 142

passional causes of belief
    defined  12, 24, 59
    as gifts of God's grace  116, 118 *n*.30
    as having epistemically rational
        aspects  198 *n*., 199–201, 212
    moral evaluation of  163–4, 165, 172,
        219
    as motivating commitment to
        evidentialism  190
    motivating faith-ventures/
        commitments  16, 74 *n*.29, 115–6,
        133, 137, 199
    as overriding rational evaluation  136
    their possibility defended  115, 121
    required for doxastic venture to be
        possible  114, 124
    scientific explanations of  16, 204–5
    subject to change  200–3
    variety of  114–5
    *see also* passional doxastic inclinations
passional doxastic inclinations
    as guides to truth  194–6, 197–8, 201–5,
        206–7, 212, 218, 221, 223, 227–8
    as a kind of evidence  198–9, 201 *n*.25,
        203–4
    and loss of integrity  191
    obligation to follow?  149, 214, 224–5
    *see also* passional causes of belief
penal substitution  202
Penelhum, Terence  102 *n*., 141
perceptual beliefs, *see* beliefs, perceptual
Percival, Philip  191 *n*.
personal relationships
    relevant to defence of Jamesian
        fideism  180–5
    trust in  145–6, 199
Phillips, D. Z.  80 *n*.3
Philosophy of Religion, purpose of  33, 48,
    52
pill, belief inducing  153
Plantinga, Alvin  2 *n*.
    on A/C (Aquinas/Calvin) model of
        Christian faith  93 *n*.27, 104
    on *de facto* and *de jure* objections to
        Christian belief  49 *n*.25
    on defining epistemological
        internalism  27 *n*.3
    on Great Pumpkin  88 *n*.
    on indirect doxastic control  31 *n*.
    on metaquestion about justifiability
        4 *n*.

    on nature of *de jure* question about
        Christian belief  93 *n*.28
    on noetic structure  80 *n*.4
    on properly basic beliefs  86 *n*., 95
    rejecting 'leap' of faith  97
    on theistic belief without evidence
        87 *n*.
    his theory of warranted Christian
        belief  93
        critiqued, as involving epistemic
            circularity  94–9
        as implicitly fideist  96–8
    on warrant  28, 49 *n*. 25, 92, 95 *n*.
pluralism
    moral  201 *n*.25
    with respect to faith-ventures  149, 199,
        210–11, 221
Pojman, Louis  110 *n*.18
politics, of toleration  213–14
practical reasoning  33–4, 36; *see also* taking
        to be true
    as involving weighting truths  36–7, 45,
        62, 63 *n*.9, 110, 119, 128, 131
pretending to believe  40, 42, 43–4, 110,
    145
Principle of Proportionality,
    Lockean  63 *n*.9
probability
    allegedly ignored by Jamesian
        fideism  129 *n*.
    not applicable to comprehensive
        world-views  142 *n*.
    *see also* Bayesianism; evidential support;
        partial beliefs
properly basic beliefs, *see* beliefs, properly
        basic
propositional attitude, *see* belief, ordinary
        and philosophical senses of
propositional-attitude-focused notions, *see*
        epistemic evaluation
puritanism  192
Putnam, Hilary  80 *n*.5

Quine, Willard van Orman  67 *n*.16
Quinn, Philip  214 *n*.

rational empiricist evidential practice, *see*
        evidential practice, rational empiricist
realism
    assuming one reality  159
    moral  166

realism (cont.)
  principled basis for integrationist doxastic
      values 159, 161–2
  in relation to beliefs, defined 54 n.
  versus non-realism, in relation to religious
      beliefs 10, 54–5, 82–4, 85 n.12,
      144–5, 159–62, 226
reason, making room for faith 162
reflective believers 6, 9, 49–50
  implications of evidential ambiguity
      for 74–5, 77, 92, 169, 176 n.
  implications of fideist/evidentialist
      impasse for 213, 214
  implications of Jamesian fideism for 148,
      167, 173, 229
  nature of their concern 53, 57, 59, 108,
      215
Reformed epistemology 2, 10–11,
      86–99
  and affectional influence on judgements
      of evidential support 74 n.29
  its appeal to epistemological
      externalism 92–9, 196–7
  both anti-evidentialist and
      evidentialist 87 n.
  compared with isolationist
      epistemology 87
  holding foundational theistic beliefs to be
      properly basic 86, 93
  implicitly fideistic 97, 196–7
  and the 'parity' argument
      88–92
  potentially satisfying moral
      evidentialism? 87–99
  use of notion of theistic doxastic
      framework 96, 142
relationship
  ethics of 201 n.24
  personal, see personal relationships
relativism, moral 213
reliabilism, epistemological 28, 60, 61 n.
religion, definition of 160
religious beliefs
  as dangerous 175, 187
  definition and varieties of 6–7
  explained by evolutionary psychology 91
  see also faith-beliefs
religious experience 172, 181, 189 n., 196;
      see also argument from religious
      experience
religious suspension of the ethical 171–2

republic, intellectual 213
responsibility, doxastic (with respect to
      beliefs), see doxastic responsibilities
right to believe 18, 117 n., 148 n., 184 n.,
      213; see also epistemic entitlement;
      James, William
Rowe, William 72 n.24
Ruben, David-Hillel 38 n.
Russell, Bertrand 129 n.

sacrifice, of child 171
scepticism
  from within theism 72
  with respect to rational empiricist
      evidential practice 68
  with respect to sensory perceptual
      doxastic practice 89
Schellenberg, J. L. 73 n.29
Schulz, Charles 88
Scriven, Michael 77 n.
self-acceptance 216–20
self-deception 32, 118, 135, 222–3
self-reference, as affecting
      evidentialism 190–2
sensory perceptual doxastic practice 88–92
sensus divinitatis 93 n.27, 99
Servetus 44 n.
sin, as blocking direct awareness of God's
      existence 96 n., 104
Smart, J. J. C. 70 n.21
Sosa, Ernest 95 n., 105 n.5
sub-doxastic venture 12, 24–5, 110–11
  as consistent with authentic faith 119–20
  counter-evidential 135, 153
  motivated by evaluative beliefs 120
  not required to accommodate evidential
      ambiguity 121
  permissible under Jamesian
      fideism 124–5
  supra-evidential 143–4
subjectivism, moral 213
suede shoes 37
supra-evidential fideism, see Jamesian
      fideism
supra-evidential venture
  defined 25
  intrinsic to theistic religious
      commitment 146–7
  see also Jamesian fideism, doxastic
      venture; sub-doxastic venture
supreme good 184–5, 188

suspension of belief, *see* belief, suspension
of
Swinburne, Richard
on definition of God 7 *n*.6
on faith as free 111 *n*.19
implicitly denying that theistic framing
principles are highest-order 141
on Plantinga's model of faith 98 *n*.
on pragmatist (sub-doxastic venture)
model of faith 110 *n*.18, 120
on Thomist model of faith 105 *n*.6,
111 *n*.19

Talbott, Thomas 44 *n*.
Taliaferro, Charles 55 *n*.
taking to be true
contrasted with holding true 8, 22, 30,
33–41, 55–6, 61 *n*., 154 *n*.
in doxastic venture model of
faith 106–7, 111, 113, 116–7
as mental action 35–41, 42, 63,
130
as morally evaluable 44–5, 63
in non-doxastic cases 39–40, 119
in sub-doxastic venture model of
faith 119–20
under utilitarianism 185
with full weight
defined 25, 110, 124
not dogmatic 120, 148–9
required for authentic faith 110,
119–20
as resolving evidentially undecidable
forced option 128–9, 143
in thesis (J$_i$) 124; (J) 147; (J+) 168
with partial weight 131; *see also* partial
beliefs
Taylor, Charles 206 *n*.29, 224
teleological argument 72
tentative commitment 148, 168, 210
Tertullian 135 *n*.
theistic beliefs
demonstrative proof of 70
evidential support of, under rational
empiricist evidential practice 68–9
falsifiability of 69
as grounding hope 226
incorporating historical claims 69, 146 *n*.
justifiability of, under evidential
ambiguity 71 *n*., 74
'mankind's most dangerous
inventions' 175 *n*.

meaningfulness of 144
properly basic, directly evident,
quasi-perceptual 86, 95, 97–8, 104,
189
*see also* doxastic frameworks, theistic;
doxastic practice, theistic
theism
classical 6–7, 168–9, 183, 188, 205,
209–11, 221
evidential ambiguity of, *see* evidential
ambiguity, of theism
restricted (generic) *versus* expanded 69,
76, 106, 146 *n*.
revisionary 17, 76, 169, 184–5,
210–11
sceptical 72 *n*.26
*see also*; faith, theistic; theistic beliefs
theists, reflective, *see* reflective believers
theology, natural, *see* natural theology
thick *versus* thin beliefs 48 *n*.23, 138
*n*.19
Tilghman, B. R. 83
Tillich, Paul 109
toleration, moral and religious 18, 211,
213–14, 217
tortoises, tendency to roam 34
trust
in passional inclinations as guides to
truth 194–5, 197–8
in personal relations 145–6, 180–1,
183 *n*., 199
related to faith 105–6, 108
*tu quoque*, strategy in defence of fideism 15,
189–90, 206 *n*.28, 207

ultimate concern 109
ultimate fulfilment 188
universalism 44 *n*.
utilitarianism 169, 185

values
commitment to 170, 226–7
integrationist, *see* integrationist values
Vanden Burgt, Robert J. 117 *n*.
venture
doxastic, *see* doxastic venture
fiducial 108
verifiability, of theistic beliefs 69, 144
post-mortem, eschatological 140 *n*.
virtues and virtue theory 31–2, 49 *n*.26,
56 *n*., 106 *n*.9, 165 *n*., 180, 226 *n*.10
voice, inner, of God 171, 172

Wainwright, William J. 74 *n*.29, 126 *n*.4,
    134 *n*., 149 *n*.28, 198 *n*.
warrant, *see* Plantinga, on warrant
weakness of will 37, 105
weight, as afforded truths in practical
    reasoning, *see* practical reasoning
*weltanschaulich* principles, *see* framing
    principles, highest-order
Williams, Bernard 30, 41 *n*., 140 *n*.
wishful thinking 114

Wittgenstein, Ludwig 80 *n*.5
Wittgensteinian fideism 80 *n*.3
Wolterstorff, Nicholas 2 *n*., 34 *n*.11,
    63 *n*.9, 81 *n*.
world, moral as well as natural
    order 226–7, 228
worship 171
Wykstra, Stephen 66 *n*., 72 *n*.25,
    87 *n*.
Wynn, Mark 115 *n*.24